THE ORIGINS OF THE ITALIAN WARS OF INDEPENDENCE

ORIGINS OF MODERN WARS
General editor: *Harry Hearder*

Titles already published:

THE ORIGINS OF THE FRENCH REVOLUTIONARY WARS
T. C. W. Blanning

THE ORIGINS OF THE ITALIAN WARS OF INDEPENDENCE
Frank J. Coppa

THE ORIGINS OF THE WARS OF GERMAN UNIFICATION
William Carr

THE ORIGINS OF THE RUSSO–JAPANESE WAR
Ian Nish

THE ORIGINS OF THE FIRST WORLD WAR (Second Edition)
James Joll

THE ORIGINS OF THE SECOND WORLD WAR IN EUROPE
P. M. H. Bell

THE ORIGINS OF THE SECOND WORLD WAR IN ASIA
AND THE PACIFIC
Akira Iriye

THE ORIGINS OF THE KOREAN WAR
Peter Lowe

THE ORIGINS OF THE VIETNAM WAR
Anthony Short

THE ORIGINS OF THE ARAB–ISRAELI WARS (Second Edition)
Ritchie Ovendale

THE ORIGINS OF
THE ITALIAN WARS
OF INDEPENDENCE

Frank J. Coppa

LONGMAN
London and New York

LONGMAN GROUP UK Limited,
Longman House, Burnt Mill, Harlow,
Essex CM20 2JE, England
and Associated Companies throughout the world.

Published in the United States of America
by Longman Inc., New York

© Longman Group UK Limited 1992

First published 1992

British Library Cataloguing-in-Publication Data
Coppa, Frank J.
The origins of the Italian wars of independence
—(Origins of modern wars)
I. Title II. Series
945

    ISBN 0–582–04045–0 pbk
    ISBN 0–582–04046–9

Library of Congress Cataloging-in-Publication Data
Coppa, Frank J.
The Origins of the Italian wars of independence / Frank J. Coppa
    p.   cm. — (Origins of modern wars)
Includes bibliographical reference and index.
ISBN 0–582–04046–9. — ISBN 0–582–04045–0 (pbk.)
1. Italy—History—1849–1870.   I. Title.   II. Series.
DG552.6.C67   1992
945′.083—dc20

Set in Linotron 202 10/12 Bembo

Produced by Longman Singapore Publishers (Pte) Ltd.
Printed in Singapore

Contents

Editor's Foreword

Of the nine volumes already published in this series, seven have dealt with twentieth-century wars, one with an eighteenth-century war, and only one with a nineteenth-century war. This, the tenth volume in the series, does something to fill the gap, and is a fine complement to Professor William Carr's *Origins of the Wars of German Unification*. The nineteenth century was, of course, rather more peaceful than the seventeenth, eighteenth or twentieth, centuries but if the wars between 1815 and 1914 were comparatively limited in time and space they were nevertheless immensely important, and to study their causes in the context of the series as a whole provides a fascinating exercise.

Professor Frank Coppa brings high qualifications to the task of studying *The Origins of the Wars of Italian Independence*. His studies of Pius IX and Cavour are well known to students of nineteenth-century Italy, and his more recent study of Cardinal Antonelli should refine historical understanding of a figure whose role has been viewed in an over-simplified manner in the past. It is precisely from his work in the Vatican archives that Professor Coppa brings a new angle on the approaches to the wars of Italian independence. In 1848 Pio Nono, with his plans for an Italian customs union, was recommending a different policy from Piedmont's war plans, but a policy which was rejected by Carlo Alberto. That rejection was one reason for the Piedmontese wars and defeats in 1848 and 1849.

The new material which Coppa has unearthed in the Vatican archives shows that the Pope was more enthusiastic for the Austrians to leave Italy in 1848 than is usually realized, even though he would not countenance the idea that he might himself go to war with Austria. In particular, Monsignor Corboli Bussi, who carried out much of the Pope's diplomacy for him, emerges as a pretty full-blooded Italian nationalist. The 1848 war was one of nationalist enthusiasm on the Italian side – an ideological war. This becomes clear when it is remembered that troops from Piedmont, Tuscany, the Papal States and Naples, as well as Garibaldi's volunteers and the Milanese revolutionaries were all fighting together against Austria. The attitude of the Italian monarchist rulers was, of course, ambiguous, and depended upon the degree to which they – in the case of the Pope, the King of Naples and the Grand Duke of Tuscany – were in the grip of revolutionary forces, or – in the case of Carlo Alberto – feared revolution. But Coppa's account provides evidence to suggest that perhaps they were all (even Ferdinando of Naples) more sympathetic to the Italian cause than is usually assumed.

The Second War of Italian Independence, in 1859, was in one respect motivated less by ideological aims than that of 1848 had been. It is true that Napoleon III spoke of fighting for 'the principle of nationality', but it would be a brave historian who would define precisely what the Emperor's motives were. Perhaps he did not have a clear idea of them himself. He would have liked to drive the Austrians out of Venice as well as Lombardy, and before the Third War of Italian Independence he was still deeply preoccupied with the acquisition of Venice for Italy. But he also wanted France to be rewarded with the acquisition of Savoy and Nice, even though Nice was undeniably more Italian than French.

Cavour's motives in 1859 were even less those of an ideologue than Napoleon's. He too wanted, of course, to drive the Austrians out of Italy, but in order to make Piedmont the dominant state in Italy rather than to unite the whole peninsula. His motives may be described as patriotic rather than nationalist. He was not working for nationalism in any ideological or general sense. While Napoleon gave diplomatic support to Romanian nationalism in these years, Cavour speculated with the idea of handing the Romanian Principalities over to Austria in compensation for an Austrian retreat from Italy. It is undeniably true that the two men planned a blatantly aggressive war at Plombières in 1858, and the Austrians can be forgiven for believing that they, for their part, fought a defensive and 'just' war.

One interesting theme that Professor Coppa mentions is the idea of the French banker, Pereire, that Austria should sell Venice to Italy for cash, at the end of 1860. Austria, in her turn, might buy Bosnia-Herzegovina from Turkey. Austria was certainly in need of funds, and the market value of the Veneto would probably be higher than that of Bosnia-Herzegovina. The idea was rejected by the Austrians.

But Coppa shows us that the Italians later took up the idea of buying Venice. La Marmora, when Italian prime minister, offered Vienna 100,000,000 lire for Venice, but again in vain. Early in the century the Americans had purchased Louisiana from France, and were later to purchase Alaska from Russia. To buy territory seems infinitely more civilized than to fight a bloody war for it, and in a market economy it could be argued that everything has its price. Yet it is an idea that has not caught on in history. The proposals are, of course, only one of the many fascinating points made by Coppa in this scholarly study of the coming of the Italian wars.

HARRY HEARDER

CHAPTER ONE

Introduction: Origins of the Italian Wars of Independence

While the Age of the Risorgimento (1796–1870), which brought both national consciousness and political union to Italy, has captured the historical imagination, various interpretations of the movement which transformed the geographical expression into political reality have emerged. One school has stressed the role of the moderates, another that of the radicals; some have noted the contributions of the bourgeoisie and the aristocracy; others have decried the failure to involve the peasantry. The part played by Cavour, Mazzini and Garibaldi, dubbed respectively the 'brain', 'heart' and 'sword' of unification, is still debated. Meanwhile Pius IX, the 'cross' of liberals and nationalists alike, has been hailed as 'the Saint of God' by conservative Catholics. Even the Contessa di Castiglione, commissioned by Cavour to seduce Napoleon III and enlist his support in a war plot against Austria, boasted that she created Italy while saving the Papacy.[1]

Despite the confusion and contradictory claims, two things are clear. First, a period of preparation preceded national consolidation. Second, a series of wars had to be fought to push the Austrians out of the peninsula before it could be united under the aegis of the Kingdom of Piedmont–Sardinia. The present book delves into the origins of the conflicts of 1848–49, 1859–60, and 1866 that led to the creation of the Italian Kingdom (dubbed respectively the first, second and third wars of Italian liberation, with the campaign of 1870 sometimes upgraded to constitute a fourth). The study includes both the internal developments and the diplomatic intrigues that unleashed the wars of Italian unification.

The precise beginning of the Risorgimento – the nineteenth-century movement that led to the unification of Italy – remains problematic, but it is widely acknowledged that its roots reach back to the Enlightenment and the revolutions which rocked the Western world at the turn of the eighteenth century. The twilight of that century, and the dawn of the nineteenth century, ushered in an age of revolutions in Europe. Intellectual, political, religious, social and economic developments contributed to shake the foundations of life on much of the Continent. The turmoil exploded into the Italian peninsula, arousing some of its people from years of slumber. The French intrusion, Napoleon's reordering of Italy's political and religious structure, and the emergence of new classes, especially in the Kingdom of Italy (1805–14), conspired to stimulate national consciousness, and the incubus which weighed down Italians was thrust aside.

By a series of decrees the French altered the basis of life in the peninsula, introducing the Civil Code, which provided for equality under the law, and making Tuscan the common language of the administration, thus assuring an increased cultural and commercial unity. The French also weakened provincialism and particularism by absorbing the smaller Italian states into their orbit. Eventually foreign domination and even religious authority were challenged. The winds of change swept away many of the illusions of Italy's *Illuminati* – her eighteenth-century reformers. The secret *Società dei Raggi* explicitly sought Italian unity, and its members were not alone. The growing realization that freedom and unity were necessary for the well-being of the peninsula and its people, inspired the Risorgimento.

The resurrection which preceded the proclamation of the Italian state in 1861 was initially a spiritual process calling for the transformation of Italian life. Only later did this literary and cultural movement assume political and military proportions. The prospects for a national political programme were not good as the Quadruple Alliance, the coalition against revolutionary France, prepared for the restoration of the petty monarchs and Austrian domination in Italy following the defeat of Napoleon. Those under the spell of Vincenzo Cuoco's *Saggio storico sulla rivoluzione napoletano* (1801), which concluded that the Parthenopean Republic had collapsed because of its failure to enlist the support of Neapolitans, sought to avoid this mistake by rousing the Italian masses. There was early and continuing controversy concerning the feasibility and advisability of a popular war of liberation, as against a traditional war of position waged by one of the dynasties bolstered by diplomacy.

In 1814 a group of patriots, which included Pellegrino Rossi, Antonio Maghella and Giuseppe Zurlo, appealed to Napoleon's Italian origins, urging him to invoke Italian nationalism as a means of arousing the people of the peninsula, and to draw upon their strength to defeat the Powers. Only say the word, they pleaded, and Italy will awake and take form. Napoleon, more of a pragmatist than a prophet, who in his public life admitted no sentiment, ignored their suggestion.[2] The Austrians, distressed by the agitation in Italy, worried about the reaction of King Joachim Murat of Naples, who they suspected would resort to extreme measures to defend himself.[3] Their assessment proved accurate.

During the Hundred Days, Marshal Murat (who was married to Napoleon's sister Caroline, and had been crowned King of Naples in 1808), appealed to national sentiments in his Proclamation from Rimini (30 March 1815). He called for an Italian state stretching from the Alps to Sicily. His invocation for a people's war, as Napoleon had foreseen, did not unleash the national energies that would have been required to defeat the Austrians at the battle of Tolentino (3rd May). The prospect of resisting the conservative, anti-national settlement vanished with the forces of Murat, and with Napoleon's defeat at Waterloo. Francesco Melzi d'Eril (1753–1816), the former vice-president of the Italian Republic under Napoleon, realised that the people of the peninsula could not determine their own fate. He invoked the aid of the Powers, pleading for autonomy, if not independence, for northern Italy. Melzi d'Eril's prayer went unanswered, however, as the European courts proved unwilling to challenge their Austrian ally, opposed to any recognition of Italian nationality.

Friedrich von Gentz, Secretary of the Congress of Vienna, admitted in a contemporary memoir that, for all its discussion of such lofty aims as the reconstruction of the social order and the regeneration of the political system of the continent, to create a lasting peace founded on a just distribution of power, the real purpose of the Congress was to divide among the conquerors the spoils stripped from the vanquished.[4] Italy, liberated from French influence, was the prize Austria coveted. The Congress thus disregarded Italian national interests, ceding Lombardy and Venetia to Austria, while placing members of the Habsburg family on the thrones of Tuscany, Parma and Modena. Although Austria considered the possession of Ferrara indispensable for the defence of her territories in Italy, the Papal States were restored to the Papacy by means of the skilful diplomacy of Cardinal Ercole Consalvi, thus effectively dividing the peninsula in two.

In order to ensure their control, the Austrians garrisoned Piacenza, Ferrara and the Commacchio, and concluded an agreement with the

Kingdom of the Two Sicilies, which stipulated that their government would not introduce principles irreconcilable with those adopted by the Austrians in their Italian provinces. The reactionary Ferdinand IV of Naples returned as Ferdinand I of the Kingdom of the Two Sicilies. His repudiation of constitutionalism alienated the liberals, while his subservience to the Habsburgs aroused the nationalists. Modena, more under the influence of the Jesuits than the States of the Church, was governed by the will and whim of Francesco IV, nephew of Leopold II of Austria. Almost everywhere in the peninsula there followed a concerted effort to reimpose the *ancien régime*, as French civil and legal codes were repealed, privileges were restored to the aristocracy and the Church, and many of the pre-war prohibitions against the Jews reinstated. National aspirations were dismissed as Italy was deemed a 'geographical expression'.[5]

To be sure, voices and hearts resisted the restoration. The poet and dramatist Vittorio Alfieri (1749–1803), whose works envisioned a free and united Italy, transmitted a legacy of pride to his countrymen. Alessandro Manzoni (1785–1873), grandson of Cesare Beccaria and author of *I promessi sposi* (1827), affirmed as early as 1815 that Italians could not be free until they were united.[6] Giacomo Leopardi (1798–1837), in his 'All'Italia', decried the plight of his homeland. This poem, as well as his 'Sopra il monumento di Dante' of the same year, inspired nationalists in the peninsula.[7] Ugo Foscolo (1778–1827), the patriotic poet and dramatist, endured exile in England rather than submit to Austrian control in Lombardy. Back home copies of his *Last Letters of Jacolo Ortis* (1802) were eagerly sought.

These poetic voices championing a national vision were echoed in the *Carboneria*, the secret society which opposed the settlement of 1815, and other radical fraternities which fostered discontent and resistance. Patriots such as the Lombard patrician, Federico Confalonieri (1785–1846), resented the terms imposed on the peninsula and schemed against them. Eventually this opposition served as a catalyst for change, provoking a number of revolutions that proved unable to overturn the Vienna settlement. A series of wars, orchestrated in part by the Kingdom of Piedmont–Sardinia, would be needed to topple the restoration and replace it with the Kingdom of Italy. Thus the 'lasting peace' envisioned by Friedrich von Gentz, Secretary of the Congress of Vienna, and architect of the Holy Alliance, proved to be of short duration.[8]

The wars which erupted in Italy in the first half of the nineteenth century led to the creation of the Kingdom of Italy (1861), as well as substantial changes in the European balance of power. The origins of the wars are complex, determined by events within the broader context of the European state system as well as specific Italian developments. The conflicts were instigated by activity within the diplomatic community, the political ambitions of Piedmont–Sardinia, the consequences of the Peace of Paris (1856) and the agitation within the radical and revolutionary camp. Thus the causes of the three wars which saw the emergence of a united Italy, and the 'fourth war', which made Rome its capital, are to be sought in Paris and Vienna as much as Turin and Rome, and flowed from the actions of the secret societies as well as the manoeuvres of the European chancelleries.

This book focuses on the causes of the Wars of Italian Independence, emphasizing the role of national forces, including the monarchical and popular ones, which competed for control in the peninsula within the framework of the Concert of Europe. It also stresses the role of the Powers, particularly the rivalry between France and Austria, and the European aspirations of Britain and Russia, as well as the impact of the Crimean War (September 1854–February 1856). Beginning with an examination of Italy in 1815, at the opening of the age of Metternich, specific chapters examine the origins of the First War of Italian Independence (1848), the Second War of Italian Independence (1859), and the Third War of Italian Independence (1866). There is also an account of the avalanche of events that eventually brought Rome under Italian control (1870). In each case the part played by the major powers, the Catholic Church and the Papacy, the Italian states, and the radicals who fostered the 'Italian Revolution', is considered.

The Italian loss of life in these wars was small in comparison, say, to the bloodletting of the American Civil War, and minuscule in comparison to the slaughter during the First World War. Indeed it has been calculated that national casualties during the three wars of independence were less than those endured in one single day of carnage during the Franco-Prussian War.[9] Nonetheless, the consequences were far-reaching politically, religiously and diplomatically.

The dramatic events of the Risorgimento have inspired a broader historical literature than any other period of modern Italy since the Renaissance.[10] The sources for the maze of European diplomatic activity that permitted, and in some instances provoked, the Wars of Italian Unification were published early on by writers who were decidedly favourable to Piedmont.[11] More recently Italian scholars have edited a series of volumes of documents shedding additional light on the diplomacy of unification.[12]

There is need for a short history of the origins of the Wars of Italian

Independence which synthesizes national developments, including the role of Cavour's Piedmont, Mazzini's *Giovane Italia*, Garibaldi's Redshirts and Manin's National Society with the aims and policies of the European powers. This has been my goal, and I hope that this work will shed light both on the causes of the Risorgimento wars and their consequences in the age of transition that led to the new balance of power. Hopefully, it will prove useful for students of Italian unification as well as students of nineteenth-century European diplomacy.

NOTES

1. Frédéric Lolilée, *Women of the Second Empire: Chronicles of the Court of Napoleon III, Compiled from Unpublished Documents* (New York: John Lane Company, 1907), p. 19.
2. Domenico Massè, *Cattolici e Risorgimento* (Rome: Edizioni Paoline, 1961), p. 28; Prince Richard Metternich-Winneburg (ed.), *Memoirs of Prince Metternich*, trans. Mrs Alexander Napier (New York: Howard Fertig, 1970), I, 283.
3. Ibid., II, p. 584.
4. Ibid., II, p. 553.
5. Countess Evelyn Martinengo Cesaresco, *The Liberation of Italy, 1815–1870* (Freeport, NY: Books for Libraries Press, 1972), pp. 16, 51.
6. Luigi Salvatorelli, *Pensiero e azione del Risorgimento* (2nd edn; Turin, Einaudi Editore, 1963), p. 13.
7. Luigi Ferrante (ed.), *Il Risorgimento* (Milan: Nuova Accademia Editrice, 1963), p. 13.
8. Antonio Monti, *La Politica degli Stati Italiani durante il Risorgimento* (Milan: Casa Editrice Francesco Vallardi, 1948), pp. 1–2.
9. Denis Mack Smith (ed.), *The Making of Italy, 1796–1870* (New York: Harper and Row, 1968), p. 11
10. For a concise and updated English survey of part of this literature see 'The conflict of interpretations and sources', in Harry Hearder's *Italy in the Age of the Risorgimento, 1790–1870* (London and New York: Longman, 1983), pp. 1–14. Also useful, particularly for the reaction of the Counter-Risorgimento see the annotated 'Selected Bibliography' in Frank J. Coppa, *Pope Pius IX: Crusader in a Secular Age* (Boston: Twayne Publishers, 1979). Journals such as the *Rassegna Storica del Risorgimento* pour out a stream of articles and book reviews on this period, presenting what is available in Italy and abroad.
11. In this regard see Nicomede Bianchi's *Storia documentata della diplomazia europea in Italia dall' anno 1814 all' anno 1861* (8 vols, Turin: Editrice tipografica editrice, 1865–72); and Luigi Chiala's *Lettere edite ed inedite di Camillo Cavour* (6 vols, plus index, Turin: Roux e Favale, 1883–87). Later works such as Franco Valsecchi's *L'Unificazione italiana e la politica*

europea dalla guerra di Crimea alla guerra di Lombardia, 1854–1859 (Milan: Istituto per gli studi di politica internazionale, 1939), and his *L'Alleanza di Crimea, Il Risorimento e l'Europa* (Milan: Mondadori, 1948) serve as important supplementary correctives to the contemporary publications. Likewise Cavour's political papers edited by the National Commission for the Publication of the Papers of Count Cavour, published by Zanichelli of Bologna, provide insights into the omissions of the earlier works, assuring a more objective selection of sources.

12. Eight volumes on Sardinian–British relations, covering the period of the three Wars of Italian Independence, have been published by the Istituto storico italiano per la età moderna e contemporanea in Rome. The Institute has published additional volumes on relations between Great Britain and the Kingdom of Two Sicilies, Austria and the Kingdom of Sardinia, Austria and the Papal States, and the Papal States and France during these same years. *I Documenti Diplomatici Italiani. Prima serie (1861–1870)* published by the Commissione per la pubblicazione dei Documenti diplomatici (Rome, 1952) helps to reconstruct the policy of the new kingdom in the decade from the formation of the unitary state to the forcible acquistion of Rome.

CHAPTER TWO

From Geographical Expression to Political Consciousness: Italy in the Age of Metternich

During his occupation of Italy, Napoleon burdened the country with heavy financial and military obligations. Thus many applauded the departure of the French, but their joy was to prove short-lived. Alongside resentment of Gallic exactions was an appreciation of their well-ordered administration, equality under the law, as well as the primacy of the civil over the religious order. For almost two decades the peninsula had benefited from the material improvements and institutional changes introduced by Paris, and although the Italian sense of nationality had not been consistently promoted or encouraged during the Napoleonic period, it was not stifled and offended as in the subsequent age of Metternich. The Austrian Foreign Minister played a crucial part in the coalition that defeated Napoleon, and a major one at the Congress of Vienna. Metternich argued that the Italians were not a people; his secretary, Friedrich von Gentz concurred, claiming that the vast majority were not prepared to accept a large Italian state.[1]

Metternich's Austria played a key role in the reorganization of Central Europe at the Congress of Vienna, where the Italians, with the exception of the Pope, were not represented. The resulting edifice rested on the Habsburg domination of Italy and Germany. These two people were denied the political existence patriots craved. In Italy, Austrian influence extended from the canals of Venice into the Bay of Naples. Lombardy and Venetia were combined into the Lombardo–Veneto Kingdom ruled by a viceroy of the Austrian Emperor, the younger brother of Franz, the Archduke Rainier. Tuscany, Parma–Piacenza, and Modena likewise had Habsburg rulers. In the small territory of the former Republic of Lucca Metternich permitted the return of the 'Spanish' Bourbons, without threat to Habsburg domination.

At the Congress of Vienna Metternich sought to extend Austrian dominion in Italy to the Legations of Bologna, Ferrara, Forli and Ravenna, by wresting them from the Papal States, and to the other side of the River Ticino – at the expense of the Kingdom of Sardinia. When both schemes failed to materialize, Metternich devised other means to expand Austrian influence in Italy. He concocted agreements with the various restored petty monarchs, and envisioned an Italian league within its headquarters in Milan. The Austrian–Neapolitan Accord of 12 June 1815 represented the Foreign Minister's first major Italian diplomatic initiative. In its two secret provisions Ferdinando pledged not to introduce changes in his state that would conflict with the principles of the Lombardo–Veneto Kingdom, controlled by the Austrians, not to enter any agreement contrary to their convention, or the proposed Austrian league.

The league never materialized, blocked as it was by the opposition of the Papal States and Sardinia, as well as the reservations of the Austrian Emperor. The Kingdom of Piedmont–Sardinia, which most resented the preponderant Austrian influence in Italy, and sought to pursue an independent course, was far from liberal or enlightened. King Vittorio Emanuele I, whose conservatism had intensified during his long years of exile, entered his capital in 1814 wearing his perruque with pigtail, determined to restore the *ancien régime*.[2] The army returned to aristocratic control, and education to the supervision of the Church. Ecclesiastical immunities were restored, and canon law enforced by the state. Across the River Ticino neither the Lombards nor the Venetians were allowed any real autonomy, as Italian civil servants were replaced by Slavs and Austrians, and German was imposed as the language of the administration. Travel to and from the region was restricted, and the press and journals screened.

Pope Pius VII, the beneficiary of a degree of popularity because of his refusal to bow to Napoleon's demands, was enthusiastically greeted upon his return to Rome in 1814. Under the influence of Cardinal Consalvi, his Secretary of State, a reform programme was drafted which sought to modernize and laicize the administration of the Papal States. The programme confronted difficulties from the first, having to deal with the Pope, who restored the Society of Jesus by a Bull of 7 August 1814, and condemned bible societies in 1817. The *zelanti*, the ultra-conservative faction of the curia undermined the position of Consalvi, and therefore his reforms. Under their pressure French legislation was abandoned, toleration terminated as the Jews were shut in the ghetto, and the clerical domination of the administration resumed.

Reformism in the Kingdom of the Two Sicilies, which constituted some three-eighths of the entire peninsula, did not fare better. True enough, Naples did not witness the excesses of the *sanfedisti*, the irregular forces of the Army of the Holy Faith, or the bloodbath of 1799. Moderation prevailed following the restoration, as the Code Napoleon and the French financial administration were preserved, if arbitrarily applied. Under the inspiration of the Duke of Canosa, prefect of police, the tone, if not the policies, of the *ancien régime* re-emerged. In the Southern Kingdom, as elsewhere, the pre-war authority, influence and almost universal presence of the Catholic Church was resurrected as the Jesuits returned to the realm, reviving old hostilities. Religious discontent, economic dislocation, and political dissatisfaction, combined with the resentment of the fierce suppression of all national sentiment to arouse discontent that soon translated into opposition to the status quo.

Although the great mass of Italians remained dormant and submissive, a minority had awoken to the plight of the peninsula. The secret society of the *Adelfi*, which organized and united various leftist groups against Bonapartism at the end of the eighteenth century, after 1814 directed its opposition against Austrian domination and the petty despotism of the conservative Italian regimes. Inspired and organized by Filippo Buonarroti (1761–1837), the *Adelfi* understood that the Italian problem had to be solved within the broader international context. Like the other societies, such as the *Filadelfi* and the *Veri Italiani*, which the Tuscan revolutionary inspired, the *Adelfi* proved strongest in northern Italy. Likewise the *Federati*, formed in 1818 from the union of nationalist and liberal organizations in Piedmont and Lombardy, concentrated in the north. The *Federati* sought independence and constitutionalism, and therefore called for the expulsion of the Austrians who blocked both programmes. In North and Central Italy, groups such as the *Cavalieri della Libertà* and the *Decisi* also demanded liberty and concessions for the oppressed Italians.

The *Carbonari*, or charcoal-burners, on the other hand, arose in southern Italy during the reign of Joachim Murat, spreading to central Italy after the restoration. They intermingled with the secret societies formed by Buonarroti, and called for unity of organization and purpose in the battle against Austria. Grouped in *vendite* (shops), the clubs with their elaborate ritual provided a place for social interaction as well as a vehicle for political change. Their membership ranged from dissatisfied aristocrats to literate peasants, but found its broadest support among the beleaguered middle classes. In Naples the *Carbon-*

ari penetrated the military, following the Bourbon restoration, so there were thousands under arms. Likewise in Piedmont, Carbonarism made headway among the younger army officers clamouring for change. Spread as it was throughout the peninsula, the diffusion and dissatisfaction of the *Carbonari* created a potentially explosive situation.

Metternich periodically received reports on the *Carbonari* and the other secret societies, but discounted the danger they represented, concluding that their divisions rendered them incapable of organized revolutionary action. Furthermore, he doubted their resolve. The Italians liked to talk but seldom acted, he confided to Gentz on 7 May 1819.[3] Nevertheless, despite his confident words, Metternich kept a watchful eye on the peninsula.

Few vehicles of protests against the status quo were permitted by the Austrians, their Habsburg satellites in Italy, or even by the independent sovereigns of the peninsula. Thus Lord Leigh's invocation to the Italians to arise but to avoid violence, proved impossible. Piedmont–Sardinia, which had an army and chafed at the Austrian domination, was not inclined to champion the causes either of constitutionalism or of national liberation. In Lombardy the weekly newspaper, *Il Conciliatore*, published between September 1818 and October 1819, ran foul of the Austrian censors, as its editor, Silvio Pellico, turned to Italian themes, providing a focus for intellectual opposition. Warned repeatedly about the political tone of its content, Pellico suspended publication, eliminating one of the few places where reform could be openly advocated. The Congregations of Lombardy and Venetia, the sole representative voice of these provinces, could only petition the court of Vienna, but were not encouraged to do so. Into the vacuum created by the Austrians stepped the *Carbonari*, who played a key role in the revolutions of 1820–21.

In 1820, the year of the first liberal revolution in Italy, the Austrians remained confident that order could be preserved. In his May 1820 report to the Emperor Franz on the State of Political Affairs, Metternich showed no concern about conditions in the peninsula.[4] Shortly afterwards, on 1 July 1820, Morelli and Silvati, two officers in the Neapolitan army, encouraged by the successful revolt of the army in Spain, demanded a constitution for the Kingdom of the Two Sicilies. As the cry 'God, the King and the Constitution' spread throughout the realm, and the Carbonarist General Gugliemo Pepe assumed control of the military, a frightened Ferdinando granted a constitution, swearing allegiance to it on 13th July. This revolution was the result of a Carbonarist–military conspiracy rather than a broad, popular movement.

News of the Neapolitan revolution shattered Metternich's complacency, and he was shocked to learn that the Carbonarist government of Naples dispatched emissaries to Piedmont to incite revolution there.[5] Metternich took immediate steps to repair the damage. Presenting Austria as the natural protector of the public peace in the peninsula, he warned that his state hoped to preserve order by legal and administrative means, but would resort to more vigorous measures if necessary.[6]

Metternich proved true to his promise, drawing the powers to Troppau in October 1820, while denouncing the revolution in Naples as the latest manifestation of a universal threat. Supported by the conservative monarchies of Russia and Prussia. Austria insisted upon its right and duty to intervene to preserve the European peace. Metternich dreaded the example set by Naples for the rest of Italy. He learned from Starhemberg, the Austrian representative at Turin, that a revolutionary ferment prevailed throughout the peninsula, and the upheaval in Naples echoed in Piedmont. Still, the Austrian Ambassador in Turin did not expect the revolution to explode there. Vittorio Emanuele I, the Piedmontese king, was less sanguine, and pressed the Austrians to reinforce their military presence in Italy. Conservatives on both shores of the River Ticino were upset by the outpouring of constitutional manifestos in Turin, allegedly encouraged, if not abetted, by the French Ambassador.[7]

Although Metternich boasted that the great European powers supported his stance *vis-à-vis* the Neapolitan revolution,[8] at Troppau the English questioned the propriety and wisdom of the proposed Austrian intervention against the constitutional regime. While Prussia and France joined Austria in condemning the Neapolitan revolution, they did not intend to abandon the entire peninsula to her control, and after consulting the Papal States and Sardinia, refused the Austrian request to occupy Alessandria, Civitavecchia, and Ancona to prevent the spread of revolution. The controversy led the powers to invite the Neapolitan king to a congress in Laibach (January 1821), to sound out his opinion. With the approval of Ferdinando and the conservative powers, the Austrians massed a large force to restore order to the disaffected region. Notwithstanding English reservations, and the Papal Envoy's argument that peaceful mediation was preferable, the Austrians marched on Naples to restore absolutism. On 7 March 1821 the forces of Guglielmo Pepe were overwhelmed by a superior Austrian force in the mountains near Rieti. Two days afterwards, the

Austrians assailed the strong position of Antrodrovoco, opening the road to Naples. Ferdinando, meanwhile, hastened to ensure that his country's institutions complied with the Austro-Neapolitan treaty of June 1815, which had belatedly been made public.

Metternich had barely put out one fire when another flared up in Piedmont, where public opinion, if not the monarchy, was clearly anti-Austrian. Encouraged by the departure of the Austrian army from the Lombardo-Venetian Kingdom to Naples, the standard of revolt was raised in Turin, Alessandria, and other cities in Piedmont. The *Carbonari* hoped to proclaim a Kingdom of Northern Italy under the Savoyards, and were supported by army officers from some of Piedmont's best families in their call for a constitution and war against Austria.[9] Almost half the Sardinian army backed the demands, which were opposed by the Powers still in congress at Laibach, who warned Vittorio Emanuele not to surrender to the revolutionaries.

Unable and unwilling to satisfy the popular call for a constitution, Vittorio Emanuele I abdicated on 13 March 1821. Since his brother and heir, Carlo Felice, was then in Modena, Carlo Alberto, his nephew, was appointed regent. Metternich hoped the regent would find the means to combat the revolution, threatening that if he proved unequal to the task, the Austrian and Russian emperors would find the means to do so. His worst fears materialized as Carlo Alberto, letting others believe he had the approval of King Carlo Felice, granted the constitution sought by the army. The Austrian Ambassador, frightened by the public animosity against his country, fled from Turin.[10]

Neither Metternich nor Carlo Felice accepted Carlo Alberto's concession of constitutionalism. Metternich claimed that the 'babel of confusion' assumed the weakness of a man of strong character (Carlo Felice), and the will of an inexperienced youth (Carlo Alberto), and were disappointed on both counts.[11] Carlo Felice, who firmly believed in his divine right to rule, ordered Carlo Alberto and those troops which had remained loyal to absolutism, to Novara. At Novara, Carlo Alberto was forced into exile in Tuscany, while the loyalist and Austrian troops overcame the constitutionalist forces. With the defeat of the revolution, liberals and constitutionalists scrambled abroad, and among them was Cesare Balbo (1789–1853), who had advised the regent during the stormy events of 1821. When he returned home in 1824, he turned to the pen rather than the sword, hoping to influence public opinion by his historical writing.

Santorre di Santarosa, the guiding spirit behind the revolution in

13

Piedmont, initially had no contacts with the *Carbonari*, or any other secret societies, which he considered the blight of Italy. Only when he realized that the Piedmontese government had neither the means nor the will to resist Austrian domination, did he seek their assistance. Santarosa concluded that a military movement would be impotent if not supported by a popular uprising, which would require the participation of the secret societies.[12] Thus, during the period of preparation for the future wars of independence, some Piedmontese patriots concluded that the public authority required the support of popular sentiment to overcome Austrian hegemony.

In Austrian-controlled Lombardy, where the military worked to suppress rather than support change, the secret societies represented the only hope for patriots. Fearful of a possible explosion, an imperial decree of 1820 provided for the confiscation of property and the death penalty for all those who joined the *Carbonari*. In the autumn of 1820, Pietro Maroncelli and Silvio Pellico were arraigned as *Carbonari*, and Count Arrivabene of Mantua was arrested as an accomplice. The noted philosopher, jurist and writer, Gian Carlo Romagnosi (1761–1833), was forbidden to teach, accused of treason and placed under house arrest. Having learned that the *Carbonari* in Milan conspired to persuade Carlo Alberto to lead his army into Lombardy, the Austrians arrested Gaetano Castiglia, the Marquis Giorgio Pallavicino, who assumed the responsibility for the abortive mission to Turin, and eventually Count Federico Confalonieri, architect of the projected uprising. The count joined Pellico in the Spielberg, the Austrian political prison in Bohemia, where Pellico gathered material for *Le mie prigioni*, a book that popularized the Italian dilemma. It revealed that Lombardy and Venetia were subjugated by the iron hand which wielded the *bastone tedesco* (German club).

Following the restoration of 1820–21, Metternich reached the apogee of his power, as princes and statesmen competed for his advice. At this juncture he again produced his proposal for an Italian league, but, as earlier, it was not favourably received. Metternich resorted to other means to combat the 'opponents of order'. The failure of the revolutionary upheaval of 1820–21 in Italy was provoked both by military weakness and an immaturity of political conception. The miscarriage proved costly, contributing to a deterioration of conditions for patriots, who witnessed trials, executions and confiscation of property. In Piedmont–Sardinia, Carlo Felice prosecuted the rebels, expanded police power and increased the influence of the Church. Even Carlo Alberto abandoned his liberal and national inclinations. Men such as Camillo di Cavour, who sought reform from above, grew increasingly disenchanted with monarchical policies, yet shunned radical alternatives as counterproductive.[13]

In Naples the liberalism of Francesco I, who succeeded Ferdinando in 1825, vanished with his youth. Corruption, inefficiency and repression marked his reign (1825–30), which culminated in the savage suppression of the uprising in Cilento in 1828. Throughout much of the South, *sanfedisti* organizations, which supported 'throne and altar' and attacked liberalism and nationalism, were encouraged. Conservatives in Rome feared that the example of Naples and Sardinia might stimulate discontent in the Eternal City, but their fears proved unfounded during 1820–21. Cardinal Consalvi believed that two developments, one internal, the other external, threatened the security of the Papal States. At home, the *Carbonari* programme worked to undermine the very basis of the Papal States, while abroad, the Holy Alliance, and especially Austria, sought to control Papal policies.

In the Papal States, the death of Pius VII in 1823 brought Annibale Sermattei della Genga to power, as Leo XII (1823–29), the *zelante* Pope. The reformism of Consalvi was officially terminated as Leo sought to restore the pre-revolutionary administration. His close alliance with conservatives at home, and collaboration with the forces of the Holy Alliance abroad, enraged liberals and encouraged revolutionary discontent. Leo XII excommunicated members of the secret societies, while his successor, Pius VIII (March 1829–December 1830), imposed the death penalty on them. Nevertheless, the *Carbonari* proliferated in the Legations, especially during the brief pontificate of Pius VIII.

For patriots in Italy, the decade 1820–30 proved discouraging. Metternich continued to pull the diplomatic strings from Vienna, and, with the collaboration of conservative princes in Italy, imposed order on the peninsula. Some, such as Francesco Lampato, the director of the *Annali Universali di Statistica*, founded in Milan in 1824, sought to address economic and technical problems, rather than the political ones, censored by the Austrian government.

From their various places of exile abroad, and especially from Paris, liberal Italians appreciated the need for assistance in containing Austria and the loyalist forces. Just as Cavour in the 1850s sought the aid of Imperial France, Italian radicals in the later 1820s counted upon the resurgence of revolutionary France. Under the inspiration of the entrepreneur and liberal conspirator, Ciro Menotti (1789–1831), a plan was conceived for the carbonarist clubs to gain control of one of the smaller Italian states, and utilize its army to spark a broader national uprising and a war of liberation. The Modenese lawyer,

Enrico Misley (1801–63), served as Menotti's agent to Italian exiles in Paris and London, and chief contact with the international revolutionary committee which served to coordinate their efforts.

Menotti and Misley, knowing that Francesco IV, Duke of Modena, had ambitions which transcended his small duchy, sought to enlist his aid in their revolutionary scheme, promising him the rule of the larger central Italian state which they envisaged. The central committee in Paris looked for simultaneous revolutions in France, Italy and Spain. Within the peninsula there would be risings in the duchies and the legations, culminating in their inclusion into a constitutional kingdom which would embrace the whole of northern central Italy. In 1830 Italian conspirators were buoyed by the outbreak of the July Revolution in Paris, followed by the French proclamation of non-intervention, which seemed to suggest that the new, constitutional regime in Paris would not tolerate Austrian interference in Italy. Even moderate Italians, such as Camillo di Cavour, were elated by the 'glorious July Revolution' but distressed by the fact that while the rest of Europe seemed to move ahead, Italy remained crushed beneath the weight of political and religious oppression.[14]

In early February 1831, as Menotti and his followers planned the final arrangements for the central Italian revolutionary upheaval, Francesco had the leadership of the group arrested. Despite this decisive action, the revolution erupted as planned. Francesco was forced to flee his duchy for Austrian-held Mantua, dragging along Menotti, whom he later had hanged. In Modena the liberal Biagio Nardi established a provisional government. Expecting French support, which would prevent Austrian intervention, the revolution spread from Modena to Parma, where Count Filippo Linati replaced Marie Louise, and to the northern tier of the Papal States. As the cardinals closeted themselves in Rome, in order to elect a successor to Pius VIII, delegates from northern central Italy convened in Bologna and proclaimed the independence of the United Italian Provinces. The Bolognese appealed to their brothers in Lombardy to follow their example and cast-off Austrian domination, but their appeal went unanswered. Tuscany, which possessed the most tolerant government in the peninsula, likewise proved immune to the revolutionary fervour of 1831.

The Papal Secretary of State, Cardinal Tommaso Bernetti, chosen by the new Pope (Gregory XVI), strove to avoid the opprobrium certain to accompany Austrian intervention, by appealing to France and Naples for assistance. Their reluctance to act, coupled with the inadequacy of Papal forces to effect a restoration, constrained Bernetti to appeal for Austrian arms. The French opposition to Austrian intervention was neutralized by Metternich who convinced Louis Philippe that the revolution in Italy was inspired by Bonapartism which threatened the French monarchy. He also claimed to have the moral, and if required, the military support of Russia and Prussia. Once the threat of French intervention was removed, Austria proved capable of crushing the revolutions and restoring the status quo. By March 1831, Modena was occupied and Bologna pacified. The events of 1831, and the continued unrest thereafter, made the Italian question a European, rather than a purely Austrian, affair. Louis Philippe, criticized for the weakness of his policy in Italy *vis-à-vis* Austria, demanded that a conference of the major powers – Austria, France, Great Britain, Prussia, and Russia – be held in Rome, to advise the Pope on the reforms required to avoid further disruption.

The Austrian Chancellor, Metternich, concurred that certain changes in the administration of the Papal States were essential, proposing the *motu proprio* of Pius VII, of 1816, as the basis for the reforms. In May 1831, the Conference of Ambassadors submitted a Memorandum to Gregory XVI, cataloguing the changes deemed essential, including the admission of lay people to all administrative and judicial functions, the revival of some of the provincial liberties which had earlier existed in the Papal States, and the maintenance of sound finance and credit by creating a board to supervise the audit of public accounts. The Memorandum also proposed the creation of a national consultative assembly to advise the Pope on governmental and administrative affairs.[15] Bernetti objected to the latter, branding it incompatible with the special nature of the pontifical regime. In July Gregory issued an edict promising to implement most of the other recommendations. In fact, the Memorandum of the Powers remained a dead letter. Only English pressure, Cavour observed, could help the Romagnols acquire a reasonable government.[16]

Gregory XVI, suspicious of revolution, identified the interests of the Church with the existing regimes in the peninsula. The 'Catechism on Revolution', published in 1831, enquired 'Does the Holy Law of God permit rebellion against the legitimate temporal sovereign?' and answered, 'No, never, because the temporal power comes from God.' It proclaimed that since one had to submit to God, likewise one had to remain subject to the prince, who was his minister.[17] Gregory's encyclical, *Mirari vos*, of 1832, condemned the entire liberal movement. This conservative attitude encouraged *sanfedisti* violence, and the outbreak of new revolutionary disturbances. Austrian forces were thus constrained to return to Bologna, and the

French, to preserve some balance, garrisoned Ancona. This dual foreign occupation of the Papal States continued until the winter of 1838. Cardinal Luigi Lambruschini, who succeeded Bernetti as Papal Secretary of State, favoured conservatism at home, and alignment with Vienna abroad. The reaction in Rome persisted throughout the Pontificate of Gregory XVI (1831–46), while conditions elsewhere in the peninsula produced little to encourage patriots.

The suppression of the revolutions of 1831, following the failures of 1820–21, brought the first stage of the Risorgimento struggle to a close. The revolutionary fires lit by the radicals proved to be fuelled by straw, rapidly sparked, but just as easily extinguished. The *Carbonari* and the other secret societies, unable to achieve their liberal and national aspirations, had kept alive the notion of national independence, and provided inspiration for the new leadership which emerged in the 1830s. Giuseppe Mazzini, who wrote for the *Indicatore Genovese* until the Turin government suppressed it, decided to accept an invitation to join the ranks of the *Carbonari*. The man who was destined to become the most influential leader of the national revolution, recognized that Carbonarism represented war to the monarchy, and little else, but deemed this better than complete inactivity.[18]

In 1830, while initiating a member into the *Carbonari*, Mazzini was entrapped by the police and imprisoned in the fortress of Savona for six months. On his release he was given the choice of internment in a small village in Piedmont, or exile abroad, and chose the latter, finding his way to Marseilles. In October 1831 he formed a new organization, *Giovane Italia*, to inspire Italians and lead the people's revolution that would liberate and unite the peninsula. The call for a republican Italy with its capital in Rome was issued in the society's journal, *La Giovane Italia*, published irregularly from Marseilles and smuggled into Italy. Finding its initial appeal in Lombardy and Piedmont in the 1830s and 1840s, Young Italy spread throughout the peninsula, replacing the *Carboneria* as the major organization of opposition to Austrian domination. Unlike the earlier secret societies, *Giovane Italia* did not place its hope in a revolutionary élite, but upon the broad nationalism of an informed Italian people.

The reorganization of Italy, Mazzini insisted, must be undertaken by the Italian masses. Revolution by and for the people, he wrote, summed up their whole doctrine. He scorned diplomatic and military solutions which required the initiative of one or another of the Italian states, which he distrusted, opting instead for a popular insurrection supported by the Italian people. Nonetheless, in April 1831, when Carlo Alberto replaced Carlo Felice on the throne of Piedmont–Sardinia, Mazzini, inspired by the accession of one 'who had been a *carbonaro* in 1821', urged the new king to lead the movement for Italian independence. He warned his enigmatic sovereign that if it did not meet his national responsibility, others would act without him, even against him.[19]

Carlo Alberto responded by ordering Mazzini's arrest, should he venture into his kingdom. Angered by the king's 'betrayal', in 1833 Mazzini planned an invasion of Savoy to correspond with an internal insurrection. The Piedmontese learned of the scheme and Carlo Alberto responded energetically to the Mazzinian threat. The police moved quickly to arrest and deliver the conspirators for trial before special military tribunals. Twelve were found guilty and executed. Jacopo Ruffini, Mazzini's long-standing friend who was taken prisoner, committed suicide. Thus the Young Italy organization in Piedmont was dealt a blow from which it never recovered.

Mazzini's attempt in 1834 to overturn the Piedmontese monarchy proved equally disastrous. Count Cavour deplored the republican conspiracies, convinced that the plots of 'confused souls' would only reinforce the government's repression and bring it into a closer relationship with Metternich's Austria. Condemning both the reactionaries and the revolutionaries, he sought a *juste milieu* between these dangerous extremes.[20] One of the few positive results of the fiasco was its impact on Giuseppe Garibaldi, who decided to devote himself to Mazzini and the national cause. Father Vincenzo Gioberti, implicated in the plot, fled to Belgium where he pondered the failure and sought a more practical means of achieving unification.

Under the banner of 'God and the People' Mazzini continued to press for education and insurrection from his second home England, scheming energetically and incessantly to effect both. His invocations struck a responsive chord in a revolutionary élite. Uprisings occurred in the Kingdom of the Two Sicilies in 1837 and 1841, but were brutally repressed by the forces of Ferdinando II. In 1843 general uprisings were planned in Naples, the Romagna and Tuscany, but the projected rebellion was stillborn. In 1844 Emilio and Attillo Bandieri, brothers from Venice who had organized a branch of Young Italy, led an expedition for the liberation of Calabria, which ended in dismal failure and their execution. Insurrections in the Papal States in Viterbo in 1837, and the Legations in 1845, proved no more successful.[21]

Moderate constitutionalists, realizing that the latter uprising in Rimini was doomed to failure, issued a 'Manifesto of Rimini' which denounced before the tribunal of Europe the political bankruptcy of the Papal regime. Massimo D'Azeglio's *Degli Ultimi casi di Romagna*

(1846) condemned both the Mazzinians, who sought to overturn the Papal government, and the reactionary policies of Rome, which encouraged revolution. The inability of Mazzini's popular insurrections to liberate the peninsula led D'Azeglio, and other moderates, to propose alternative means of realizing their national ambitions.

The moderate constitutional party deplored the abortive revolutions of the *Carbonari* and Young Italy, which, they maintained, only increased repression. Other forces and means were needed to effect the regeneration of Italy. Figures such as the Lombard Carlo Cattaneo preached the need for economic preparation and integration to pave the way for eventual unification. Likewise, the Venetian Daniele Manin believed that economic and educational changes had to precede political initiatives. Their technical approach was implemented by the annual scientific congresses which were initiated by the Tuscan government in 1839, drawing representatives from most states of the peninsula. Meeting first in Pisa (1839), they subsequently convened in Turin (1840), Florence (1841), Padua (1842), Lucca (1843), Milan (1844), Naples (1845), Genoa (1846), and Venice (1847). Only the Duke of Modena and Pope Gregory XVI prohibited their subjects from attending, fearing the meetings would inspire nationalist unrest.

Cesare Balbo described the eighth congress held in Genoa as the first real Italian parliament. Branding it inconsequential in its scientific mission, Balbo perceived it as a serious school of preparation in the political realm. Other means were found to spread the gospel of the moderates. *L'Antologia Italiana*, initiated in 1846, had the collaboration of a large number of moderate liberal writers in Piedmont. It advanced not only scientific and literary progress, but an awakening and nourishment of national sentiments, and its moderate message was echoed in a series of books.

As early as 1836, Nicolò Tommaseo, in his *Delle nuove speranze d'Italia*, urged priests and princes in the peninsula to participate in the national movement. Those who relied upon the princes to assume leadership came to be known as secular moderates, while those who looked to the priests, and above all to the Pope, were dubbed Neo-Guelphs. The latter movement came to the fore with the publication in 1843 of Vincenzo Gioberti's *Del primato morale e civile degli Italiani*.

While in exile in Paris and Brussels, Gioberti abandoned his Mazzinian and revolutionary leanings, turning instead to history and philosophy for a better understanding of the plight of his country. Influenced by Daniel O'Connell (the Irish nationalist known as 'The Liberator' who founded the Catholic Association which opposed the Act of Union) and Félicité de Lamennais (the French Catholic priest who sought to reconcile Catholicism and political liberalism), he dedicated himself to achieving national aims by peaceful and legal means. In 1843 he submitted his conclusions to the princes and the public in his *Primato*, which called for the creation of an Italian confederation under the aegis of the Papacy and with the military cooperation of Piedmont–Sardinia. Offering as it did an alternative to the 'insanities' of the radicals, while satisfying national sentiments by the peaceful formation of a confederation, the book and programme gained wide approval. However, not all were convinced.

Cesare Balbo, who favoured a federal over a unitary solution, explained that the Papacy could not provide either national liberation or political unification for the Italians. Profoundly Catholic, and dedicated to the Papacy, Balbo, in his *Delle Speranze d'Italia* (1844), insisted that Piedmont–Sardinia, rather than the Pope, had to assume the initiative on behalf of the nation, once Austria was diverted by diplomacy into the Balkans. Massimo D'Azeglio and Cavour – fellow Piedmontese – concurred, sharing the conviction that only the Piedmontese monarchy possessed the military and diplomatic clout to liberate Italy. If he were Carlo Alberto's minister, Cavour prophesied, he would know what to do, making Austria tremble while astonishing the world.[22]

The Piedmontese, or at least Carlo Alberto, seemed to lack the will to implement the liberal and national programme, as his soul and psyche were torn between the conflicting sentiments of religious mysticism and towering national aspirations. The reformism which the king began in 1837 represented something of a break with the conservative course he had pursued since 1831, but no one was certain of his final destination. Some believed that the Albertine Codes were the precursors of the long-awaited Piedmontese national initiative. Others argued that only the death of the conservative Gregory XVI would usher in a new Pope and a new age. Thus, in the 1840s the clash between those who championed Piedmont and those who looked to the Papacy for national liberation continued. The competition would be resolved only during the course of the First War of National Independence.

NOTES

1. Golo Mann, *Secretary of Europe: the life of Friedrich von Gentz, Enemy of Napoleon*, trans. William W. Woglom (New Haven: Yale University

Press, 1946), p. 220; G. de Bertier de Sauvigny, *Metternich and his Times*, trans. Peter Ryde (London: Darton, Longman and Todd, 1962), p. 190.

2. Antonio Monti, *La politica degli stati italiani durante il Risorgimento* (Milan: Casa Editrice Francesco Vallardi, 1948), pp. 30–1; E.E.Y. Hales, *Revolution and Papacy, 1769–1846* (Notre Dame: University of Notre Dame, 1966), p. 237.
3. Prince Richard Metternich-Winneburg (ed.), *Memoirs of Prince Metternich*, trans. Mrs Alexander Napier (New York: Howard Fertig, 1970), III, pp. 99, 279.
4. Ibid, III, p. 432.
5. Narcisco Nada (ed.), *Le relazioni diplomatiche fra l'Austria e il Regno di Sardegna. I Serie: 1814–1830, Volume Secondo* (Rome: Istituto Storico Italiano per L'Età Moderna e Contemporanea, 1968), p. 65.
6. Metternich, III, p. 434.
7. Nada, pp. 23–5, 36–7.
8. Ibid, p. 51.
9. Ibid, pp. 82–3, 148.
10. Ibid, pp. 168–9, 176.
11. Metternich, III, p. 493.
12. Piero Gobetti, *Risorgimento senza eroi e altri scritti storici* (Turin: Einaudi, 1969), p. 237.
13. Metternich, IV, pp. 182–3; Pasquale Villari, 'The Youth of Count Cavour', in *Studies Historical and Critical*, Chiala (ed), *Lettere edite ed inedite di Camillo Cavour* (Turin: Roux e Favale, 1883–87), V, pp. 21–2.
14. Villari, p. 122.
15. Angelo Filipuzzi, *Pio IX e la politica austriaca in Italia dal 1815 al 1848* (Florence: Felice Le Monnier, 1958), pp. 100–5; Luigi Rodelli, *La Repubblica Romana del 1849* (Pisa: Domus Mazziniana, 1955), pp. 35–6; Alexandre de Saint-Albin, *Pie IX* (Paris: E. Dentu, 1860), p. 35.
16. Carlo Ghisalberti, 'Il Consiglio di Stato di Pio IX: Nota storia giuridica', *Studi Romani, anno,* I (1954), p. 56; Edgar Quinet, *La question romaine devant l'histoire. 1848 a 1867* (Paris: Armand Le Chevalier, 1868), p. 16; Chiala, V, p. 22.
17. Catechismo Sulle Rivoluzioni (1832), *Archivio Segreto del Vaticano. Fondo Particolare Pio IX, cassetta 5, busta 4.*
18. Giuseppe Mazzini, *Note autobiografiche,* ed. Mario Menghini (Florence: Felice Le Monnier, 1944, 2nd edn), p. 12.
19. Giuseppe Mazzini, *Life and Writings of Joseph Mazzini,* 6 vols (London: Smith, Elder and Co., 1864–70), I, pp. 60, 106.
20. Villari, p. 126.
21. Giacomo Antonelli to Filippo Antonelli, 7 September 1837, *Archivio di Stato di Roma, Fondo Famiglia Antonelli, busta 1, fascicolo 125; Posthumous Papers of Jessie White Mario,* ed. Duke Litta Visconti-Arese (New York: Scribners, 1909), p. 67.
22. Frank J. Coppa, *Camilli di Cavour* (New York: Twayne Publishers, 1973), pp. 51–3.

CHAPTER THREE
The Origins of the First War of Italian Independence

The death of Pope Gregory XVI in early June 1846, during the sixteenth year of his pontificate, compounded the threat of revolutionary upheaval. Fearing disorder, Metternich's ambassador assured the Papal government that it could rely upon Austrian assistance, should it be required; meanwhile measures were taken to reinforce the army in Lombardy. When the conclave to elect a successor to Gregory opened on the evening of 14 June 1846, Cardinal Luigi Lambruschini, the former Secretary of State, and the first choice of the conservatives as well as the Austrians, emerged as the leading contender. During the course of the next three ballots, however, Lambruschini's vote declined, while that of the Archbishop of Imola, Giovanni Maria Mastai-Ferretti, increased. On 16 June 1846 Mastai-Ferretti was elected Pope, assuming the name Pius IX (or Pio Nono in Italian), in memory of Pius VII.

Metternich and his government, recognizing the need for reform in the Papal States, did not attempt to veto this selection, as some later charged. Nonetheless, some questioned the choice of a figure untrained in statesmanship amid the present political complications. Thus, while the press in London, Paris, Madrid, Brussels, Florence and even Constantinople exalted the merits of the new Pope, Vienna had reservations. Whereas the Pope's affability, warmth and spontaneity fanned his own subjects' ardour, north of the Alps it caused a chill.[1] Metternich criticized the first actions of Pius IX, which confirmed the new Pope's liberal reputation. Above all, Metternich feared the consequences of his general amnesty of 16 July 1846, which provoked a collective delirium in Rome, paving the way for Pio Nono's portrayal as an apostle of liberty and an angel sent to regenerate the country of Caesar. Comparing the amnesty to an invitation to thieves to enter one's home, Metternich considered the Pope's political leniency a mistake, noting that God pardoned, but did not grant amnesties. Vienna's qualms intensified as the demonstrations and jubilation greeting reforms in Rome assumed a decidedly patriotic and anti-Austrian tone. Increasingly, the cry 'Long live Pius' was coupled with the call for 'Death to the Germans', and 'A free Italy'. Giuseppe Garibaldi, from Montevideo, proclaimed Pius the political Messiah of the peninsula, and the Pope was deemed the figure heralded by Gioberti to liberate Italy. Indeed, the latter declared that with the reign of Pio Nono a new age had begun for the peninsula and the world.[2] The Austrians, wedded to the status quo, looked with suspicion upon developments in the Eternal City.

Pio Nono loved Italy and prayed it would be regenerated gradually. Considering himself a priest with a religious mission, rather than a Washington or Bolivar, he was surprised at the enthusiasm which his election and early reformism unleashed. Oblivious to the consequences of his cordiality towards the liberals and nationalists persecuted by his predecessor, he in fact had no intention of launching the crusade for the liberation and unification of the peninsula so desired by the patriots. He assured the French Ambassador, Pellegrino Rossi, that he could not plunge into such utopian schemes. Still, his selection of Cardinal Pasquale Tommaso Gizzi as Secretary of State, lionized as a liberal by Massimo D'Azeglio in his *Degli ultimi casi di Romagna*, heartened the liberals and nationalists alike. Carlo Alberto praised the appointment, mistakenly assuming that the Pope would begin a war against Austria.[3] The awakening of Italian national aspirations distressed the Austrians.

In Vienna Metternich resented the unbounded enthusiasm generated by the election of Pius IX and the agitation it aroused in Piedmont. The Austrian Chancellor recollected that Piedmontese writers such as Vincenzo Gioberti and Cesare Balbo had long sought to inspire Italians by contrasting the splendour of their past with the alleged degradation of the present. At the moment Massimo D'Azeglio had assumed first place among those Piedmontese writers holding Austria responsible for the peninsula's plight, and championing its regeneration. He saw little difference between figures such as Balbo, Gioberti and D'Azeglio, who attacked the peace with the poison of their words, and Mazzini and his followers who had recourse to the dagger. The protection which Carlo Alberto afforded these writers convinced Metternich more than anything else, that the king might abandon the conservative course that had characterized the first fifteen years of his reign.[4]

Increasingly, the anti-Austrian, pro-Italian sentiments of the Piedmontese king unfolded. During the course of a private interview granted D'Azeglio a year earlier, he posed no objections when his visitor insisted that without force nothing could be achieved in Italy, and Piedmont represented the only force in the peninsula. Indeed, the king surprised D'Azeglio by promising that at an appropriate moment he would devote his life, his children's lives, his sword, his treasury and his army to champion the cause of Italy.[5] By the end of 1846, the tension between Turin and Vienna became public, as the two states disagreed about the Austro-Piedmontese Trade Treaty of 1751 and the salt trade with Switzerland. Despite Austrian protests, and their steep increase in the custom duties on Piedmontese wines sent to Lombardy, Carlo Alberto would not be cowed, and his resistance aroused the expectations of patriots. Thus a series of misunderstandings had emerged between Vienna and Turin, as well as Vienna and Rome.

Metternich charged that Italian revolutionists sought consolidation and confederation as a means of pushing out the Austrians and achieving unification. He accused Pellegrino Rossi, who was then the French Ambassador to Rome, of conspiring with the nationalists, and perhaps placing the support of his government behind the radical schemes. Vienna looked askance at Pio Nono's overtures to the other princes, and Piedmont in particular, to forge a tariff league to preserve the tranquillity of the peninsula. Although Pio Nono's aims were pacific, he did see the league as a means of sustaining the rights of the princes.[6] While the Pope may have had the domestic situation in mind, Metternich feared that the Piedmontese would exploit the proposed league to extend their influence in Italy at Austria's expense. His assessment proved accurate.

Vienna perceived Piedmontese ambitions in its 'pandering' to national sentiments. The Turin government allowed the members of the Italian congress, meeting in Genoa in September 1846, to make a series of patriotic pronouncements, virtually proclaiming Carlo Alberto co-director with Pio Nono of the national movement. In order to further arouse the Austrians, the Genoese were permitted to publicly commemorate the centenary of their expulsion of the Austrians. The Lombards did not escape the anti-Austrian contagion, expressing their national sentiments in Milan in December 1846, during the funeral of Count Federico Confalonieri, who had been imprisoned in the Spielberg prison. Italian patriots debated as to how far they could go without provoking a premature Austrian intervention.

From London, 'the Master', Giuseppe Mazzini, pressed for a radical solution, urging his friends to unite the masses in patriotic rallies to make them aware of their potential power. They need not meekly accept what had been accorded, he argued, but should demand more fundamental change. Eventually Mazzini hoped this would inspire a people's war against Austria, which was the precondition for the Italian republic he envisioned. The moderate Massimo D'Azeglio, who had begun his political career in the 1840s under the guidance of his cousin, Count Cesare Balbo, disagreed. He cautioned the population of the Romagna not to push the Pope too far, lest reform lead to revolution, and then reaction. He advised avoiding any pretext for Austrian intervention and the occupation of additional Italian territory. Italians had to behave like thieves in the countryside, he wrote, going as far as they could without waking the watchdog.[7] Unfortunately for the peninsula's patriots, the Austrians were wide awake, monitoring the Italian situation, and determined to preserve their dominance in the region.

Thus, with the encouraging developments in Rome and Turin, the year 1847 opened with the promise of further progress. Even Mazzini, sceptical of the promises of princes, wrote to Pio Nono, urging him to champion Italian rights. Not all, however, were inebriated by the popularity of Pio Nono, the increasing daring displayed by Carlo Alberto, the frantic demonstrations and the prospect of impending change. The national current was opposed by the dukes of Parma and Modena, closely associated with the Habsburg Empire, and Ferdinando II of Naples, who resisted the call for constitutional government and national reorganization.

Austria, profoundly distrustful of Italian intentions, stood poised for action. Cardinal Gizzi, whose undeserved liberal reputation did not reflect his true centrist and quasi-conservative leanings, shared the Austrian Chancellor's concern. Distressed by the disorders in Rome, and the government's loss of authority, he confided to the Sardinian representative, Domenico Pareto, that if things spiralled out of control any further, he would feel constrained to call for Habsburg intervention. Shortly thereafter Gizzi informed the Austrians that since the Pope had consented to the creation of a national guard, which he deemed of dubious loyalty, and therefore dangerous, the Papal government might find itself in the unfortunate position of having to invoke Austrian assistance. Later the Secretary of State absolved Pius of any responsibility for the unpopular step by claiming he took this action on his own initiative, without consulting the Pope.[8]

The British did not share the apprehensions of the continental conservatives. Richard Cobden, travelling in Italy, urged reforms and the promotion of a tariff union. His views were, in part, shared by the British Foreign Office, which deemed Austrian hostility to Italian reformism understandable, but unfortunate. The British believed reformism the best means of averting revolution. To encourage the Piedmontese to resist Austrian opposition, and encourage constitutionalism in Florence and Rome, Lord Minto, the British Lord Privy Seal and member of the Cabinet, was sent on a special mission to Italy in 1847. His task was to remind the Sardinian king that he could rely upon Her Majesty as a 'true and disinterested friend'. At the same time, however, Minto was to caution prudence to avoid exciting the apprehension of the great powers, and above all, Austria.[9]

In the summer of 1847, the Austrian Commander in Italy, General Johann Josef Radetzky decided to reinforce his troops. By the terms of Article 103 of the Treaty of Vienna, Austria had the right to maintain forces in the 'place' of Ferrara, and since 1815 had garrisoned some thousand soldiers in its fortresses. On 17th July a corps of over 800 Croats crossed the Po in full war regalia, giving the Cardinal Legate only a day's notice. The surprised residents, convinced that Metternich wished to intimidate the Pope, discourage further reforms and encourage the conservatives, revealed their displeasure. The Austrian military responded by occupying the areas surrounding the barracks, outside the citadel. This promoted a protest from the Cardinal Legate, Cardinal Luigi Ciacchi, which the new Secretary of State, Cardinal Gabriele Ferretti, had published in Rome. Massimo D'Azeglio hastily drafted a pamphlet denouncing the Austrian action, which apparently had the approval of the Pope. Although he perceived himself a prince of peace, Pius recognized his responsibility to preserve the independence and integrity of the States of the Church. In Turin, Carlo Alberto let it be known that if providence provoked a war for the independence of Italy, he was prepared.

Metternich realized that the recent events and public excitement threatened the status quo in Italy, and called upon England, France, Russia and Prussia to join with Austria in maintaining the territorial division of the Italian peninsula resolved at Vienna. Charging that the party in control in Rome sought to establish a unitary state in Italy, Metternich indicated that the Austrian Emperor, determined to preserve his Italian territories, would not permit Italian unification. Palmerston, disturbed by Austria's attitude and actions, submitted a stern note to the Austrian Ambassador in London. He revealed that England regarded the independence and integrity of the Roman states as essential for the independence of the Italian peninsula, and opposed any invasion or infringement of its sovereignty which would compromise its position. Asserting that he had no information concerning a scheme for uniting the various states of Italy into a Federal Republic, Palmerston attributed the recent discontent not to utopian ambitions, but the real abuses plaguing the Italian states.[10] London's assessment that limited reformism would eliminate the agitation in Italy did not reassure Vienna. Metternich assumed that the Italians wanted more, and were plotting a war against Austria.

During the course of 1847, the Powers differed on the Italian question. Division existed not only among the conservative, eastern powers, but also between the more liberal, Western states of England and France. Metternich complained that under the guise of administrative reforms the sects sought to subvert the existing order and create an Italian state. The British government disagreed, Palmerston claiming that the reforms granted or contemplated in Rome and in Tuscany, tended to counteract any dangerous delusions.[11] Both the Austrians and the British sought to influence the position of the French in this matter, with Metternich proving more successful than Palmerston.

Although Guizot pledged his support for reformism in Rome before the French Chamber, Metternich's request to uphold the status quo in Italy was seconded by the French. In the Franco-Austrian agreement concluded in the spring of 1847, the two powers promised to maintain the territorial status quo, to oppose revolutionary agitation, and to approve administrative, but not far-reaching political innovations. France no less than Austria deemed the Italian states and people too immature for constitutional government. This Vienna–Paris axis, which discouraged political change, understandably led to frustration in the peninsula. The Piedmontese, appraised of the French position, resented the rumours that Pio Nono's reformism was stimulated by the French, when the opposite was the case.

Rossi, the French Ambassador in Rome, was instructed to prevent Pius from taking steps which might displease Austria. Guizot alerted his ambassador that their government required good relations with Austria, predicting that conflict would lead to a general upheaval in Europe. The Piedmontese, in turn, were warned to abandon any expansionist design in Italy, lest they provoke a watchful Austria, whom they would have to confront without French help. Regarding the Ferrara incident, France tacitly recognized Habsburg rights and stood shoulder to shoulder with them against the transformation of the Papal States into a constitutional regime.[12]

French support of the anti-reformist Austrian policy disturbed the liberal English Cabinet. Palmerston suspected that Austria secretly encouraged disturbances of the public peace in the peninsula to produce a pretext for intervention against the progressive changes initiated in Rome and Turin. Her Majesty's Government remained convinced that the Italian states should pursue a series of timely reforms to eliminate the evils that bred discontent. Thus Lord Minto in his mission to Turin, Florence and Rome, was instructed to counterbalance the aggressive Austrian interference in the internal affairs of the states of the peninsula. In Turin Minto informed Carlo Alberto that the British government felt 'surprise and regret' at Austrian interference, and approved of Sardinia's friendly attitude towards the reformism of Pio Nono. Minto promised his government would block any Austrian action that compromised the independence of the States of the Church. Carlo Alberto, in turn, vowed that he and his sons would defend the cause of the Holy Father with their blood, should circumstances warrant such action.[13]

The prospect of Austrian intervention against reformism in Italy promoted closer collaboration between Piedmont and the Papal States. In July 1847 the two consolidated their commercial relations by means of a reciprocal trade agreement. Rome also appreciated Piedmontese support during the Austrian occupation of Ferrara. Pius confessed to Pareto, the Piedmontese Ambassador in Rome, that he considered the Habsburg action arrogant and illegal. The Pope divulged that he would despatch troops to the area to observe the Austrians, but not to wage war, while awaiting the outcome of his diplomatic initiative. Massimo D'Azeglio was among the patriots who marched north with the Papal Volunteers to assume their watchful waiting. Should the Austrians prove obstinate and refuse to end their illegal occupation, Pius threatened to launch all the spiritual weapons at his disposal against them.[14] Nationalists applauded the Pope's resolution and recourse to spiritual arms; nevertheless, they invoked material means to counter Austrian pretensions.

Pius, who lacked a dependable military force of his own, looked for closer cooperation among the various Italian states. A memorial of the Secretariat of State stressed that the individual Italian states had succumbed to foreign influence due to their divisions. While they were sovereign and completely independent under international law, in reality they fell under the sway of the great powers. This led to the situation, alluded to by Metternich, whereby Italy had deteriorated into a geographic expression. Only Italian cooperation could remedy the situation. A tariff league was proposed by the Pope, and seconded by the Marquis Pareto, the Sardinian Minister in Rome. Pius apparently perceived the tariff league as the first step towards a more far-reaching political agreement, and looked forward to having the strongest state in the peninsula sustain the rights of the weakest.[15]

Pius commissioned the pro-Italian Monsignor Giovanni Corboli Bussi to undertake a special mission to the courts of Florence and Turin, to secure their adherence to the projected league. Corboli Bussi found the Grand Duke Leopoldo of Tuscany receptive to the papal initiative, claiming that the proposed league would help separate the moderates from Mazzini's Young Italy, giving satisfaction to the reasonable request for some form of unity, without falling prey to the utopian schemes of the radicals. Perhaps to counter the conclusion of the league, Vienna offered to place 5,000 soldiers at the Grand Duke's disposal. It was an offer that was not accepted. Instead Leopoldo agreed to enter the tariff league and, following his decision, showed himself more frankly Italian at court. Corboli Bussi, wishing to reconcile religion and liberty, wrote to the Pope informing him of the anti-Austrian feeling in the peninsula and stressing that the tariff league, by its concessions to national sentiments, would perhaps help to mitigate the discontent. The papal emissary then moved to Turin to secure Carlo Alberto's adherence to the league.

Following his first conference with the Piedmontese king, Monsignor Corboli Bussi concluded that Carlo Alberto had an agenda of his own, and would be more difficult to bring on board than the Grand Duke of Tuscany. In response to Carlo Alberto's queries about the Pope's policies, Corboli Bussi indicated that Pius aimed to make revolution unlikely. Noting that the revolutionaries wished to push all of Italy into a unitary republic, he disavowed the plan, but observed that there was something noble in the nationalist aspiration. A prudent prince, he continued, knew how to satisfy reasonable requests, leaving the radicals with what was manifestly impossible. Early on, the moderate decision to champion Italian interests reflected not only national aspirations, but the need to frustrate radical designs.

The Piedmontese king, distressed by the pressure for concessions placed on him by the Roman example, blurted out that the Pope had done enough for his subjects. However, he was willing to consider entry into the Pope's tariff league, referring to his pledge to place his forces at the disposal of the Holy Father, should Austria prove difficult. Monsignor Corboli Bussi, assessing the king's attitude and behaviour, surmised that Carlo Alberto wished to avoid making concessions to his subjects and preferred to preserve his liberal reputation by championing the Pope's independence *vis-à-vis* Austria. The Monsignor also sensed that the Piedmontese king sought to expand his state at the expense of the small Austrian-dominated duchies of north central Italy.[16]

It was an accurate assessment of Carlo Alberto's thoughts and intentions. The enigmatic king voiced his opposition to anything contrary to the maxims of his Catholicism, but confessed that his heart quickened its beat at the thought of Italian independence from the foreigner.[17] His present actions did not, however, match his words. His vacillations, hesitation in liberalizing the administration, and painfully cautious approach towards Austria provoked criticism. Vincenzo Gioberti noted early in October 1847, that there was an increasing dissatisfaction with the pace of Carlo Alberto's reformism and his continuing irresolution. Gioberti decried the fact that while Austria insulted Rome and threatened the independence of all the Italian princes, the Piedmontese did nothing. When the Piedmontese king violently suppressed a popular demonstration in Turin which aimed to praise the king and Pius IX, one of the demonstrators wrote a poem denouncing 'The Vacillating Monarch'.

Monsignor Corboli Bussi, who still pressed for the conclusion of the tariff league, witnessed first-hand the tortuous course of the king. During his second formal interview with Carlo Alberto, the Piedmontese ruler boasted that he and His Holiness were the only two princes in the peninsula that were really Italian, but unfortunately their states were not contiguous, being separated by a series of Austrian bases. The king recounted that his forces were at the disposal of the Pope, pledging that his people would rise *en masse* on behalf of his noble and just cause. On the issue of the tariff league, the king reported that his minister, De Revel, was studying its financial considerations prior to examining the political implications. Carlo Alberto promised that everything possible would be done to secure its approval and implementation.

In his campaign to draw the Piedmontese into the League, Monsignor Corboli Bussi reported that Italian unity and independence was now so much in the minds and hearts of the Italians that it was impossible to extinguish the flame. The Monsignor argued that the real question was who would assume direction of this inevitable movement; the princes or the agitators? Would it be effected in such a manner as to assure peace and stability for the Italian thrones, or would it be undertaken as a destructive force? The Monsignor argued that the Pope's projected league had brought the immense benefit of taming Italian nationalism, placing it under the direction of the princes, rather than the demagogues. The Papal envoy warned that time was of the moment, and the channelling of this nationalism by means of the league, presently possible, might not be viable in six months. If the Italian princes listened to the voice of their common father, they could avert the disaster which might topple their thrones.[18]

Despite the exhortations of the Monsignor, Carlo Alberto remained irresolute. The Marquis Emanuele Pes Di Villamarina confided to Corboli Bussi that the king purposely kept his ministry divided into diverse political factions, retaining the option of moving in one direction or the other. The Monsignor wrote to Pius that not only was the Piedmontese ministry divided, but the country as well. One part was conservative and Catholic, the other liberal, with Solaro della Margarita reflecting the Catholic and conservative sentiments, and Villamarina the liberal ones. Paradoxically the liberal elements supported the Pope's league, while the Catholic conservative bloc had reservations.

The king, meanwhile, remained indecisive. In the light of French reluctance to support an Italian war of independence against the Habsburgs, and his realization that the Piedmontese army alone would not suffice, Carlo Alberto appreciated the need for a measure of popular enthusiasm. A crusade on behalf of Pio Nono and the Church could arouse the dormant masses without endangering the peninsula's social order. Hence he insisted that Piedmont and Italy required more than a tariff league, pressing for the conclusion of a political union with a decidedly anti-Austrian bias. The Papal Envoy, discussing the king's proposal with the Tuscan representatives, wondered if Carlo Alberto's complaint that the league did not go far enough, was an expedient to reject the Papal overture while retaining his position in the liberal camp. The Piedmontese continued to push the Romans and the Tuscans to go further than they had originally intended, emphasizing the need for a political league in the light of the circumstances afflicting the peninsula.

Monsignor Corboli Bussi, questioned about his instructions on the conclusion of a political league, responded that common political principles, a unity of action in reform and a system of reciprocal security, were benefits the Pope believed would flow from the tariff agreement. The Papal Envoy noted that a fusion of financial interests would have far-reaching implications, admitting he had not received instructions on rendering explicit what he believed was implicit in the projected tariff league. He personally felt that upon the approval of this agreement, there might be a codicil specifying that the signatory princes respectively assured the quiet and integrity of their states from internal and external disturbances. Clearly the Pope's representative recognized the political implications of the Pope's projected agreement, claiming that the King of Piedmont was being offered a position in Italy which Prussia would love to have in Germany. Not only the fate of the league was at issue, but who should be supreme in Italy – Austria or Piedmont. The Pope as arbiter was offering the mantle of leadership to Piedmont, warning the king that if he chose not to assume it, then the opportunity might vanish.[19]

Carlo Alberto moved cautiously, waiting for the chance to wage his war against Austria, rather than for an invitation to enter a nebulous economic agreement. Furthermore, he had reservations about joining with some of the other princes whom he considered Austrian in sentiment, especially his brother-in-law, Leopoldo of Tuscany. While he appreciated the advantage of having the Italian princes coordinate their concessions to their subjects, he perceived this as only a first step. In exchange for his adherence to the Pope's tariff league, the king insisted on the formation of a political union to assure the preservation of Italian reformism against all possible opposition. Meanwhile, a clear signal that the Piedmontese king was prepared to pursue a more liberal and national policy was given on 9 October 1847, when Carlo Alberto dismissed the cautious, conservative and peaceful Count Solaro della Margarita, who had directed Piedmontese foreign policy for the past twelve years.

Monsignor Corboli Bussi, much more sympathetic to the national cause than his sovereign, recognized that the Piedmontese offer of a political agreement for the independence of Italy, placed the Papal States in a difficult position. Should Italians learn of the Piedmontese offer, and suspect a Papal rejection, this would undermine their moral position in the peninsula. Furthermore, his instructions from the Secretariat of State to negotiate among the Italian Princes, in order to satisfy the honest desires of their populations as well as to compromise the disorderly movements, led the Monsignor to conclude that he could simultaneously negotiate a political as well as a tariff league. This broad interpretation of his instructions, which met the conditions of the Piedmontese, was corrected by a despatch from the Secretariat of State (9 October 1847) that he negotiate only the economic accord.[20] Although disappointed, Corboli Bussi adhered scrupulously to the Pope's instructions.

Carlo Alberto was also disappointed, but did not end negotiations for the league, having finally committed himself to the liberal and national cause. The Earl of Minto wrote to Palmerston on 8 October 1847 that Carlo Alberto had personally assured him of his determination to proceed on the path of reform, enumerating the measures already matured or in progress.[21] On 30 October 1847, the king issued the decree containing a number of long-awaited reforms, including the election of communal and provincial councillors, increased equality in the penal and judicial system, and greater freedom of the press. The last provision inspired political journalism in Piedmont, as had a similar concession earlier in Rome. Vienna's remaining illusion that Carlo Alberto could be kept on a conservative course was shattered. Anticipating the opening of a national war of liberation against Austria, the Piedmontese sought to prepare the political and military ground for the impending conflict.

The negotiations for the tariff league continued, and in mid-October Carlo Alberto agreed to its conclusion. Although the Piedmontese king finally accepted the narrower trade agreement, he expressed the expectation that it would also advance matters in the political realm. The Papal representative responded that implementing what was presently practical and useful for Italian unity, would prove highly political. This reassurance was insufficient for the Piedmontese king, who indicated his intention of informing the Austrian Minister that he would brook no interference in the states of Italy.[22] While Pius IX perceived the league primarily as a means of averting revolutionary agitation, Carlo Alberto thought in terms of his military confrontation with Austria.

On 3 November, 1847, the Customs League Treaty was signed by representatives of the States of the Church, Piedmont–Sardinia and the Grand Duchy of Tuscany by Monsignor Corboli Bussi, domestic prelate of His Holiness, Count Emolao Asinari di San Marzano, the Foreign Minister of Piedmont, and the Cavalier Giulio Martini, Chamberlain of the Grand Duke of Tuscany and Duke of Lucca. They favoured the well-being of Italy by the fusion of the material interests of their respective populations. Article 3 of the agreement made provision for the appointment of representatives from the three contracting powers to discuss the implementation of the agreement, following the adherence of the King of Sicily and the Duke of Modena. These last two rulers, who were invited to join, replied evasively. Perhaps their reticence stemmed from their realization that the Customs League Treaty was perceived as a first step towards federation.

From the moment the Piedmontese and the Romans joined in the customs union, they thought of forming a political league that would serve as a nucleus for Italian nationality, while providing Italy with the means for its defence. With that aim in mind, a draft proposal was produced for the consideration of the contracting parties. The first article of the projected political alliance called for a perpetual confederation among the States of the Church, the Grand Duchy of Tuscany, and the Kingdom of Sardinia, guaranteeing the territories of the participating powers while assuring their perpetual and peaceful development. The second article provided that the Holy Father, mediator and initiator of the league and the confederation, and his successors, would serve as presidents of the confederation. Article 3 noted that a month after ratification, representatives of the three confederated states would meet in Rome to establish a federal constitution.

Article 4 of the proposed political agreement stipulated that the federal constitution would create the organization of a central power in the form of a permanent diet in Rome. Among the principal duties of the diet were the power to declare war and peace, and to supervise the forces of the member states required either for internal security or for external independence. These measures were included to satisfy Carlo Alberto who anticipated a war against Austria. Additionally, the diet was charged with regulating the tariff of the confederation, while providing an equitable distribution of the expenses and entries among the states. It was also entrusted with directing the negotiation and conclusion of treaties of commerce and navigation with outside powers, while creating a mechanism for the mediation and resolution of conflicts among the member states. Finally, the diet was to assure the uniformity of monetary systems, weights and measures, and military discipline, while safeguarding the conformity of political, penal, civil and procedural legislation.[23]

The projected Italian political league was supported by *Il Risorgimento*, the newspaper founded in December 1847 in Turin by Camillo Di Cavour, Cesare Balbo, Pietro Di Santarosa and other liberal moderates. Their programme called for independence and a league of Italian princes. In January 1848, Cavour, the editor of the journal, arguing that the salvation of the fatherland could only be achieved by her legitimate monarchs, urged Carlo Alberto to grant a *Statuto* or constitution. Giacomo Durando, who returned from his exile to Piedmont and founded the journal *L'Opinione*, supported Cavour's request. Disturbances in Sicily, public discontent in Lombardy, a growing anti-Jesuit agitation following the publication of Gioberti's *Gesuita Moderna* and the pervasive hatred of Austria troubled conservatives and led them to question whether reform prevented or encouraged revolution.

The year 1848 opened with turmoil in Milan, where the boycott of tobacco and the state lottery provoked disturbances and led to a cavalry charge upon the unarmed citizenry. The Lombard Congregation, having little power beyond the right to petition the Crown, called for an investigation. At the other end of the peninsula in Palermo, tremors erupted from the volcanic soil of Sicily. Initially calling for a civic guard, in January 1848 protesters in Palermo escalated their demands. An ultimatum was transmitted to Ferdinando to restore the constitution of 1812 by 12th January, his birthday – or face the consequences. When the women of the city approached the viceroy's palace on the morning of 12th January, it was to learn that their demands had been rejected. An uprising ensued which soon engulfed other parts of the island. Resorting first to repression, the government soon changed its tune, and on 29 January 1848, Ferdinando published the bases of a common Constitution for Naples and Sicily. The City of the Vespers lit a torch threatening to ignite all of Italy, and to the Austrians the Italian situation looked serious indeed.

In Turin Carlo Alberto responded to the petitions of the municipal council and the pleadings of Cavour in the *Risorgimento* by his proclamation granting a *Statuto*. Metternich was hardly reassured by the assertion in the *Risorgimento* of 9 February 1848 that the king, in granting his people a constitution, had increased his influence in Italian and European affairs more than had he doubled the size of his army. On 11th February, the Grand Duke of Tuscany found he could no longer deny his people a constitution, and the next day the Pope created a new government dominated largely by laymen. Even in Rome there was talk of constitutionalism. Metternich was shocked that the Pope permitted celebrations in his capital for the triumph of constitutionalism in Naples, concluding that the Papal government endured such festivities, because it lacked the power to prohibit them.[24]

Metternich predicted that the age of liberalism in Italy, and the reforms passed under its veil, would soon end, and the radicals and revolutionaries would emerge undisguised. He did not second Guizot's suggestion that Austria intervene in Italy, fearing that this would lead her into an ambush. Imperial forces would respond if the Pope appealed for assistance and if there were a general consensus among the powers that Austria should move to preserve order. Nonetheless, Austria remained alert to the danger in Italy, reinforcing her troops there, while the energetic Field Marshal Radetzky, despite his eighty-two years, prepared to confront all who challenged Habsburg authority. On 22nd February, he declared a state of siege in Venice, and leaders of the national party, such as Daniele Manin and Nicolò Tommaseo, were thrust into prison.

Metternich discarded the possibility of a peaceful Italian liberalism, forecasting anarchy, revolution and war.[25] As Austrian hostility to Italian developments became increasingly apparent, there was the call for the princes of the peninsula to prepare for military measures to defend their position. Massimo D'Azeglio argued in the columns of the *Risorgimento* that even the Pope, as a temporal sovereign, had the obligation to defend his territory and people against Austrian pretensions. As Pope he was minister of charity, justice and peace, but as a prince he assumed the responsibility of defending the public order against its enemies. Cavour concurred, noting that in the past Pius had protested against Austrian aggression, and in the process defended the principle of Italian independence.[26]

Within his own state, Pius found a mounting fear of Austrian intervention, prompting the call for military readiness. When the independence of a state was menaced by a potent enemy, the *Circolo Romano* (a radical club) petitioned the *Consulta,* to allow the people had the sacred right to assure their own defence.[27] The *Consulta* agreed, and asked the government to organize a military force, calling upon Carlo Alberto to supply an expert to assist the pontifical regime. Pius, however, advised calm and cautioned restraint, denouncing the attempt to agitate the people of Italy into a foreign war. He reassured his subjects that if he were threatened, Catholics worldwide would spring to his defence, providing a safeguard for Italians as well. Within this framework he blessed Italy, and her most precious gift – the Catholic faith. However, this benediction was taken out of context, and given a nationalist and anti-Austrian tone which the Pope had not intended.

As the clamour for war against Austria mounted, Pius looked for increased cooperation with the other constitutional monarchs in the tariff league. The ministers of Austria, Prussia and Russia, he informed his friend, Cardinal Amat, had expressed their displeasure to those monarchs who had granted constitutions. Now, more than ever, the Holy Father appreciated the need to act in concert with the states of the Italian League.[28] He wrote to Leopoldo of Tuscany that from the first he believed that the customs union would evolve eventually into a political league whose objectives were defensive rather than offensive. These were the instructions he provided his diplomatic representatives in Turin, Florence and Naples, charged with completing the accord. Realizing that he, too, could not avoid constitutionalism, Pius indicated that the political league would be formed by the main Italian powers: the Papal States, Naples, Tuscany and Piedmont, which little by little were being transformed into constitutional regimes.

The Grand Duke of Tuscany shared the Pope's vision, and wrote to Carlo Alberto imploring him to conclude the political union which the Piedmontese king had earlier proposed. Like Pius, Leopoldo believed that the constitutional regimes could best defend themselves by means of a defensive league, and urged its immediate approval. However, Carlo Alberto, having more aggressive aims, gave a tardy and evasive response. Psychologically committed to a national war of liberation against Austria, and coveting part of the territories of the duchies, the Piedmontese king could not afford to be burdened by a defensive alliance under the Pope's leadership.

The vacillations of the Italian monarchs were, however, overtaken by events. On 24 February 1848 there was a revolution in Paris which resulted in the flight of King Louis Philippe to London. The provisional government which followed declared its peaceful intentions, but indicated that should a number of oppressed nationalities seek to remove the chains which bound them, France reserved the right to guard their legitimate aspirations. Italians had no sooner learned of developments in France, when word spread of the students' revolution in Vienna and the flight of Metternich, the high priest of the status quo and the arch-enemy of Italian independence. Soon after, the people of Milan rose in rebellion against their occupation, triggering the First Italian War of Independence.

NOTES

1. *Mémoires, documents et écrits divers laissés par le Prince de Metternich*, ed. Prince Richard Metternich with the papers arranged and classified by M.A. de Klinkowstroem (Paris: Plon, 1880–84), VII, 246–8; Angelo Filipuzzi, *Pio IX e la politica austriaca in Italia del 1815 al 1848 (nella relazione di Ricardo Weiss di Starkenfels)* (Florence: Felice Le Monnier, 1958), p. 131.
2. Dispatch of Apostolic Nuncio in Vienna to the Papal Secretary of State transmitting Metternich's report on Central Italy, *Archivio Segreto del Vaticano, Archivio Particolare Pio IX, Ogetti Vari*, no. 412; *Mémoires . . . Metternich*, VII, p. 255; Giovanni Maioli (ed), *Pio IX da vescovo a Pontefice, Lettere al Card. Luigi Amat. Agosto 1839–Luglio 1848* (Modena: Società Modenese, 1943), p. 59.
3. George F. Berkeley and Joan Berkeley, *Italy in the Making, 1815–1848* (Cambridge: Cambridge University Press, 1932–40), II, p. 44.
4. *Mémoires . . . Metternich*, VII, pp. 298–300, 407–8.

5. Massimo D'Azeglio, *I miei ricordi* (Milan: Rizzoli, 1956), p. 475.
6. Political Report on Central Italy sent by Metternich to Cardinal Gizzi (1846), *ASV, Archivio Particolare Pio IX, Ogetti Vari*, no. 412; Pius IX to Carlo Alberto, 6 October 1846, *ASV, Archivio Particolare Pio IX, Sovrani, Sardegna*; *Mémoires . . . Metternich*, VII, pp. 331, 339.
7. Luigi Rava (ed.), *Epistolario di Luigi Carlo Farini* (Bologna: Zanichelli, 1911), p. 570.
8. Romolo Quazza, *Pio IX e Massimo D'Azeglio nelle vicende romane del 1847* (Modena: Società Editrice Modenese, 1954), I, p. 168; II, p. 5.
9. *Parliamentary Debates*, 3rd series, vol. 95, 1059, 14 December 1847; *Posthumous Papers of Jessie White Mario: the Birth of Modern Italy*, ed. Duke Litta-Visconti-Arese (New York: Charles Scribner's Sons, 1909), p. 114.
10. Giacomo Martina, *Pio IX (1846–1850)* (Rome: Università Gregoriana Editrice, 1974), 146–150; Quazza, II, 148–9; Great Britain, *British and Foreign States Papers (BFSP), 1847–48)*, XXXVI, 1228–33.
11. Palmerston to Viscount Ponsonby, 13 August 1847, *BFSP, (1847–48)*, XXXVI, 1234.
12. Quazza, I, pp. 20, 120; Martina, p. 150; Filipuzzi, p. 176.
13. Lillian Parker Wallace, 'Pius IX and Lord Palmerston, 1846–1849', in L.P. Wallace and William C. Askew, *Power, Public Opinion and Diplomacy* (Durham, N. C.: Duke University Press, 1959), pp. 20, 30; Quazza, II, p. 156; Carlo Alberto to Pius IX, 26 September 1847, *ASV, Archivio Particolare Pio IX, Sovrani, Sardegna*, no. 63.
14. 'Convenzione conchiusa tra la Santità di Nostro Signore e Sua Maesta Carlo Alberto re di Sardegna sul commerio reciproco di ambi gli Stati,' *Atti del Sommo Pontefice Pio Nono. Felicement Regnante. Parte Seconda che comprende i motu-propri, chirografi, editi, notificazioni, ec per lo Stato Pontificio* (Rome: Tipografia delle Belle Arti, 1857), I, pp. 109–20; Quazza, II, pp. 81–2; 91–2.
15. Memorial Containing Considerations for the Project of a Confederation Among the Italian States, 1847, *ASV, Archivio Particolare Pio IX, Ogetti Vari*, no. 368; Quazza, II, pp. 148–9.
16. Monsignor Corboli Bussi to Pius IX, 30 August 1847, and 10 September 1847, *ASV, Archivio Particolare Pio IX, Sovrani, Stato Pontificio*; Palmerston to Ponsonby, 20 April 1847, *BFSP (1847–48)*, XXXVI, 1204–5.
17. Pietro Orsi, *Cavour and the Making of Modern Italy 1810–1861* (New York: G.P. Putnam's Sons, 1914), p. 85.
18. Monsignor Corboli Bussi to Pius IX, 16 September 1847 and 21 September 1847, *ASV, Archivio Particolare Pio IX, Sovrani, Stato Pontificio*.
19. Monsignor Corboli Bussi to Pius IX, 29 September 1847, *ASV, Archivio Particolare Pio IX, Sovrani, Stato Pontificio*.
20. Monsignor Corboli Bussi to Pius IX, 8 October 1847 and 14 October 1847, ASV, *Archivio Particolare Pio IX, Sovrani, Stato Pontificio*.
21. Earl of Minto to Palmerston, 8 October 1847, *BFSP (1847–47)*, XXXVI, 1293.
22. Monsignor Corboli Bussi to Pius IX, 16 October 1847 and 19 October 1847, *ASV, Archivio Particolare Pio IX, Sovrani, Stato Pontificio*.
23. Considerations on the project of a Confederation Among the Italian states, *ASV, Archivio Particolare Pio IX, Ogetti Vari*, no. 368.

24. 'Programma', *Il Risorgimento*, 15 December 1847: *Il Risorgimento*, 8 February 1848; *BFSP (1848–49)*, XXXVII, 856–857; *Mémoires . . . Metternich*, VII, pp. 592–3.

25. *Mémoires . . . Metternich*, VII, pp. 558–64.

26. *Il Risorgimento*, 14 January 1848 and 19 January 1848.

27. Luigi Carlo Farini, *Lo Stato Romano dall'anno 1815 al 1850* (3rd edn, Florence: Felice Le Monnier, 1853), I, p. 322.

28. *BFSP (1848–49)*, XXXVII, 866–7; Maioli, p. 116.

CHAPTER FOUR
The Revolutionary Upheaval and War of 1848–49

News of the students' revolution in Vienna of 13 March 1848, the paralysis of Austria and the resignation of the arch-enemy of Italian nationalists, Metternich, electrified Lombardy and Venetia. On the morning of 18th March, demonstrations for reform in Milan exploded into violence as barricades mushroomed against General Radetzky's occupying forces. The entire population of Milan, over 150,000 strong, seemed to turn against the general's garrison of 12,000. At the end of five days of fighting, the famous 'Cinque Giornate', Radetzky abandoned the capital of Lombardy. The Austrians fared no better in Venice where Daniele Manin, released from prison, secured control of the arsenal and the city of canals. Under the banner of 'Saint Mark and Italy' the Venetians pushed the Austrians out. As the Republic was proclaimed in the Great Piazza of Venice, the people in the duchies of Parma and Modena frightened their princes into departure, and the national programme suddenly triumphed.

The Austrian decision to evacuate Milan, and their setback in Venice, served as a signal to the rest of the peninsula, setting all Italy ablaze. Few remained calm in the midst of this cataclysm as the old world fell to pieces and the rock of absolutism splintered. Turmoil rocked the Italian Tyrol, and even the Habsburg Grand Duke of Tuscany felt constrained to raise the Italian standard. In Rome, where the double-headed Austrian eagle was stripped from the Palazzo Venezia, the Council of Ministers opened enlistment for volunteers for the impending war against Austria, and in the course of a few hours, thousands enscribed. Pio Nono, personally reluctant to sanction war against Catholic Austria, looked to the courts of Sardinia, Naples and Florence to regulate the Italian movement. While the Pontiff shied from a declaration of war, there were hints that he might be drawn into the conflict by the Italian League he had long promoted.[1]

Attention turned to Carlo Alberto of Piedmont who had assumed a new importance in the liberal movement by his publication of the *Statuto* on 4th March, and selection of Cesare Balbo as head of the first constitutional ministry, on 16th March. When General Franzini issued orders placing the Sardinian army on a war footing, word spread that the enigmatic monarch would soon redeem his pledge to champion the national cause against Austria. The Milanese counted on his support, and the very day their rebellion erupted, entreated immediate Piedmontese intervention. Carlo Alberto, weighing the advantages of victory against the dangers of making common cause with the democrats and revolutionaries of Milan, hesitated.

The King had to consider the national enthusiasm which the five days had unleashed, Piedmont's anti-Austrian sentiments and expansionist ambitions, as well as the prospect that his inactivity might lead to the creation of a republic in Lombardy, so jeopardizing the future of the House of Savoy. The Duke of Savoy, who later succeeded his father as King Vittorio Emanuele, pressed for war, as did the editors of the newspaper *Il Risorgimento*. Aroused by the heroism of their neighbouring Lombards, and the prospects for the creation of a unified kingdom of northern Italy, Camillo di Cavour called upon Carlo Alberto to wage war:

> The supreme hour for the monarchy of Savoy has arrived – the hour of firm decision, the time which will determine the fate of empires and people. In light of developments in Lombardy and Venetia, hesitations, doubt, delay are no longer possible; these of all policies, would be most calamitous. As men of cool judgment, accustomed to paying attention to the dictates of reason rather than the impulse of passion, we feel bound in conscience to declare, after carefully weighing our every word, that only one road is open to the nation, the government, the King. That way is war – immediately, without delay.[2]

On 23rd March, Carlo Alberto's forces crossed the River Ticino into Lombardy. While Piedmont's ambassadors sought to convince the conservative powers that the move into Lombardy was mandated by the need to preserve order and prevent the formation of a radical republic, a conflicting message was broadcast to the people of the peninsula. In his proclamation to the Lombards and Venetians, written by his minister, Federigo Sclopis di Salerano, the king promised to support their aspiration for independence. Revealing his intention of arousing the religious instincts of the peasantry, the king placed his trust in the God who had bestowed them with Pio Nono and provided Italy the opportunity to fulfil its destiny. His statement was altered to 'L'Italia farà da se' or 'Italy will do it alone', which became the national slogan in 1848.

At the end of March and early in April 1848, Italy appeared capable of achieving its national programme without foreign assistance. The Piedmontese forces, swelled by volunteers from Lombardy and Tuscany, advanced against the Austrians from the west. In Rome there was an explosion of enthusiasm for the national cause as the cry 'Out with the Barbarians!' resounded on its squares. The constitutional ministry of Cardinal Giacomo Antonelli decreed the formation of an army, under the Piedmontese General Giovanni Durando, permitting it to march northward. These regular forces were assisted by more than 12,000 volunteers, including two nephews of the Pope, led by Colonel Andrea Ferrari. Although Pius had not declared war against Austria, his proclamation of 30th March to the people of Italy, sounded like a prelude to a formal declaration. 'The events of these past two months, which have succeeded and pressed on each other with such rapid change, are not the work of man', wrote Pius. 'Woe to him who in this agitating wind which splits and breaks to pieces cedars and oaks, does not heed the voice of the Lord!'[3] Pio Nono's words were bolstered by actions as he and the religious congregations made generous donations to the Italian cause.

Naples, too, witnessed enthusiasm for the war of liberation. On 27th March, during the course of a public demonstration in favour of Italian independence, Ferdinando II pledged himself to the national cause. In his proclamation of 7th April to his countrymen, Ferdinando expressed his dedication to the liberation of the peninsula, committing his forces to the campaign. General Guglielmo Pepe, after twenty-seven years of exile, led a contingent of 14,000 Neapolitans to fight the Austrians. Leopoldo II of Tuscany also hastened to identify himself with the Italian crusade. Asserting that the cause of Italian independence would be decided on the plains of Lombardy, he contributed a Tuscan corps of 6,000 men.

In 1848 the diplomatic situation turned favourably towards the Italian cause. Tsar Nicholas, expected to make common cause with the Austrians, did not categorically oppose Italian autonomy, or even a Gallic extension of territory, so long as France allowed Russia a free hand in the east. The Parisian Assembly voted in favour of Italian independence, supporting a confederation of Italian states. Meanwhile Palmerston did not deem it convenient, if indeed possible, for Austria to preserve her Italian possessions to keep the French out of Italy. The creation of a liberal kingdom in northern Italy might better serve as a barrier and buffer. The English Foreign Secretary Palmerston perceived the Italian provinces not as a shield for the Habsburg Empire, but its Achilles heel.[4]

The military campaign likewise initially proceeded well for the Italians. On 26th March the vanguard of Carlo Alberto's army entered Milan, reaching Pavia a few days later. In early April General Bava crossed the Mincio to assume control of the right bank of the river. Nonetheless, errors were made. The first allowed General Radetzky to retreat from Milan without any hindrance, enabling him to seek refuge within the quadrilateral of the fortresses of Verona, Peschiera, Mantua and Legnano. Here he found security and supplies. Still matters might have been saved if an immediate attack had been launched against Mantua, at first defended by only a small force, and therefore vulnerable to a determined invasion. Unfortunately Carlo Alberto and the Piedmontese procrastinated, allowing Radetzky to transport reinforcements. Finally political – military errors were made in keeping a large part of the Piedmontese force in reserve, discouraging the use of volunteers and converting the national movement into a religious crusade. The latter assumed the compliance of Pio Nono, who proved absolutely opposed to converting the war of liberation into a religious struggle.

Although Pio Nono sensed the end of Austrian domination in Italy, from the first he had reservations about launching an attack upon that Catholic power. Minister of a God of peace, he hesitated lighting a torch that might well set all of Italy, and Europe, ablaze. The troops which the Pope permitted to march north were commanded to defend the frontier of their state, and warned against assuming an aggressive posture. Pius confessed to those around him that he would never allow his forces to cross the frontier; he had no legitimate reason for declaring a war against Austria. The Pope's ministers, who considered his participation in the war of national liberation crucial, believed it could be effected only through the Italian political league.

Carlo Alberto, bearing the brunt of the fighting against Austria, did not wish protracted negotiations to conclude a political league during the course of a decisive war. He invoked immediate military assistance, indicating that they could negotiate a political accord once the enemy had been beaten. The most he would concede was the conclusion of a straightforward military convention for the joint prosecution of the war, which did not satisfy Rome. Monsignor Corboli Bussi pleaded that Pius required the formation of a political league before entering a war which he was unwilling and unable to declare unilaterally. The Piedmontese, for their part, anxious to fulfil their century-old dream of extending their dominion over the entire valley of the Po, refused to tie their hands by the formation of the political union. Piedmont's reluctance for the federal solution, which the Neapolitans readily accepted, led the Pope to suspect her motives and ambitions.[5]

In April, as the war settled into one of position, and the need to dislodge Radetzky and the Austrians from the Quadrilatral loomed large, Carlo Alberto focused on military matters to the detriment of cementing a political alliance. The Piedmontese expected that the Pope could be cajoled into the war by popular pressure, ignoring his qualms of conscience and his primary concern of protecting the ship of Saint Peter. Perhaps with this thought in mind, on 5th April the Piedmontese commander of the Papal forces, General Giovanni Durando, issued a proclamation to his troops, claiming that the Holy Father blessed their swords, which, united with those of Carlo Alberto, would exterminate the enemies of both God and their country. Such a war, Durando concluded, was not only national but Christian, giving the war cry 'God wills it.'

When the Pope learned that Durando was leading his troops across the Po, contrary to his explicit instructions, and proclaiming him the principal author of the war, by giving it the semblance of a crusade, he was outraged. Pius determined to raise his voice to quiet the protests in Germany, avoiding the threat of a disastrous schism. In order to soothe the conscience of the Pontiff, and quiet his fears, his ministers inserted an article in the official gazette. 'A proclamation of April 5, to the soldiers in the field, expresses ideas and sentiments as if they emanated from the Pope', it read. Correcting this impression, the article made clear 'that when the Pope wishes to make a declaration of sentiment or position, he does so for himself, never through the words of a subaltern.'[6]

Pio Nono, caught between the dictates of his conscience, and the popular demand that he join the war of national liberation, looked to the league for deliverance. It could allow his state to participate in the war, absolving him of the responsibility of declaring or waging it. The pressing circumstances again led Pius to send Monsignor Corboli Bussi to Carlo Alberto to hasten the conclusion of the Italian league. Expressing doubts about which course to pursue, Pius found himself torn between the welfare of Italy and the needs of the Church. Meanwhile little progress was made in concluding the political league. Carlo Alberto exhorted the Pope to declare war against Austria, arguing as Durando had done, that their common aim was the independence of the *patria* and the triumph of their holy religion, both of which were oppressed.[7]

The Austrians sought to persuade the Pope to publicly denounce the notion that the national struggle was a religious crusade, and they found Pius sympathetic. The Pope confided that while delighted by the prospect of Carlo Alberto's success and the expansion of his realm, he resented the abuse of his name and the Holy Faith for secular designs. To set matters straight, Pius wished to reveal the religious scruples which prevented him from entering the war, but was momentarily restrained by his ministers, who feared the political consequences. As a wave of Italian nationalism swept over the peninsula, the Pope felt the need to resist the current that would embroil him in a conflict that jeopardized the welfare of the Church.[8]

Nationalists sought to persuade Pius to join the cause. On 26th April, Monsignor Corboli Bussi warned Pius that the Austrian Ambassador's presence in Rome and the Papal Nuncio's in Vienna conflicted with his mission to the Piedmontese. The patriotic priest encouraged the Pope to reveal his support for the War of Italian Independence, predicting that otherwise either the Austrians or the factions would triumph. The Monsignor implored the Pope to speak on behalf of the national cause, contending that Carlo Alberto could not succeed without his benediction.

Corboli Bussi presented the Pope with a plan of action, advising him to write to the Emperor of Austria pleading for an end to the war. Should his mediation prove futile, the Pope could then reveal to the world his exhortation for peace and the reasons why he, as an Italian sovereign, could not restrain his people from taking part in the common struggle of the Italians against the Austrians. The Monsignor suggested the Pope propose the following: (1) a recognition of Italian nationality without offending German nationalism; (2) an exhortation for peace without having the Pope serve as mediator of specific transactions; (3) a clear distinction between the Pope's role as common father of all Catholics and that of sovereign of the Papal States. Corboli Bussi predicted that if Pius restored the peace, he would be blessed by both Italians and Austrians.[9]

Terenzio Mamiani, who would soon succeed Cardinal Giacomo Antonelli as the Pope's chief minister, recognized that Papal reluctance to declare war on Austria stemmed from the intermingling of spiritual and temporal power. Mamiani proposed to spare the conscience of the Pope by having his constitutional ministers declare war, but the Pope refused to follow his plan. Marco Minghetti, Minister of Public

Works in the Pope's Cabinet, feared for the future of Italy should His Holiness abandon the national cause.

On 19 April 1848, Pius spoke to the Tuscan representative, Scipione Bargagli, explaining his distress at the diffusion of demagogic ideas and the threat of schism among the German Catholics. He discussed the central ideas of an allocution he planned to present to the Cardinals. On 27th April he wrote to his confidant, Monsignor Corboli Bussi, of his intention of letting the world know that he could not wage war against anyone.[10]

Pius made his position public on 29th April in an allocution which revealed that as common father, he could not declare war, although he could not prevent his subjects from entering the conflict as volunteers. Reaction in the Papal States and Italy was immediate and negative. The conservative, anti-nationalist Cardinal Lambruschini was one of the few in the peninsula to applaud the allocution, claiming that finally Pius had spoken like a Pope. Understandably, north of the Alps the allocution was received with relief, as the Austrians scrambled to bring it to public attention.[11] Perhaps to counter the Austrian attempt to use the allocution to influence Italian public opinion, Pius insisted in his clarification of 1st May that his position was neither anti-nationalist nor a betrayal of the Italian cause. He repeated the denial in his letter of 8th May to Cardinal Luigi Amat, insisting that he had not condemned Italian nationalism nor branded the war unjust, and complaining that he had been misinterpreted.

The Italians understood the consequences of the Pope's actions if they misjudged his intent. The Senate and the Council of Rome, in its special session of 3rd May, observed that the agitation which followed the allocution stemmed from the fact that all believed that the Pope, whatever his intentions, had delivered a fatal blow to the Italian cause. Constitutionalism in the Papal States was also jeopardized, as the Cabinet resigned over the war issue. The Council noted that Catholics listened reverently to the words of their spiritual leader, but they expected him to defend the temporal power. The ministers did not demand that the Pope, Nuncio of Peace, declare war upon Austria; rather they asked only that he should not stand in the way of those entrusted with temporal power.[12] To restore order, Pius accepted the liberal and pro-Italian Terenzio Mamiani's ministry on 4 May 1848.

While the allocution precipitated a crisis in Rome, the Piedmontese, on 30th April, scored their first major success in the Battle of Pastrengo (fought near Peschiera), pushing the Austrians back to Verona. Increased pressure was placed upon Pius to join the effort, and the Pope responded by sending a letter to the Austrian Emperor on May 3, imploring him to withdraw from a struggle in which he could not win the hearts of the Lombards. He did not threaten to enter the conflict should the Austrians refuse his initiative, nor did he promise Carlo Alberto that he would join him in the campaign, as Corboli Bussi suggested. Nonetheless, the Austrians resisted the Papal peace effort. Pius's liberal advisers urged him to allow his new ministry, under Mamiani, to declare the war the Pope could not himself initiate. Complaining that Carlo Alberto had acted unilaterally against the Austrians, the Pope did not feel committed to enter the conflict. Like other Italians, the Holy Father questioned the intentions of the Piedmontese troops who had as their war cry, 'Sempre avanti Savoja'.

The Mamiani Ministry in Rome continued to believe that the political league was the sole means of effecting Papal participation in the war, expressing this sentiment to the first Piedmontese parliament which opened on 8th May. It was a sentiment shared by Monsignor Corboli Bussi who seconded the efforts of Mamiani, including his distinction between Pius' actions as sovereign, and as head of the faith.[13] Turin, however, believed the war would shortly be won with or without the Pope's benediction. In mid-May this prospect seemed probable to the Austrians as well. Vienna considered invoking an English diplomatic effort to secure an armistice with Carlo Alberto on the basis of the renunciation of Lombardy, which had fallen, but not Venetia, which Radetzky's forces still controlled.[14] The Turin Cabinet rejected the offer, and the war continued.

At the end of May the Piedmontese won a second victory at Goito, during which the twenty-year-old Marquis Augusto Cavour, Camillo's nephew, died on the battlefield. Michelangelo Castelli, who went to pay his condolences to the Count, found him rolling on the carpet of his room crying desperately, refusing to respond to the consolation of his friend. Later, Cavour had his nephew's uniform, revealing the traces of his mortal wound, placed in a cabinet in his room – a constant reminder of the first war of liberation. The victory at Goito was accompanied by the fall of Peschiera, and for some the two victories signalled the end of the struggle and the liberation of northern Italy. Parma and Modena, which had fused with Piedmont in May, were joined by Lombardy in June, to be followed by Venetia in July. Camillo di Cavour, elected to the Piedmontese Chamber in the by-elections of June, considered the fusion and talk of a constituent assembly premature. Thus Cavour's maiden parliamentary speech of

4 July 1848, on the proposed electoral law, was not well received and the aristocratic Cavour was booed from the gallery.[15]

In London, Palmerston applauded the efforts of the people of Italy to obtain free and constitutional governments, making it clear that the policy of Her Majesty's Government was not to interfere in Italian developments. Vienna thought otherwise, and the Austrian minister in London complained that the entire English Cabinet had adopted the views of the Italian Revolution, and was seeking the creation of a great kingdom in northern Italy formed by Piedmont, Lombardy, Venetia, Parma and Modena, under the direction of Carlo Alberto.[16]

The Austrians, discouraged by events in Italy and at home, unsuccessfully sought an armistice with the Piedmontese. Radetzky, entrenched in Verona, believed that the Austrians would eventually triumph, and his optimism proved prophetic as cracks began to emerge in the Italian camp. In Naples, where the republicans attempted a coup, the army suppressed the disorders and Ferdinando reacted by revoking the constitution and closing the newly elected Chamber of Deputies. The 14,000 troops under General Pepe, poised to cross the Po and join Carlo Alberto in the war, were recalled by the king. Pepe refused to follow Ferdinando's orders, but less than 2,000 of his men crossed the Po with him to fight the Austrians. There were also defections in the Papal ranks after the April allocution, so Durando placed his troops under Piedmontese command. The war, no longer national in scope, was reduced to a Piedmontese campaign.

The Piedmontese by themselves proved unequal to the task of liberating Italy, as reinforcements reached Radetzky, who resumed the offensive. Under these circumstances, Papal support again appeared crucial, and from Turin Gioberti urged that broader military forces be entrusted to Carlo Alberto and the Papal contingent enlarged. Above all, some word from the Pope to rouse the masses was needed to reinvigorate the Italian effort. Pius, pondering the feasibility of issuing a proclamation on the Dogma of the Immaculate Conception, proved unreceptive to the pleas from Turin. 'Even though the desire grows for the greatness of the Italian nation and its liberation, the entire world must again know that for us war cannot be the means of achieving these objectives', he responded on 10th July, to the urging of his Chamber for participation in the national struggle. 'It was for us a great surprise to learn that the Council had discussed the subject,' Pius added, 'in spite of our public declarations, and at a time when we had assumed peace initiatives.'[17]

As Carlo Alberto prepared to besiege Mantua, Radetzky broke

through his line in the battle of Custozza (22nd–25th July) forcing the Piedmontese to fall back first to Villafranca, and then to Milan. The outnumbered and dispirited Piedmontese, realizing they could not defend the city, sued for peace. The initial proposal for an armistice was spurned by Radetzky, to the dismay of the Austrian ministers who feared a possible French intervention. A temporary agreement was concluded early in August, providing for a suspension of fighting for three days, Piedmontese withdrawal beyond the Ticino within two days, and the Milanese who wanted to leave able to do so within twenty-four hours.

On the night of 5th August, the Piedmontese retreated from Milan, followed by over 60,000 of its inhabitants, fearing the wrath of Radetzky, who entered the half-deserted city the next day. On 9th August, the Salasco Armistice was signed, which provided for a cessation of hostilities for six weeks, the Piedmontese evacuation of Venetia, Parma and Modena, together with their surrender of Peschiera. While the French and Russians opposed territorial changes in Italy, Britain announced that she would not interfere to help Carlo Alberto avoid the consequences of his violation of the European peace and the treaties of Vienna. Nonetheless, in mid-August Carlo Alberto secured the mediation of England and France concerning the final peace terms with Austria, refusing to negotiate directly with the Habsburg Empire.[18]

Following the armistice of Salasco, Italians wondered why the campaign which began so promisingly should have ended so disastrously. Nationalists and liberals, democrats and conservatives sought scapegoats, and the two men who had provided much of the initiative for change, Pio Nono and Carlo Alberto, were charged with betrayal, if not treason. Cavour's newspaper, *Il Risorgimento*, now placed little trust in the 'Liberator-Pope', fearing that the Roman government would prove unable to move him to wage war. Garibaldi found Carlo Alberto's conduct equally appalling. Stung by the criticism, in his proclamation of 30th August, the Piedmontese king spoke of reopening the war with Austria after the expiration of the armistice. Cavour considered such action, without French assistance, to be madness.[19] Events had shown that 'Italy could not do it alone.'

Both Piedmont and the Papal States saw the emergence of new governments in August, that of the Marquis Alfieri in Turin and that of Edoardo Fabbri in Rome. Some still hoped that Pio Nono could be persuaded to wage war, most likely through the mechanism of the political league. In August, Carlo Alberto wrote to Pius expressing his desire both for a new concordat between Piedmont and the

Papacy, and a political alliance between their sovereigns. Subsequently, the Piedmontese government sent Father Antonio Rosmini to Rome to effect the league, but this patriotic priest found that Turin and Rome had different visions of the league and its mission. Pius persisted in his opposition to war against Austria, while the Piedmontese pressed for its reopening. The Pope, fearing disorders in his state, negotiated with the French to send two or three thousand troops to Rome 'to prevent honest liberty from degenerating into licence.'[20]

In mid-September, when Count Pellegrino Rossi became Minister of the Interior and effective head of the Papal government, prospects for the political league diminished considerably. Rossi, determined to preserve the temporal power of the Papacy, considered the war against Austria a mistake, and Papal participation impractical. At any rate, it was noted in the *Risorgimento*, what Italy required was not Papal military power, which was negligible, but the moral authority of the Pope to rouse the masses. Pius had already announced in his allocution that he would not declare a crusade against the Austrian oppressor, so that the promise of the league was simply an illusion.[21]

Paris and London, fearing that the reopening of the war in Italy might embroil all of Europe, urged the Piedmontese and Austrians to extend their armistice and conclude a permanent peace. Their mediation proved fruitless as the Austrians determined to preserve their rights in Italy, while the Piedmontese still nourished the hope that Lombardy, if not Venetia, could be obtained. Pushed by the radical opposition which insisted on the reopening of the war, the new Piedmontese government of General Perone, replacing that of Marquis Alfieri in October, leaned in that direction. Rosmini, still in Rome, was told to negotiate an alliance for war first, concluding the league later.[22] These instructions precipitated Rosmini's resignation and the termination of talks on the political union.

Nationalists blamed the Pope for the failure of the negotiations, but Pellegrino Rossi challenged their analysis. In the *Gazetta Ufficiale* of 4 November 1848, Rossi charged the Pope had been criticized for refusing to follow unquestioningly the Piedmontese proposals. Rossi reported that Turin simply wanted arms and men, but the Papal Minister stressed that Rome and Florence needed to ascertain their purpose and aim. The enlargement of Piedmont and the autonomy of Italy were not identical matters, Rossi reminded Italians. Piedmont could not drag the rest of Italy to fulfil her own dynastic aims. He found it ironic that while the Piedmontese negotiated peace, they were pressing the other Italian states for men and money to wage war. In Turin, rather than Rome, Rossi charged, duplicity prevailed.

Count Rossi's spirited response to the accusations of the Piedmontese and determination to protect the Pope from the radicals of the war party roused the clubs in Rome, which put a price on his head. Pietro Sterbini, who presided over the Popular Club, denounced Rossi in the columns of his *Contemporaneo* as an enemy of the Italian cause. A revolution against his ministry erupted on 15th November, the day the Roman Chamber reopened. As Rossi walked into the Palace of the Chancellery, where the Assembly was housed, a dagger slashed his throat, and within five minutes he had bled to death. Thus opened the Roman revolution.[23]

The next day's demonstrations in Rome degenerated into violence, as an unruly crowd, led by some of the Deputies, marched upon the Pope's residence, the Quirinal Palace, demanding the promulgation of Italian nationality and the convocation of a federal constituent assembly, while insisting on the Deputies' right to decide the issue of participation in the war of national liberation. When the Pope refused to sanction this programme, the crowd began the siege of the Quirinal Palace, threatening to raze it to the ground, and kill all its inhabitants, apart from the Pope. In order to avert this slaughter, on 17th November, Pius accepted the Ministry demanded by 'the people' – albeit with considerable reservations – thus declaring himself a virtual prisoner.

Rumours trickled out of Rome that the Pope, protected only by the diplomatic corps and advised by Cardinals Soglia and Antonelli, might abandon his capital. The Austrians knew of the Pope's intentions by 24th November.[24] That evening, assisted by the French, Spanish and Bavarian ambassadors, Pius fled the Papal States for Gaeta, in the Kingdom of Naples. Offered asylum by the French, Spanish and even the Piedmontese, Pius decided to remain in the Neapolitan Kingdom. From Gaeta, on 27 November 1848, he sent a letter to his subjects, explaining the chain of events that had led him to flee from his state. Vienna, which had been brought back under imperial control in November, reacted positively to the Papal pronouncement to the Roman public.[25]

The Piedmontese and the national party were less pleased by the Pope's flight. Cavour's *Risorgimento* reported that the Pope's behaviour exposed a problem that had long troubled Italian minds: the need for a separation of the temporal and spiritual power of Rome.[26] Carlo Alberto wrote Pius offering his mediation between the Holy Father and his subjects, but discouraging any attempt to impose a solution.

The Piedmontese king foresaw that military measures would only aggravate the already tense situation in the peninsula. In the light of his impending resumption of hostilities with Austria, Carlo Alberto confessed he could not send troops to assist the Pope. He cautioned Pius not to call upon the assistance of the Catholic powers, predicting it would provoke a foreign intervention detrimental to Italy, the Holy See, and even the cause of religion.[27]

Carlo Alberto's pleas went unheeded. Pio Nono and his Prosecretary of State, Cardinal Giacomo Antonelli, were encouraged by the Spanish–Austrian proposal to convene a congress attended by the representatives of Spain, Austria, France, Portugal, Bavaria, Sardinia, Naples and Tuscany to examine the most opportune means of restoring the Pope to Rome. Palmerston, considering the move to be an Austrian intrigue, argued that the Pope did not require a state to assure his spiritual independence. Pius disagreed. In early January the new Piedmontese Prime Minister, Gioberti, wrote to Antonelli protesting against the Spanish plan to restore the Pope to Rome. Gioberti called for a reconciliation between the Pope and his subjects.[28]

The prospects for a reconciliation were slim. On 5 January 1849, Pius issued a virtual excommunication of those responsible for the radical ministry of mid-November, denouncing the proposal at the end of December to call a General Assembly to reorder the political structure of the Papal States. The Assembly's arrogation of full sovereign power, and the proclamation of the Republic on 9 February 1849, infuriated the Pope, who believed he was being punished for his liberal past. He now relied on the Catholic powers, and Austria, in particular, to rescue him from the dilemma which he perceived a threat to both his political and spiritual power. Pio Nono's appeal to the Austrians offended national sensibilities, confirming the opinion that the earlier Papal refusal to enter the war represented an act of betrayal, dooming the temporal power.

Resentment of Rome's pro-Austrian posture proved greatest in Piedmont, which planned to reopen the war of national liberation. In preparation for the resumption of hostilities, on 18 January 1849, the Piedmontese concluded a secret agreement with the 'sacrilegious' Roman junta. Under its provisions, as soon as Turin declared war against Austria, its troops would be allowed to enter the Papal States to coordinate strategic actions *vis-à-vis* the enemy. The Roman government also promised to take part in the holy war, placing a force of 15,000 men at Carlo Alberto's disposal. The Papal decision to appeal for the armed intervention of Austria, Spain, France and

Naples against a potential ally understandably upset the Piedmontese. Gioberti sarcastically observed that his government's peaceful mediation should have been more pleasing to the Pope of peace than the bloody recourse to arms. Likewise he would have supposed that as an Italian sovereign, the Pope would have preferred the assistance of a fellow Italian prince rather than relying upon German troops.

At the opening of parliament in February, Carlo Alberto consecrated his life and that of his sons to the well-being and independence of his country. On 12 March 1849, the king denounced the armistice with Austria. In the eight-day truce before the resumption of hostilities, while the Piedmontese forces, some 100,000 strong, sought to accustom themselves to the techniques, style and language of their new commander, the Polish General Chrzanowsky, General Radetzky secretly planned to surprise the Piedmontese by assuming the offensive. His strategy caught the Piedmontese off-guard in the Battle of Novara (23 March 1849), leading to the Austrian victory.

Following Novara, Carlo Alberto sought terms from the Austrians. General Hess, chiding the Sardinian king for his lack of good faith, responded that the Piedmontese would have to permit the Austrians to occupy a considerable portion of their territory and transmit the Crown Prince to them as their hostage. Recognizing the Austrian animus towards himself, Carlo Alberto abdicated in favour of his son, Vittorio Emanuele. The next day, 24th March, the young king met with General Radetzky, who granted to the son the armistice denied his father. Radetzky's conditions for peace called for Piedmont's return to its borders of 1815, the recall of its fleet from the Adriatic, the disbanding of the Lombard Legions, and the abandonment of all claims to the duchies of Parma and Modena. Piedmont was to admit an Austrian force into the city of Alessandria and, finally, to pay an indemnity for the cost of the war.[29]

The Princess Melanie, Metternich's third wife, complained that the terms were too lenient. Radetzky had promised to dictate peace terms in Turin, but had broken that promise after the abdication of Carlo Alberto to help the new King, Vittorio Emanuele. The Princess considered the General's leniency a mistake, doubting that the son would behave any better than the father. The Piedmontese as well as the Austrians considered the peace a temporary solution. Even the moderate Cesare Balbo noted that under the circumstances the Piedmontese could not conclude a definitive peace with the Austrians, only a truce that would last ten years. His prediction proved prophetic. Cavour shared Balbo's sentiment, noting that they would learn from their errors and do better next time.[30]

Massimo D'Azeglio, who became the Piedmontese Prime Minister in May 1849, recognized that the country needed at least a decade of preparation to resume the conflict with Austria. His sensible approach was not appreciated by the Chamber selected in the third general elections held in July 1849, in which the most liberal elements carried the day. The new parliament, which named the radical Marquis Pareto president, proved reluctant to approve the peace treaty concluded between Piedmont and Austria at the end of July. This created problems for Vittorio Emanuele, who had sworn allegiance to the Albertine Constitution at the end of March, and wished to govern constitutionally. However, he steadfastly refused to renew the war at that time, noting that the internal and European situation were not propitious.

At the Conference of Gaeta, which opened in March, the Catholic powers of Spain, Austria, Naples and France agreed on the need for joint action to restore the Pope to Rome. Meanwhile, the Austrians, having defeated the Piedmontese at Novara, opened the path to central Italy. Fearing a massive Habsburg intrusion into the peninsula, the National Assembly in France, at the end of March, passed an order of the day supporting a French intervention in Italy. However, Paris coordinated its actions with Vienna as the Second Republic sought the recognition of Austria. An arrangement was made assuring Vienna that Paris would not intervene in Lombardy or the Kingdom of the Two Sicilies, and in return Austria recognized the French Republic. Regarding Italy, the Austrians permitted a French intervention in Rome, while Austrian forces secured the Legations. Tuscan affairs were to be left in Austrian hands. Since France and Austria agreed to return to the territorial settlement of 1815, prospects for its unilateral revision by the Piedmontese were not promising.

As Habsburg forces marched inexorably towards Rome, a French expedition landed in Civitavecchia in April, and Spanish and Neapolitan forces marched from Gaeta towards Terracina, the debate continued in the Piedmontese parliament about the prospect of renewing the war. In June Rome fell, despite the valour of Garibaldi and the leadership of Mazzini. In August, Venice, plagued by famine and cholera, and weakened by heavy bombardment, capitulated. Under the circumstances, Cavour's *Risorgimento* considered the Chamber's refusal to approve the peace, and the prospect of an immediate renewal of the war, a grave threat to the existence of constitutional Piedmont.[31] Massimo D'Azeglio shared his concern, persuading the king to dissolve the Chamber and issue a statement urging his subjects to select a moderate replacement.

On 20 November 1849, the same day that he dissolved the Chamber elected in July, Vittorio Emanuele issued a proclamation from the royal château of Moncalieri calling upon his subjects to choose responsible deputies in the forthcoming elections for the new house. The need for peace was pressed. Although the 'Proclamation of Moncalieri' was an extraordinary – some claimed an extraconstitutional – measure, it was in many ways a necessary step to preserve the peace and the constitutional system of Piedmont. It proved effective, for in the elections of December 1849 the D'Azeglio Ministry, which favoured an immediate acceptance of the peace, was vindicated. On 9 January 1850, the new Chamber quickly approved the treaty with Austria by a vote of 112 to seventeen, with seven abstentions. Shortly afterwards the Senate approved the treaty by a vote of fifty to five. The First Italian War of Independence had finally ended. Some immediately began planning for the second.

NOTES

1. *Mémoires, documents et écrits divers laissés par le prince de Metternich*, ed. Prince Richard Metternich with the papers arranged and classified by M.A. de Klinkowstroem (Paris: Plon, 1880–84), II pp. 544–5; Pier Silverio Leicht, 'Memorie di Michele Leicht', *Rassegna Storica del Risorgimento*, anno XXII (July 1935), II, 83.
2. *Il Risorgimento*, 23 March 1848.
3. *Il Risorgimento*, 7 April 1848.
4. Luigi Carlo Farini, *Lo Stato Romano dall' anno 1815 al 1850* (3rd edn, Florence: Felice Le Monnier, 1853), II, pp. 22, 27, 31; Alois Simon, 'Palmerston et les États Pontificaux en 1849', *Rassegna Storia de Risorgimento*, anno XLIII (July–September 1956), III, 539–44.
5. Narration of events of 16th November and considerations leading Pius IX to abandon Rome, *Archivio Segreto del Vaticano, Archivio Particolare Pio IX, Stato Pontificio*, no. 19; Marco Minghetti, *Miei Ricordi* (3rd edn. Turin: Roux, 1888), I, pp. 363–4; Farini, II, pp. 28, 52–3; Luigi Rodelli, *La Republica Romana del 1849* (Pisa: Domus Mazziniana, 1955), pp. 64–5.
6. *Gazzetta Ufficale*, 10 April 1848; Minghetti, I, pp. 366–7.
7. Pius IX to Carlo Alberto, 7 April 1848 and Carlo Alberto to Pius IX, 18 April 1848, *Archivio Segreto del Vaticano, Archivio Particolare Pio IX, Sovrani, Sardegna*, no. 1.
8. Giovanni Maioli (ed.), *Pio IX da Vescovo a Pontifice. Lettere al Card. Luigi Amat, agosto 1839–luglio 1848* (Modena: Società Tipografico Modenese, 1943), pp. 117–18.
9. Monsignor Corboli Bussi to Pius IX, 26 April 1848 and 27 April 1848, *ASV, Archivio Particolare Pio IX, Sovrani, Stato Pontificio*, no. 33.
10. Luigi Rava (ed.), *Epistolario di Luigi Carlo Farini* (Bologna: Zanichelli,

1911), II, p. 216; Giacomo Martina, *Pio IX e Leopoldo II* (Rome: Pontifica Università Gregoriana, 1967), p. 113; Pius IX to Corboli Bussi, 27 April 1848, *ASV, Archivio Particolare Pio IX, Sovrani, Stato Pontificio*, no. 33.

11. Great Britain, *British and Foreign State Papers*, XXXVII (1848–49), 1062–5; Carlo Minocci, *Pietro Sterbini e la Rivoluzione Romana (1846–1849)* (Naples: Edizioni La Diana, 1967), p. 75; Angelo Filipuzzi (ed.), *Le relazioni diplomatiche fra L'Austria e il regno di Sardegna e la guerra del 1848–49*, Vol. I: *24 marzo 1848–11 aprile 1849* (Rome: Istituto storico italiano per la storia moderna e contemporanea, 1961), pp. 40–1, 94.

12. Farini, II, p. 108; Maioli, p. 118; *BFSP*, XXXVII (1848–49), 1071–1072; Antonio Monti, *Pio IX nel Risorgimento Italiano con documenti inediti* (Bari: Laterza, 1928), p. 101.

13. Monsignor Corboli Bussi to Pius IX, 22 May 1848, *ASV, Archivio Particolare Pio IX, Sovrani, Stato Pontificio*, no. 33.

14. Filipuzzi, I, pp. 99–104.

15. Guiseppe Massari, *Il Conte di Cavour. Ricordi biografici* (Turin: Botta, 1873), pp. 35–6; Luigi Chiala (ed.), *Il Conte di Cavour. Ricordi di Michelangelo Castelli* (Turin: Roux e Favale, 1886), p. 27; *Il Risorgimento*, 20 June 1848.

16. *Mémoires . . . Metternich*, VIII, p. 450.

17. 'Riposta della Santità di Nostro Signore Papa Pio IX all' indirizzo del Consiglio dei Deputati', *Il Risorgimento*, 17 July 1848.

18. Filipuzzi, I, pp. 205–7, 213, 222–3, 234.

19. *Il Risorgimento*, 31 August 1848; Chiala, *Ricordi di Michelangelo Castelli*, p. 127.

20. Carlo Alberto to Pius IX, 10 August 1848, *ASV, Archivio Particolare Pio IX, Sovrani, Sardegna*, no. 15; Pius IX to Foreign Minister, *ASV, Archivio Particolare Pio IX, Francia, Particolari*, no. 3.

21. 'Del probabile ordinamento di una Lega Politica Italiana', *Il Risorgimento*, 11 September 1848.

22. Filipuzzi, I, p. 244; William Lochart (ed.), *Life of Antonio Rosmini Serbati* (London: Kegan Paul, Trench e Co., 1886), I, p. 352.

23. Farini, II, 344–8; *Il Risorgimento*, 21 November 1848; *Il Contemporaneo*, 12 November 1848.

24. Narration of events of 16th November, *ASV, Archivio Particolare Pio IX, Stato Pontificio*, no. 19; Filipuzzi, I, p. 345.

25. 'Pius Papa IX. Ai Suoi dilettisimi sudditi', 27 November 1848, *Atti del Sommo Pontefice Pio IX Felicemente Regnante. Parte seconda . . .* (Rome: Tipografia delle Belle Arti, 1857), I, p. 252; Archbishop of Cartaginia to Cardinal Giacomo Antonelli, 28 December 1848, *ASV, Segreteria di Stato Esteri, Corrispondenza da Gaeta e Portici, 1848–1850, Rubrica 247, sottofasccoli 85–6*.

26. *Il Risorgimento*, 30 November 1848.

27. Carlo Alberto to Pius IX, 24 December 1848, *ASV, AP Pio IX, Sardegna, Sovrani*, no. 17.

28. Gioberti to Antonelli, 12 January 1849, *ASV, Segreteria di Stato Esteri, Corrispondenza da Gaeta e Portici, Rubrica 165, fascicolo 23*.

29. Farini, III, 265–6; Edgar Quinet, *La question romaine devant l'histoire, 1848*

à *1867* (Paris: Armand Le Chevlier, 1868), pp. 55–7; Filipuzzi, I, pp. 411–12, 423–6; 442–3.

30. *Mémoires . . . Metternich*, VIII, p. 49; Massari, *Il Conte di Cavour*, pp. 45, 47.
31. Filipuzzi, II, 441–2; *Il Risorgimento*, 23 July 1849.

CHAPTER FIVE
The Italian Question during the Second Restoration

During the second restoration, following the failure of the First War of Italian Independence, nationalists in the peninsula watched their dreams of self-determination and unification shatter. In Italy, as in most of Central Europe, the status quo was championed by Austria, which remained anchored to the past. In their quest for stability, the Habsburgs found conspicuous and valuable allies in Tsar Nicholas of Russia and Pope Pius IX who had been respectively frightened and disillusioned by the turmoil of the 1840s, pursuing decidedly conservative courses in the aftermath. Queen Victoria, with her German connections and English desire to avoid continental commitments, likewise proved sympathetic to Vienna's goal to preserve the existing boundaries.

Louis Napoleon, nephew of the great Napoleon, overwhelmingly elected President of France at the end of 1848 (he gained three and a half million more votes than all his rivals combined), remained something of an enigma. The twists and turns of his mind and heart were difficult, if not impossible, to chart. His unpredictability frightened the Austrian government. Frederick William of Prussia, infected by nationalist ambitions in Germany, represented another obvious danger to Austrian hegemony. Vittorio Emanuele's Piedmont, though less potent than Prussia, had grandiose ambitions in Italy that also threatened the Austrian position. It was thus not surprising that the French ruler considered Prussia and Piedmont potential allies against his Habsburg rival.

Recollecting his revolutionary experiences of the 1830s, Louis Napoleon regarded the Italian question not only as a political issue but a national one as well. Following his election, when Italian patriots in the French capital enquired what he would do for their *patria*, Napoleon quietly responded that he was a Bonaparte who understood the obligations the name imposed. Moderates in the peninsula, as well as their more radical confrères, sought French support. Liberals in Piedmont seconded Napoleon's contention that Pius IX should be restored as a constitutional monarch, maintaining that the struggle in Italy was between absolutism and moderate reformism. Lord Palmerston warned that Austria retained Italy only so long as Louis Napoleon allowed, predicting that the French would seize the first opportunity to push the Habsburgs out of Lombardy and Venetia. Clearly, Vienna could no longer rely on French acquiescence in their domination of northern Italy and widespread influence throughout the peninsula.[1]

On the issue of the liberalization of the Papal States, Paris and Turin concurred, sharply disagreeing with the Austrian stance. France, no less than Piedmont, resented the *Motu proprio* decree of 12 September 1849, which failed to provide for public participation in political affairs, thus re-establishing a paternalistic regime. In turn, Pius IX and his Secretary of State, Antonelli, resisted the calls for reforms emanating in Paris and echoed in Turin. Austria, on the other hand, while approving the broad conservative sweep of the Papacy, feared the consequences of its political intransigence, and therefore encouraged the Pope to make some concessions, lest Napoleon champion constitutionalism and the national cause to the detriment of the European peace and the Habsburg position in Italy. The Austrians sought to isolate the Piedmontese who were expected to resume their acquisitive policies.[2]

Even moderate Piedmontese longed for a second round against Austria, but learning from the mistakes of 1848–49, demanded better preparation for the next war. Insisting that the cause of Italian liberalism and nationalism was tied to the progress made by Piedmont, Cavour's *Risorgimento* championed the creation of a progressive, well-ordered state to set an example.[3] Cavour's strategy found broad support in Paris and London, which contrasted the efficiency of Piedmont with the backwardness of the Papal States and Naples. While Napoleon considered revisionist Piedmont a likely ally against the conservative eastern bloc, liberal England was impressed by her reformist bent and free trade bias.

Capitalizing on the Papacy's identification with the Austrian enemy since the allocution of April 1848, Massimo D'Azeglio, who assumed power in May 1849, proposed radical changes in Church–state relations, and a restriction of the role of the Church in Piedmontese affairs. Both Turin's initial legislative proposals on altering

Church–state relations, as well as the critical tone of their press towards Rome, antagonized Pius IX. Accusing the Piedmontese of expansionist designs, he appreciated that its ambitions worked to undermine the Papal States and his own position.[4] The reformism that distressed Rome impressed Protestant England, which perceived it as the initiation of a second Reformation. Whatever the motivation behind its policies, Piedmont was increasingly hailed in Italy and abroad as the only oasis in the sandy desert of political absolutism which comprised the peninsula.

The same year that Pio Nono returned to Rome – his hair having turned grey during the ordeal of his exile – in Turin the forty-year-old Camillo di Cavour entered the Cabinet of Massimo D'Azeglio as Minister of Agriculture, Industry and Commerce. Firmly convinced of the advantages of economic liberalism and free trade, he inspired the government to sign a series of agreements with England, France and Belgium, providing for a lower tariff and a freer economy. His customs reform had political as well as economic advantages, linking Piedmont to England and France, the more enlightened powers in Europe, against the conservative bloc of Austria and Russia. Cavour constantly sought to contrast Piedmontese progressivism with the rigidities imposed by the imperial systems of the eastern powers; in so doing, he hoped to create a European climate favourable to Turin and critical of Vienna.

Part and parcel of his strategy of liberal affirmation was Cavour's support of ecclesiastical reform. Unable to resolve the national problem swiftly on the battlefield, Cavour encouraged the country to look inward, solving a host of problems long neglected. Piedmont's constitutionalism, parliamentary life and religious liberty served as beacons to the oppressed of the peninsula, casting a shadow upon Austria and her Italian satellites. In 1850 he supported the Siccardi Laws, which abrogated various forms of ecclesiastical jurisdiction hitherto enjoyed by the Piedmontese Church, eliminated the Church's right of asylum, provided for the suppression of mortmain, and sought to regulate the civil aspects of marriage. 'I believe this reform should clearly manifest what the real sentiments of the Crown are, and by whom it is counselled,' Cavour pleaded in the Sub-alpine parliament. 'This consideration is of such gravity for me, of so high an importance, that it would suffice to decide my vote, were there no other considerations in favour of the proposed legislation.'[5] By this ecclesiastical policy Cavour sought to attract national elements in the peninsula, while winning liberal, anti-Catholic England to his cause.

Vienna quickly perceived the political implications of Piedmont's religious policies. The official gazette observed that Turin wished to differentiate herself from Catholic Austria by antagonizing the Papacy which had wounded national sentiment during the course of the recent war. The Austrians concluded that they should not bend or alter their policy in the face of Piedmontese opportunism, but rather show themselves increasingly Catholic as Piedmont betrayed her 'heretical' sentiments. The Habsburgs had other reasons to remain loyal to the Church, and above all the need to preserve their position in Germany. Prince Schwarzenberg suspected that the King of Prussia had granted religious freedom to his Catholic subjects to attract wider support in Germany, with the thought of eventually exercising dominion over the entire nation. Austria could not allow the Prussian initiative to succeed, and therefore had to outbid the Prussians for Catholic support in Germany.[6]

Vienna monitored the aims and actions of the French and Piedmontese as well as the Prussians, Russians and the English. It also confronted massive internal problems, and most notably those associated with the Hungarians, who like the Italians in 1848, challenged Habsburg control. The Papal Nuncio in Vienna, writing to Cardinal Antonelli, Papal Secretary of State, identified Italy and Hungary as the two cancerous bodies currently disturbing Austria, containing forces of insurrection prepared to explode should the opportunity arise. He predicted that if things remained quiet in Europe, and France was crucial in this matter, then the Austrian army could preserve the peace and maintain the viability of the Habsburg Empire.[7] Nonetheless, the situation remained perilous. The Austrian position was precarious, menaced not only by French and Piedmontese intrigues, but also by Prussian ambitions in Germany, leading Prince Schwarzenberg to fear the outbreak of war. For this reason, the Nuncio informed the Pope that the prince courted the goodwill of Russia, while improving his diplomatic relations with France. However, his success in this was to prove partial and temporary.

France remained crucial to the diplomatic situation in Europe, and Louis Napoleon the key to Gallic policy. Consequently the *coup d'état* of 2 December 1851 created consternation in the conservative camp. Cavour understood the importance of Napoleon's coup at the end of 1851, appreciating the possible advantages that Piedmont and Italy could draw from this development.[8] Cavour, who in 1851 had been entrusted with the portfolio of finance in addition to that of agriculture already held, further strengthened his internal position early in 1852 by forming an alliance with Urbano Rattazzi of the centre-left. During the course of the parliamentary debate on the revision of the country's press law, Count Ottavio di Revel, noting the similarity of position between the followers of Cavour and Rattazzi, dubbed their alliance a *connubio* or marriage. Cavour considered this alliance of the centre-right and centre-left the most important act of his political career – and so it was.[9] It offered him the parliamentary support that enabled him first to challenge and later to replace D'Azeglio as prime minister.

Cavour, confirmed in office in November 1852, did not assume the Ministry of Foreign Affairs, which was assigned to General Giuseppe Dabormida. Another General, Alfonso La Marmora, was named Minister of War, and later Cavour's political ally, Rattazzi, took the Ministry of the Interior. Conscious of the importance of economic and financial issues, which he deemed prerequisites for Piedmont's political expansion, Cavour retained the Portfolio of Finance in his own hands. Determined that the country be adequately prepared for the second war of Italian Independence, the king and La Marmora reorganized and modernized the army following the disastrous defeat of 1848–49. Cavour pressed for more, recognizing that the country could not achieve its national objectives without additional assistance, and therefore sought the support of a powerful ally in the crusade.

As in 1848, Cavour looked to Paris for reinforcement. He remained convinced that Napoleon was moved by Italian interests, regretting the resistance of Pio Nono and Antonelli to reformism, and the pressure placed upon him by the ultramontane party in France. Cavour believed that Napoleon, no less than Rattazzi, sought to keep the court of Rome in check. These convictions were confirmed during the course of his visit to Paris and interview with Louis Napoleon, prior to assuming power in Piedmont. On that and subsequent occasions, Louis Napoleon revealed his desire for an Italian federation under the honorary presidency of the Pope, but effectively directed by Piedmont. Thus Cavour reacted favourably to the overwhelmingly popular vote cast for converting the French Republic into the Empire at the end of 1852, and the proclamation of the Empire in December. He had reason to rejoice, for that very year Napoleon promised General Collegno, the Piedmontese Minister in Paris, that at an appropriate moment his country could expect French help. The two would find themselves companions in arms on behalf of the Italian cause. Similar promises were made later to the general's successor, the Marquis Villamarina.[10] Paris thus assured Turin that it would not wage the second war of liberation alone, as it had the first.

The conservative powers, on the other hand, regretted Napoleon's re-establishment of the Empire. Vienna, St Petersburg and Berlin feared that the proclamation of the Empire signalled the prelude to the return of imperial ambitions, leading France to challenge the treaties of 1815 and the status quo in Europe. The fact that Louis Napoleon termed himself Napoleon III was perceived as portentous, providing recognition of the Prince of Rome as Napoleon II, and thereby questioning the agreements made by the powers in the Peace of Paris and the Congress of Vienna. Having reviewed the unfortunate consequences of refusing to accept the French Empire, the conservative empires did not block its recognition. Speaking on behalf of the eastern powers, Prince Schwarzenberg pronounced that they would not intervene in internal Gallic affairs, so long as France respected the peace and the treaties.

The Vatican, like the Ballplatz, scrutinized developments in Paris as well as Turin. The Papal Nuncio in the French capital, commenting on the Emperor's insistence on marrying Eugénie in the face of considerable opposition, concluded that the same stubbornness might later create problems for Rome.[11] Perhaps this played a part in Pio Nono's refusal to travel to Paris to crown Napoleon – a slight which, while it offended Napoleon, nevertheless won Austrian approval. Napoleon also disliked the Austrian form of address towards his person, which differed somewhat from the usage towards Louis Philippe. Although word spread that the French Emperor was angry with Nicholas of Russia, who had remained consistent in his approach, the Papal Nuncio reported that Austria rather than Russia had upset Napoleon.[12] In fact the Emperor was also offended by Nicholas's refusal to refer to him as a cousin or brother, rather he called the French ruler his good friend. Napoleon made the best of the situation, and on receiving the credentials of the Russian representative commented that one had to accept one's relatives, but could choose one's friends.

Napoleon knew that Russia, as well as Britain, Austria and Prussia feared possible French aggression and disruption of the peace; thus he sought to reassure them for the time being. At Bordeaux he proclaimed that the Empire did not mean war, but peace, asserting he would respect both Europe's boundaries and treaties. Thus the proclamation of the Empire did not lead the eastern courts to break off relations with Paris, and Prince Schwarzenberg hoped that the Emperor could be persuaded to pursue a conservative course. To be sure, Russia, Prussia and Austria, as well as England, were alarmed by the publication of the article entitled 'Les limites de la France', which called for French expansion and its absorption of Belgium. Napoleon quickly denied the expansionist ideas expressed therein, indicating that they reflected neither his sentiments nor those of his government. Many inside and out of France questioned the sincerity of Napoleon's peaceful pronouncements, distressed as they were by his nationalist rhetoric and schemes.

In April 1852, Prince Schwarzenberg, who followed a conciliatory but cautious policy towards Napoleon, died, to be succeeded by Count Buol-Schauenstein, the former Austrian Ambassador in London. Like his predecessor, Buol wished to cooperate with Napoleon, preventing him from championing liberal and nationalist programmes in Europe. Unfortunately Buol lacked the ability of his predecessor as well as the confidence of Franz Josef enjoyed by the prince. Furthermore, Vienna had other problems. In 1853 the indefatigable and roving Mazzini, then based in Lugano, sought to orchestrate a revolutionary upheaval in Milan. The rebellion attracted little support, and with the information provided by the Turin government, equally suspicious of the republican revolutionary, it was easily suppressed. Not content with their success the Austrians overreacted, and in February 1853 passed a decree sequestering the property of exiled Lombards. Cavour's country, a refuge for over 20,000 Lombard families, protested against the Austrian action which violated international law. Despite almost universal condemnation, the Austrians refused to rescind their decree, providing Turin with a moral victory. The Piedmontese Minister, Adriano Thaon de Revel, was recalled from Vienna. Cavour gloated that rather than hurting or humiliating Piedmont, Austria had antagonized all the Cabinets of Europe. He predicted that Piedmont would profit from the blunder by crossing the Ticino and opening the Second War of Independence, sooner rather than later.[13]

With Turin and Vienna still embroiled in the sequestration confrontation, the peace of Europe was troubled by the differences between France and Russia in the Near East. Although these two empires sanctimoniously claimed to defend the rights of the Catholic and Orthodox Churches in the Ottoman Empire in general, and Constantinople in particular, the overriding issue remained that of Russian pressure upon Turkey, and the French determination to prevent the Tsarist regime from dismembering the Ottoman Empire. Russian expansionism pressed for the disintegration of the Ottoman Empire, assuring the Tsar control over the Dardanelles and ready access to the Mediterranean. The prospect alarmed Britain, which worked to preserve the Porte. Suspicious of the Russians since they had proposed a partition of the Ottoman Empire, Britain deemed the Russian plan dangerous for the stability of the region and the peace of the Continent.

Napoleon's objectives were neither conservative nor cautious. Having been frustrated in his desire to summon a congress of the great European powers to revise the treaties of 1815, settling a number of disruptive matters in the process, he sought other means to effect territorial change. Increasingly, the impenetrable and impulsive Emperor envisioned a war against Russia as the mechanism for disrupting the Holy Alliance, which he perceived as the main barrier to his reorganization of Europe along national lines. Inklings of his revisionist plans could be gleaned from the Emperor's disinclination to reaffirm the treaties of 1815 *vis-à-vis* Italy, as well as his broad policy towards Germany. He steadfastly refused to sanction the Habsburg attempt to include the entire Austrian Empire in the *Bund* (German Confederation), deeming it detrimental to French power and prestige in Europe.

The Emperor anticipated that a defeat of the conservative collossus would undermine the status quo, allowing him to implement his nationalist schemes. Indeed he encouraged his trusted journalist Granier de Cassagnac to explain his programme in a pamphlet entitled 'La Révision de la Carte d'Europe'. Napoleon's ministers, sensing the alarm the piece would provoke in the chancelleries of Europe, persuaded him to suppress its distribution, but not before some copies were circulated. Furthermore, during the course of his conversations and discourses, the sphinx-like ruler scattered hints of the outline and gist of his grand design. The Napoleonic plan called for pushing Russia out of the Near East, forcing the Romanovs to cede not only the Black Sea area, but Poland and Finland as well. Thus the Russian pressure upon the Balkans and eastern Mediterranean would be eradicated.

Though autocratic in his domestic policies, Napoleon pursued a liberal and dynamic policy abroad. In his partition plan, which formed part of his greater reorganization scheme, Finland would go to Sweden, while Poland was to be placed under the control of a German prince, perhaps the King of Saxony. Austria might be compensated by acquiring Bessarabia and other Balkan territory, but constrained to cede Lombardy, and perhaps Venice as well, to the Kingdom of Sardinia. Prussia, in turn, would be allowed to strengthen her base in Germany and to preside over a stronger, pro-French German confederation. For France, Napoleon determined to gain the left bank of the Rhine, Nice and Savoy – territorial ambitions which he nourished secretly, unwilling to alienate the

English, whose support he courted in his campaign against Russia and the Holy Alliance.

The actions of the Eastern Colossus facilitated Napoleon's ploys. Early in 1853 Tsar Nicholas dispatched a mission to Constantinople and ordered the mobilization of his army. The Russians also occupied the principalities of Moldavia and Wallachia, rousing Britain as well as Austria. Palmerston, who still influenced English foreign affairs, continued decidedly hostile to Russia. Russian pressure upon the Porte might have sufficed, but for the support the Turks received from Britain and France. Thus the Turkish declaration of war against the Russians in October 1853 was followed by the allied entry of the Anglo-French fleet into the Black Sea. In the light of the stance assumed by France and Britain on the one hand, and Russia on the other, little ground remained for diplomatic manoeuvring.

Franz-Josef, concerned about the impact of the Russian–Turkish quarrel on the situation in Europe in general and on conditions in Hungary and Italy in particular, implored Tsar Nicholas to resolve the dispute. However, his attempted mediation proved abortive. By March 1854 the Austrian fears of a European conflict materialized, as France and England were ranged alongside the Turks against the Russians. In September the allied armies landed in the Crimea. Both the Western allies and the Russians expected Austrian support, but Vienna distrusting Piedmont's machinations, refused to enter the fray. In Turin Cavour, the Piedmontese Machiavelli, plotted for a confrontation with the occupying Habsburgs and a struggle for the mastery of Italy.[14] The Austrians, pressed by both sides, satisfied neither. A state of the centre, Metternich wrote, could not allow itself to be drawn either to the side of the West nor that of the East.[15] Cavour, on the other hand, appreciating that the struggle between East and West would inevitably influence Italian affairs, foresaw an active role for Piedmont.

Cavour longed for Austria to join her conservative ally so that a progressive bloc of Piedmont, England and France could not only wage war upon the Russians in the Near East, but also dislodge the Habsburgs from northern Italy. The French, for their part, sought to draw Austria into the anti-Russian coalition, reassuring them that they would uphold the status quo in Italy so long as the fighting continued in the east. Despite this commitment, the Ballplatz stopped short of declaring war against Russia, content to have the Russians evacuate the principalities, followed by an Austrian occupation of the area. Cavour, however, pledged to drag Piedmont into the war in return for some territorial advantage or even the promise of support for the termination of the Austrian sequestration decree against the Lombard exiles. The allies refused to make any commitment, and Cavour's Cabinet rejected entry into the conflict under these circumstances. Even Rattazzi, Cavour's political ally, opposed participation without any concrete inducement.

Cavour, knowing that Vittorio Emanuele had assured the English and French he would join them in the war, and personally anxious to preserve Napoleon's goodwill, engineered a political arrangement to achieve the necessary support to bring his country into the conflict. Cavour would bolster Rattazzi's Law of Convents, which envisioned the suppression of over 300 religious houses and their orders, in return for Rattazzi's unconditional support for Piedmont's participation in the Crimean War. On this basis the left–centre alliance survived, committed to continuing restricting the privileges of the Catholic Church at home, and joining the allies in waging the war against Russia. In April 1855, an expeditionary force commanded by General La Marmora left for the Crimea. Cavour surmised that their efforts would determine what advantages, if any, the country would draw from the war. If this army performed well, as he believed it would, Piedmont would see its authority and credit grow and the allies would eventually be forced to support and second its aims. Some of the officers shared Cavour's opinion, with one of them predicting that out of the mud of the Crimea, Italy would emerge.

During the course of 1855, relations between Turin and Vienna steadily deteriorated. The favourable concordat which Franz-Josef accorded the Church during that year contrasted sharply with the policies pursued by the Piedmontese *vis-à-vis* Rome. Furthermore, while Austria vacillated between war and peace, attempting to retain the goodwill of both Russia and the Western allies, Piedmont closed ranks with France and England in the war against Russia. To cement relations with her allies, Cavour accompanied Vittorio Emanuele and Massimo D'Azeglio to London and Paris in November 1855.

In London Cavour tried to translate British admiration for Piedmontese progress into active support for their confrontation with Austria. King Vittorio Emanuele, in his own gruff manner also sought to elicit British support, but cautioned that a king had to be certain that a war was both necessary and just before breaking the peace. Queen Victoria neither appreciated nor agreed with the king's rejoinder that God was prepared to pardon a mistake. Cavour realized the responsibility he had assumed when he brought his country into the war, but remained certain that he had done the right thing.[16] The attempt to win the active support of Britain in remaking the map of

Italy failed, for while British public opinion generally sympathized with the patriots of the peninsula, her statesmen were committed to preserving the peace and the treaties of Vienna.

The Piedmontese found a more receptive climate in Paris, where Napoleon III envisioned a radical revision of the map of Europe, largely at Turkish expense. Above all, the object of the Emperor's eastern policy was to benefit Italy and Poland. Although Russia no longer seemed capable of blocking his plans, Austrian obstinacy remained. Napoleon looked to Piedmont and Prussia as his two swords against the champion of the status quo, Austria. The British, Prussians, and even the Austrians, were given hints of Napoleon's dreams and designs. While the European courts tended to dismiss Napoleon's revisionist suggestions, they were applauded by the Piedmontese. Thus when the Emperor asked Cavour and D'Azeglio, what he could do for Italy, they were quick to give an answer.[17]

By the end of 1855 Napoleon sought to close the eastern war, convinced that its continuation would not lead to his projected territorial changes. The fall of Sebastopol secured French honour and Napoleon confided to Queen Victoria that he would be willing to continue the conflict, which had cost some 100,000 French lives, only if it would assist the national liberation of the oppressed peoples of the continent. Thus when the French Foreign Minister, Walewski raised the spectre of a revolutionary war to frighten both his ally England, and his adversary Russia to bring them to the peace table, he reflected Napoleon's thought.

In mid-January 1856 Tsar Alexander II, who had succeeded Nicholas I in the previous spring, accepted in principle the Austrian ultimatum and the four points that the allies had imposed. They included: (1) the Russian rejection of any pretension *vis-à-vis* Serbia and the Principalities; (2) the assurance of free navigation on the River Danube; (3) a revision of the treaties of 1841 relating to the Black Sea and the Dardanelles in the interest of the European 'balance of power'; and (4) Russian abandonment of any attempt to establish a protectorate over the Sultan's Christian population.

On 1st February, the representatives of Austria, Russia, France, England and Turkey agreed in a protocol upon the terms which would serve as the basis of the final peace to be decided at the Congress of Paris, which was scheduled to open within three weeks. It opened on 25 February 1856, and the envoys of the major powers and Piedmont–Sardinia met in the French capital to frame the peace. The presidency of the Congress by diplomatic tradition fell to the French Foreign Minister, Count Walewski.

Cavour persuaded the elder statesman, Massimo D'Azeglio, whose aid he had earlier enlisted to respond to Napoleon's query as to what he could do for Italy, to represent his country at the Congress of Paris. There were three main reasons for Cavour's decision. Firstly, Cavour, directing the ministries of commerce and finances, did not have much experience in diplomacy, having assumed a role in foreign affairs only when his Foreign Minister refused to bring the country into the Crimean conflict. Secondly, D'Azeglio was well liked in London and Paris, and could be expected to exercise considerable moral influence. Thirdly (and in the eyes of some, most importantly), Cavour did not expect any tangible concession to come out of a conference largely orchestrated by the Austrian peace initiative. Hence he preferred to have D'Azeglio at Paris rather than tarnish his own prestige by the expected disappointment.

Vittorio Emanuele remained more sanguine, having been assured by the enigmatic Emperor that he would protect his interests at the Congress.[18] His optimism was not justified, for unbeknown to the Piedmontese king, Napoleon had made similar vows to Pio Nono. Furthermore, the Emperor had raised no objection to the notion that the Piedmontese representative should sit in only those sessions involving the country's direct interests, excluded from those sittings which tackled broader themes. Cavour had withheld this information from his projected emissary, who nonetheless discovered the condition. D'Azeglio, still bristling over the fact that Cavour had not utilized his long letter in response to Napoleon's enquiry about what he could do for Italy, dispatching his own brief response instead, was further scandalized by the subordination of his country at the Congress. Asserting that he would humiliate neither himself nor Piedmont, he rejected Cavour's entreaties to attend.

Following D'Azeglio's eleventh-hour refusal to represent his country at the Congress, Cavour had no alternative but to place his own position in jeopardy by going to Paris. Convinced of the need to reinvigorate the Emperor's resolve to champion the Italian cause, he enlisted the aid of his 'cousin', the sultry Contessa di Castiglione.[19] The contessa, who was commissioned by Cavour to seduce and incite Napoleon to war against Austria, succeeded in the first endeavour and, according to her own accounts, played a major role in the second. Cavour, who left for Paris on 13th February, almost immediately commenced the political seduction of the representatives of the allies, and even sought to win the goodwill of the recently defeated Russians. Thus before the opening of the Congress at the Palais D'Orsay on 25th February, Cavour had extracted a promise from

Clarendon to speak on the Italian issue should it be brought before the body. Napoleon, in turn, affirmed that Italian matters would be aired prior to the departure of the representatives.

During the negotiations which led to the peace signed on 30 March 1856 (the 42nd anniversary of the fall of Paris in 1814), Cavour and Villamarina tactfully remained aloof from the broader discussion that did not impinge upon their direct interests. In order to ingratiate himself with the French and defend the principle of nationality, Cavour supported Napoleon's plan to unite the Principalities into a single Romanian state. In addition, behind the scenes, Cavour quietly sought some tangible concession to bring home, such as the acquisition of Parma or Modena, but proved unsuccessful. To make matters worse, he soon discovered that Walewski did not share the Italophile sentiments of his cousin, Napoleon. The latter, meanwhile, seemed more preoccupied by the impending birth of his first child than the fate of the Congress, and being anxious to enlist the Pope as godfather, was reluctant to antagonize him. Still, Cavour did manage to persuade the English representatives of the need for an airing of the Italian situation, earn the goodwill of Orloff and Brunnow (the Russian representatives) and establish communication with the Emperor by means of Henri Conneau, the latter's personal physician.

During the session of 8th April, Walewski, at his Emperor's behest, proposed an exchange of ideas on a number of problems that had the potential for disturbing the peace. Among other things the President of the Congress referred to troubling developments in Greece, Belgium and Italy. Clarendon, fulfilling his pledge to Cavour, spoke on the Italian question, denouncing the policies of Papal Rome, which required the military presence of Austrian and French forces to preserve itself, and the abuses of the Neapolitan regime. Walewski then proceeded to ask the other representatives to present their views. Count Buol, visibly angry, observed that his Emperor had not provided instructions on these matters, and he could not discuss them. His position was echoed by Count Orloff of Russia, likewise citing his lack of instructions.

Cavour, who had precipitated the discussion, was prepared. Conscious of addressing the tribunal of public opinion as well as the representatives of the powers, he assumed a moderate stance. He could adopt a tranquil pose, because Clarendon had already cited the abuses plaguing the peninsula. Nonetheless, Cavour did assess the cause of Italy's problems, placing much of the blame on Austria's occupation and pernicious political influence. Cavour's public denunciation of the Habsburg position in Italy, and his insistence that his comments be inserted in the protocol, represented a moral victory of sorts, although he had hoped for more.

On 16th April, Cavour, in similar notes to the English and French, elaborated on the Italian question, arguing that the status quo in Italy worked not to protect the peace, but to precipitate revolution and war. If Cavour had entertained the illusion that the British would rush to remake the map of the peninsula at Austria's expense, this was dispelled during his visit to London following the close of the Congress. There he learned that Her Majesty's Government would neither abandon its Austrian ally, nor precipitate a continental war to cure the abuses cited by the Piedmontese and the British in the Congress. More than ever, Cavour realized that only Napoleonic France was willing and able to wage war to alter the map of Europe, but not all Italians or even Piedmontese shared his views.

Cavour's role and achievement at the Congress was debated by contemporaries and is still contested. When the Count returned to Turin without even the smallest duchy in his pocket, his reception proved lukewarm. Early in May, when he analysed the work of the Congress before the Chamber of Deputies, the most he could report was there had been no *rapprochement* between Piedmont and Austria, which moved along different tracks. Nevertheless, the Italian question had been aired in an international setting, the conservative alliance of Austria, Russia and Prussia had been smashed, and Napoleon's France, which sought revision in Europe, had a greater voice. This new fluidity in international relations worked to the detriment of Buol and Austria and to the advantage of Cavour and Piedmont. It encouraged Cavour to plan in earnest for the Second War of Italian Independence.

NOTES

1. *Il Risorgimento*, 21 February 1849; 3 July 1849; 13 August 1849.
2. *Archivio Segreto del Vaticano, Segreteria di Stato, Corrispondenza da Gaeta e Portici, 1849, Rubrica 242, sottofascicoli 24, 76–81.*
3. *Il Risorgimento*, 23 July 1849.
4. Pius IX to Archbishop Dupont, 10 June 1849, *Archivio Segreto del Vaticano, Archivio Particolare Pio Nono, Francia, Particolari*, n. 18.
5. *Legge Siccardi sull' abolizione del foro e delle immunita' ecclesiastiche tornate del Parlamento Subalpino* (Turin: Pomba, 1850), p. 77.
6. Michele Viala Prela to Antonelli, *Archivio Segreto del Vaticano*, 19 April

1849, *Segreteria di Stato Esteri*, Corrispondenza da Gaeta e Portici, *Rubrica* 247, *sottofascicoli* 197–8, 214–15.

7. Viala Prela to Antonelli, 31 January 1850, *ASV, SSE, CGP, Rubrica* 247, *sottofascicolo* 222.

8. Marco Minghetti, *Miei Ricordi* (3rd edn; Turin: Roux, 1898), III, p. 14.

9. Michelangelo Castelli, *Ricordi di Michelangelo Castelli*, ed. Luigi Chiala (Turin: Roux, 1888), p. 66.

10. Ibid., pp. 176–7; Minghetti, III, p. 84.

11. French Nuncio to Antonelli, 20 January 1853, *ASV, Segreteria di Stato Esteri, Rubrica* 242, *fascicolo* 6, *sottofascicolo* 40.

12. Ibid., *sottofascicoli* 124–5.

13. Giuseppe Massari, *Il Conte di Cavour, Ricordi biografici* (Turin: Botta, 1873), p. 93; *Mémoires, documents et écrits divers laissés par le Prince Metternich*, ed. Prince Richard Metternich, VIII, p. 143.

14. Arthur Irwin Dasent, *John Thadeus Delane, Editor of 'The Times'. His Life and Correspondence* (London: John Murray, 1908), I, p. 165.

15. *Mémoires . . . par le Prince Metternich*, VIII, p. 376.

16. Massari, *Il Conte di Cavour*, pp. 108, 125.

17. Ibid., pp. 130–1.

18. Charles W. Hallberg, *Franz Joseph and Napoleon III, 1852–1864* (New York: Octagon Books, 1973), p. 109.

19. Frédéric Loliée, *Women of the Second Empire: Chronicles of the Court of Napoleon III, Compiled from Unpublished Documents* (New York: John Lane Co., 1907), p. 16.

CHAPTER SIX

The Origins of the Second War of Italian Independence: 1856–59

Cavour returned from Paris determined to take advantage of the anti-Austrian, pro-Italian sentiments of Napoleon III to reopen the Piedmontese conflict with the Habsburgs and wage a Second War of National Liberation. Convinced that the Emperor nourished a secret rancour against Austria, and vividly remembering the revolutionary events of 1831, in which he had taken part, Cavour concluded that the interests of France and Piedmont were compatible. For this reason he sought to conciliate the enigmatic Emperor while strengthening his resolve. He cautioned Italian journals such as *Il Fischietto*, which were critical of the French Emperor, to cease their attacks upon him, as he seemed to hold the key to the Italian solution. Cavour placed his confidence in such men as Benedetti, the political director of foreign affairs in France, who was Corsican by birth but Italian at heart. He was reassured by Napoleon's prediction that the peace would not last long, and did all within his means to fulfil the Emperor's prophecy.[1]

Cavour's anti-Austrian stance encouraged some of the revolutionary party to look to Piedmont for leadership. Daniele Manin, leader of the Venetians against the Habsburgs in 1848–49, was among the first to denounce sporadic violence and break with Mazzini. Assured that the House of Savoy would risk the throne of Piedmont for the sake of gaining that of Italy, he accepted collaboration with Cavour. Manin convinced the Marquis Giorgio Pallavicino, who initially feared the intrigues of Cavour even more than those of Mazzini or Murat, that Cavour's intelligence and ambition were necessary to fulfil Italian aspirations. Garibaldi, in England in 1856, likewise appreciated Cavour's role. The general pronounced that the signal for the second round against Austria would have to be given by Piedmont. By this time the defender of the Roman Republic referred to Cavour as 'our great friend'. Even Mazzini belatedly, if reluctantly, agreed that Piedmont had a role to play in the national liberation.

Cavour hesitated to openly court the former radicals and republicans who were willing to compromise their ideals to attain national unity under the aegis of the House of Savoy. He worried that any official connection between himself and the revolutionary party would alarm England and alienate the goodwill of Napoleon. Nonetheless, the obvious limits of diplomacy at Paris convinced him to meet with Manin. Although he had reservations about Manin's ultimate ends, and questioned his means, Cavour recognized the need to bolster his diplomatic policy by garnering popular support.

Subsequently Cavour met secretly with the former Sicilian revolutionary, Giuseppe La Farina, who later wrote for the radical *Piccolo Corriere d'Italia*. According to La Farina, the meeting of 12 September 1856 in the Palazzo Cavour, was the first of many clandestine encounters. During the course of these secret sessions the man who posed as the enemy of the revolutionary party, covertly encouraged their organization and courted their support in the projected war against Austria. Indeed, Cavour instructed Marco Minghetti to remain in continuous contact with those revolutionaries who in 1857 formed the National Society, without necessarily joining their ranks. Metternich, unaware of the depth of Cavour's involvement with the revolutionaries, denounced his Cabinet's policy as one of lies and deceit.[2]

The Vienna government resented the press campaign against Austria that the Turin government tolerated, even if it did not promote it. When Franz-Josef visited Milan at the end of 1856, Cavour prevailed upon the Lombards to resist Habsburg blandishments, suggesting even extra-legal means to frustrate the attempt to achieve conciliation. His efforts proved successful as public ceremonies were ignored and receptions boycotted. To further antagonize and humiliate the Austrians, Cavour chose the occasion of Franz-Josef's entry into Milan early in 1857 to have the press announce that city's decision to build a monument to the Piedmontese army. He maliciously insinuated that Felice Orsini's extraordinary escape from an Austrian prison lent some credence to the suspicion that Austria secretly supported the revolutionary cause. Cavour's propaganda campaign proved successful, provoking the Austrians to sever diplomatic relations between Vienna and Turin. Cavour countered that Austria's declared enmity rallied honest men of all parties round his government.[3]

Although patriots increasingly looked to Cavour and Piedmont, rather than to Mazzini and his party of action, the 'soul' of Italian unification remained neither silent nor inactive. The small Mazzinian uprising in Sicily at the end of 1856 was followed in the summer of 1857 by the expedition of the Neapolitan Carlo Pisacane against the Kingdom of the Two Sicilies, aimed to coincide with 'spontaneous' uprisings in Leghorn and Genoa. The expedition to the south ended disastrously. The Neapolitan Count shot himself at Sapri rather than be hacked to pieces by the *Sanfedisti* peasantry, and only the arrival of the Neapolitan army stopped the slaughter of his followers. The risings in Leghorn and Genoa were suppressed with less bloodshed, but proved no more successful than the Pisacane expedition.

Cavour, angered and embarrassed by Mazzini's actions, was humiliated by the fact that the Piedmontese police proved unable to arrest Mazzini, who remained in hiding in Genoa. His government worked to discourage revolutionary agitation and useless uprisings, he proclaimed in the Piedmontese Chamber. He also worried about the impact the abortive revolutions would have upon Napoleon III and his commitment to the Italian cause, complaining to the Marquis Villamarina, his Minister at Paris, that French suspicion of Piedmontese complicity with the revolutionaries was unjustified, and that he would welcome Napoleon's assistance in capturing the elusive Mazzini. The Piedmontese Minister could not gauge the impact of the latest Mazzinian outburst upon the French Emperor or his Italian plans. Word spread that the revolutionary action discouraged the French ruler, but Cavour privately believed that the Mazzinian actions might have the opposite effect, spurring Napoleon to move more quickly and decisively on their behalf.[4]

Internally, the abortive revolutions helped Cavour and strengthened the Piedmontese cause throughout Italy by further eroding Mazzini's support. Agostino Bertani, who had taken part in the Milanese uprising against the Austrians in 1848, and later worked with Mazzini and Garibaldi in defence of the Roman Republic of 1849, questioned the republican's tactics. He and other former Mazzinians argued that the master was mistaken in his assumption that the masses of Italy were prepared to initiate and support a revolutionary upheaval. They denounced these 'fatal delusions' which had led many of Mazzini's former followers to turn to other parties and policies. Bertani and others cautioned Mazzini not to impose action without adequate preparation, but to wait until men and money had been gathered to counter and confront their well-organized enemies.

In the minds of an increasing number of Italians, adequate preparation for a confrontation with Austria meant that Italian liberation must rely on Cavour and the Piedmontese state. This was the programme of the National Society, formed by Daniele Manin, Giorgio Pallavicino and Giuseppe La Farina in July 1857. It channelled the support of former radicals, revolutionaries and republicans into Cavour's camp, acknowledging his leadership in the national movement. The credo of the new organization subordinated the issue of eventual political formulation to the more pressing need for independence, and supported the House of Savoy so long as it worked on behalf of Italy. Garibaldi's adherence to the party proved crucial for its success in working in tandem with the Piedmontese to undermine the established order in the peninsula. In response to those who questioned his association with the radical National Society, Cavour responded that it worked to erode the position of the Mazzinians and therefore he could not, and would not, oppose it.[5] He also recognized its potential as a useful ally when the conflict with Austria and her Italian allies resumed.

Although anxious for a second round with Austria, Cavour avoided provoking it prematurely. While energetic and firm, he shunned imprudence.[6] During the course of 1857 he proposed, and the Subalpine parliament passed, legislation improving the fortifications of Alessandria while moving the military arsenal from Genoa to La Spezia. Determined not to repeat the errors of 1848–49 during the first War of Italian Independence, Cavour recognized that Italy could not 'do it alone' and required allies. By 1857 he despaired of British assistance, conscious of the fact that while public opinion in Britain was favourable to the Italian cause, her men of affairs remained pro-Austrian. More than ever he relied on Napoleon III as the sole sovereign in Europe able and willing to champion the Italian cause. Piedmont therefore had to march with Napoleon, or not at all. Not surprisingly, Cavour's Turin showed itself sensitive to criticism from Paris, and very likely Rattazzi's removal from the Cabinet early in 1858 was orchestrated to satisfy Napoleon.[7]

Although some questioned Cavour's 'prudent audacity' and determination to secure the support of France, by the beginning of 1858 even Garibaldi appreciated the need to wait for Turin's signal. Cavour, for his part, did not discount the need for internal as well as international preparations for the inevitable conflict. Contacts with La Farina's National Society were preserved and patriotic committees in Tuscany were encouraged to undermine the ducal regime. Similar organizations, seeking internal subversion, were funded in the duchies of Parma and Modena, while Cavour's diplomacy openly criticized the Habsburg policy of intervention in central Italy.

Cavour waited anxiously for Napoleon to fulfil his promise to do something for Italy; meanwhile Italian revolutionaries and Mazzinians grew impatient, questioning the Emperor's resolve and commitment. In June of 1857 three Italians, Tibaldi, Bertolotti and Galli, arrived in Paris with the intention of assassinating the reluctant revolutionary, who was accused of abjuring his carbonarist faith. Their plot was frustrated by the police who apprehended the trio before the apartment of the Contessa di Castiglione, whom Napoleon often visited clandestinely. However, other revolutionaries assumed the burden of assassinating the Emperor, and on 14 January 1858, Felice Orsini, Antonio Gomez, Carlo di Rudio and Giuseppe Pieri were responsible for hurling bombs at the Imperial carriage which wounded or killed some 150 guards and spectators. Although physically unharmed, the Emperor was psychologically shaken by this latest attempt to take his life.

Cavour, striving to cement an alliance with the French, was dismayed to learn of Italian involvement in the terrorist plot. He expected Napoleon to react to the attempt on his life, and indeed he did. The assassination attempt, and the ensuing public debate, were instrumental in prompting Napoleon to make two decisions: firstly, to persuade, and if needs be pressure, the Piedmontese to take stronger measures against the radicals in their state; secondly, to take steps to provide a solution to the Italian problem. The two measures were interrelated in the Emperor's mind as his letter of 8 February 1858 to Vittorio Emanuele clearly illustrates. If the Piedmontese government showed itself liberal but firm in dealing with radical journals, incendiary groups and the demagogues, the Emperor promised, it could count on the full support of France. If, on the contrary, it encouraged or even tolerated outrageous behaviour, then he would have to regard Piedmont as a dangerous source of agitation.[8]

Cavour recognized the need for some concessions to assuage the Emperor's anger. At the end of January he wrote his friend and supporter, Michelangelo Castelli, that the times were dangerous and difficult, the sects grew more unrestrained, and steps were needed to curb their excesses. At the same time he instructed the intendant at Genoa to curb the press there, and if at all possible, in order to preserve the goodwill of France, to silence Mazzini's *Italia e Popolo*. Although insisting that Piedmont would continue to pursue a liberal path, Cavour introduced legislation which defined the crime of political assassination, imposing penalties for conspiring against the life of foreign sovereigns and heads of government.

Cavour's tokens of goodwill mollified Napoleon as was manifest during the trial of Felice Orsini, whose defence was assumed by Jules Favre. The latter portrayed Orsini as a patriot and a martyr, whose life was dedicated to the liberation of his country. From his prison cell, Orsini wrote a latter (11 February 1858) to the Emperor whom he had tried to assassinate, pleading for the Italian cause. Orsini did not ask that French blood be shed for his country, only that he prohibit the German *Bund* from supporting Austria in the war for Italian independence expected to erupt shortly. Free Italy, he concluded, and the benediction of twenty-three million Italians would enshrine the French ruler in posterity. On 3rd March, Orsini penned a second letter to Napoleon, thanking him for having had his first letter read in open court, and concluding that his patriotic pleas had found an echo in the heart of the Emperor.

The publication of these letters aroused fears in Vienna that they reflected the French Emperor's sentiments. Austria's concern was compounded when the Piedmontese were encouraged by Napoleon to publish them in the *Gazzetta Piemontese*, the official journal of the Turin government. Cavour, delighted by the turn of events, decided to capitalize further on the publication. He suggested an introduction to the correspondence, indicating where and how the documents were obtained, emphasizing the role played by Napoleon. He wanted Italians as well as Austrians to see who was behind them. He compared the publication of these letters to another bomb, that would fall on Vienna while pleasing patriots at home.[9] This represented the first Franco–Piedmontese action against the Austrians; others were to follow.

Through several intermediaries, including his cousin Prince Jerome Napoleon, son of the ex-King Jerome of Westphalia, and his half-Italian personal physician, Dr Henri Conneau, Napoleon let Cavour know that he wished to discuss privately the Italian situation. Concomitantly Cavour learned from his agent Alessandro Bixio that the Piedmontese Minister in Paris had obtained little from the French Foreign Minister, advising Cavour to deal directly with the Emperor outside ordinary diplomatic channels. Cavour welcomed a direct contact with Napoleon, but expressed reservations about a meeting until such time as a definite agreement seemed probable, if not certain. Fearing the international reverberations certain to follow such an encounter, Cavour hesitated to arouse suspicions until these could be counterbalanced by the prospect of an Franco–Piedmontese accord.

To prepare the groundwork Cavour sent his private secretary, Costantino Nigra, to Paris. In May his emissary telegraphed Turin that Napoleon had confirmed three essential points: a marriage uniting his house with the Savoy dynasty, a Franco-Piedmontese war to be waged against Austria for the liberation of northern Italy, and the Piedmontese formation of a Kingdom of Northern Italy. At the end of May, Napoleon sent Dr Conneau to Turin to talk with Vittorio Emanuele and Cavour. The Italophile physician reported that the Emperor planned to spend a month in Plombières, near the Piedmontese border, and would be disposed to meet with Cavour to discuss the Italian situation. Discounting the Emperor's lack of appreciation of the distances involved, Cavour acknowledged the political signal transmitted and agreed to venture to Plombières.

Turin reported officially that Cavour had left for Switzerland and was stopping in Savoy to examine work on the railways there. Only the king and General Alfonso La Marmora knew his eventual destination and intended mission. Cavour travelled to Plombières as Giuseppe Benso, accompanied only by a young undersecretary of the Ministry of Foreign Affairs, de Veillet. The two reached Plombières on 20th July, intending to stay in a hotel, but a messenger from the Emperor invited them to stay with him. During the course of their momentous meeting of 21 July 1858, Napoleon informed Cavour that he had decided to champion Piedmont's cause against Austria, provided the conflict were undertaken to create stability in the peninsula and could be justified before the courts of Europe.[10]

Following the meeting, Cavour compiled a short report of the discussion to brief Vittorio Emanuele, despatching a longer account on 24th July, when he left Plombières for Baden-Baden. These are the only direct reports of what transpired in July as the prime minister of Piedmont and the Emperor of France plotted war against Austria for the reorganization of Italy. According to Cavour's narrative, Napoleon insisted that the Pope and the King of Naples be treated with circumspection. Cavour agreed, replying that Pius IX could be assured of the possession of Rome, by the presence of the French garrison there, while the provinces of the Romagna revolted. As for the King of Naples, he would be left unmolested so long as he did not attempt to aid the Austrians.

Regarding the ultimate objective of the war, Napoleon agreed with Cavour on the need to push the Habsburgs out of the Peninsula, leaving them without even an inch of territory south of the Alps or west of the River Isonzo. The two conspirators had a lengthy discussion concerning the subsequent reorganization of Italy, the details of which Cavour spared his monarch. The gist of their compromise called for the formation of four states that would form an Italian Confederation, similar to the German *Bund*. Specifically the valley of the Po, the Romagna and the Legations would constitute a Kingdom of Upper Italy, under the House of Savoy, while Rome and its immediate environs would be left to the Papacy. The remaining provinces of the Papal States would be absorbed by Tuscany to form a Kingdom of Central Italy. The Kingdom of the Two Sicilies would continue unchanged.

Napoleon insisted that the presidency of the confederation be conferred upon the Pope, as partial compensation for the loss of the greater part of his territory. Cavour had reservations both about the efficacy of the confederation and the leadership of the Pope, but raised no objections. His willingness to accept these terms flowed from his appreciation of the importance of the French alliance and the inclusion of an escape clause within the agreement. The latter stipulated that the principle of reorganization the two outlined was subject to modification dependent on the course of the war. Cavour and Napoleon examined the prospect that the thrones of the new Kingdom of Central Italy and Naples might be left vacant if their rulers should retire to Vienna. Although no definite decisions were concluded to cover the possibility, Napoleon suggested Murat for Naples, and Cavour proposed that the Duchess of Parma might be compensated by occupying the Pitti Palace.

Napoleon pondered both the diplomatic and military aspects of the conflict, which he perceived were interrelated. It was necessary that Austria should be the sole enemy, and she would therefore have to be isolated as such. Consequently, Napoleon continued, the *casus belli* was of crucial importance, while the fears and jealousies of the continental powers had to be addressed. Napoleon believed that Britain would remain neutral, but prudently pressed Cavour to court British public opinion to assure their non-intervention. Alexander of Russia, the Emperor continued, had promised on numerous occasions, both formally and informally, not to interfere with the French reorganization of the peninsula. Finally he counted on the Prince of Prussia's antipathy towards Austria to prevent any assistance from that quarter.

Napoleon speculated that, even alone, Austria was a formidable foe who would have to endure several defeats before evacuating Italy. The Emperor estimated that their victory would require an army of at least 300,000 front-line soldiers, proposing that France supply two-thirds of this force, and Piedmont and her Italian allies, the remaining third. The French army would be commanded by Napoleon personally, the Italian army by King Vittorio Emanuele. So far as financing the war was concerned, Napoleon promised to provide the Piedmontese with whatever weapons they required, facilitating loans in Paris. Napoleon encouraged Cavour to solicit contributions of money and material from the other Italian provinces, but to do so cautiously. Cavour, for his part, approved these stipulations.

In compensation for his services Napoleon wondered whether Vittorio Emanuele would cede Savoy and the county of Nice. Cavour responded that since his king adhered to the principle of national self-determination he was prepared to sacrifice the cradle of the dynasty which should be united to France. Nice, far more Italian than French, was another matter, and Cavour suggested that its cession to France violated the very principle which prompted the projected conflict with Austria. Having no immediate rejoinder, the Emperor nervously stroked his moustache, indicating that there were secondary issues which could be resolved later. Although Napoleon did not make an issue of the cession of Nice, he persisted in his acquisitive scheme.

The Emperor again raised the issue of the dynastic connection between his house and the dynasty of Savoy to be effected by the marriage of his cousin, Jerome Napoleon, to Princess Clotilde, daughter of the Piedmontese king. Cavour tried tactfully to convey his king's reservations, citing his reluctance to give his young daughter away in marriage and his determination not to impose an unwelcome choice upon the child. Napoleon, undismayed, stressed that the marriage, which would seal the dynastic alliance, was very important to him. Cavour, in his correspondence with the king, noted that the Emperor did not go so far as to make the marriage a *sine qua non* of the military alliance and the waging of the war against Austria. Nonetheless, Cavour warned his king that Napoleon, being highly sensitive, would never forget a service or a slight, and would perceive the rejection as a blood insult. Thus Cavour reported that to accept the alliance while rejecting the marriage would be an immense political error, posing grave consequences.[11]

The Plombières agreement delighted Cavour. Upon his return he explained to Marco Minghetti that initially Napoleon had been reluctant to touch the states of the Church, and only upon his insistence had the Emperor eventually relented. Napoleon consented to have the Legations up to Ancona included within the projected Kingdom of Upper Italy, but insisted this be kept quiet. Likewise, the Emperor did not wish the planned cession of Nice and Savoy to leak out. Cavour recognized that there were those who questioned the Emperor's motives and commitment, but he did not share their suspicions. He assured another close associate, Michelangelo Castelli, that during the course of his recent conversations with Napoleon, it was clear that the French ruler's attitudes towards Austria, the Roman question, and even the future of Italy, approximated his own. Cavour confided that at Plombières, he had the distinct feeling that he was not dealing with the Emperor of the French, but an Italian liberal.[12]

Following his departure from Plombières, Cavour visited Germany, where he met a number of princes, most important of whom was William, prince regent of Prussia, and future King of Prussia and German Emperor. William was delighted to make the acquaintance of Cavour, finding him quite different from the turbulent revolutionary he had anticipated. Cavour, likewise, was impressed with William's resolve, and from that moment envisioned an alliance with Prussia to complement that with France. Cavour considered it compatible with the Napoleonic connection, but before making any proposals determined to approach the Emperor through the intermediary of the Marquis Gioacchino Pepoli of Bologna. Napoleon responded enthusiastically, indicating that should Prussia join France and Piedmont against Austria, she would not only be associated with the just Italian cause, but would assure the future of German nationalism. Prussia, however, could not be persuaded to join the coalition.

Despite the cloak of secrecy, word immediately leaked out of Cavour's visit to Napoleon. Indeed, while the two were in conference, the Emperor received a telegram and then turned to his co-conspirator, reporting that Walewski, his Foreign Minister had learned of Cavour's presence at Plombières. Small wonder that Count Hubner, the Austrian Ambassador at Paris, was haunted by the thought of what Cavour and Napoleon had concluded. Walewski could tell the Austrian little, knowing nothing about the meeting, but hoping to learn something soon. Walewksi no less than Hubner had few kind words for Cavour, accusing him of employing deceit, intrigues and trickery to wring concessions from the French Emperor.[13]

The Austrian apprehension was shared by the British, who were alarmed by the prospect that the peace might be shattered. As long as Cavour remained Minister of the King of Sardinia, Austrian diplomats complained in London, Austria would have no peace and the tranquillity of Europe would be constantly threatened. Cavour's rejoinder that he was only doing his duty, did not calm the courts. While the government of Lord Malmesbury, Lord Derby and Disraeli supported Cavour's internal reformism, it decidedly opposed his efforts to revise the map of Europe by belligerent means. Lord Malmesbury indicated that, wishing Piedmont to preserve its position in Europe, he counselled it not to become embroiled with Austria or threaten the peace. Nor did the British appreciate Turin's overtures to Russia.

British fears were confirmed when Cavour informed the Cabinet, via Hudson, that the Piedmontese were determined to push the Habsburgs out of Italy – even at the cost of razing their own cities. Austrian diplomats in London and Vienna were quick to take advantage of British misgivings, and Cavour's agents reported that London and Vienna remained in close communication, adding that Count Buol lost no opportunity to denounce Sardinian actions. English hostility to his foreign policy objectives disturbed but did not deter the energetic Cavour. There were, he calculated, three major powers in Europe interested in disrupting the status quo: France, Prussia and Russia; while two powers, Austria and England, wished to preserve it. Though it distressed him that the first three were not the most liberal, self-interest dictated a close association with those favouring change. Cavour complained that London did not understand that Italian liberals had few choices available; since Russia opposed Austria she had good reason to support Piedmont.[14]

The British were upset by Cavour's machinations for war, but even more so by the news from Paris. French relations with Austria were as poor as those of Sardinia and prominent voices in the French capital foresaw war as inevitable. Napoleon made no secret of his intentions. He informed Palmerston, who visited Paris in the autumn, that the present situation in Italy could not continue and would provoke a crisis detrimental to Austrian interests. He might have added that the crisis would also undermine the Pope's temporal power, which he was committed to preserve. Small wonder that Filippo Antonelli, the older brother of the Cardinal Secretary of State, and his confidant, questioned French foreign policy. Cavour alone was pleased. Reading an anti-Austrian article in *La Presse*, which supported a French war against Austria, he commented that if he were the Austrian Ambassador he would immediately request his passport.[15]

Rome was alarmed by the anti-Austrian tone of the French and Piedmontese press. Articles appeared in Paris expressing sympathy for the Italian nation and were widely known to be inspired by the government. Word reached Rome that Napoleon had even subsidized the establishment of a new journal to champion his Italian policy. The Papal Nuncio in Paris, Sacconi, reported to Antonelli that public personages in Paris, even some members of the Imperial family, spoke unkindly of the Papal government, and there was a growing sentiment that the Pope's territory should be restricted so he would have fewer problems. The Papal Nuncio urged Antonelli to move expeditiously to eliminate the foreign troops which continued to occupy parts of the Papal territory. In this fashion, Sacconi explained, the enemies of the Pope could no longer claim that his regime survived only by means of foreign bayonets. Meanwhile Cavour's memorandum to the Cabinets of London, Berlin and St Petersburg, suggesting that much of the anti-Austrian sentiment in Lombardy–Venetia flowed from Vienna's concordat with the Papacy, aroused and angered Pius IX, who denounced Turin's policies.

Back home, Cavour hastened preparations for the war that had been planned at Plombières. Preliminary to the formal alliance was the marriage proposal, and Cavour pressed both the king and his daughter to please Napoleon on this matter. By the end of August 1858 his will had prevailed. Even before Clotilde has given her formal consent, Cavour despatched a note to his co-conspirator outlining what had been agreed at Plombières, beginning with the fact that a treaty of offensive and defensive alliance was to be concluded between the Emperor of the French and the King of Sardinia for the liberation of Italy. Further articles detailed the contribution of each partner, the means of provoking and financing the war, and the subsequent reorganization of the peninsula. Cavour indicated that he would use recruits and volunteers, but they would be incorporated into the Sardinian army.[16]

Cavour sought to implement the last provision by means of Garibaldi and the National Society. Using La Farina and Pallavicino of the National Society as intermediaries, Cavour informed Garibaldi he had important matters to discuss with him. In December the 'brain' and the 'sword' of Italian unification met, and the former appraised the latter of part of his discussion with Napoleon at Plombières. In preparation for the impending war, Cavour asked Garibaldi to enrol and command a volunteer force for the struggle, and the latter accepted. Cavour thus established the base for Garibaldi's 'Cacciatori delle Alpi' and his commission as major-general in the Royal Army of Piedmont. Conservatives in Turin questioned Cavour's contacts with the National Society and Garibaldi, but he was neither dismayed nor dissuaded by their arguments, replying that many instruments were needed in an orchestra. However, he was determined to remain conductor. No one else had the means and the nerve to coordinate the campaign.

Cavour was assisted in provoking the war by his co-conspirator who dropped a bombshell during his reception for the diplomatic corps on New Year's Day. During the festivities, Napoleon turned to Baron Hubner, the Austrian Ambassador to the Tuileries, expressing regret that relations between their countries were strained. The veiled threat did not come as a complete surprise. Indeed, since mid-November 1858, the Austrians had considered mobilization plans. The Papal Nuncio, fearing the consequences of a Franco-Austrian conflict, left the reception 'pale as death'. Although the Emperor sought to soothe the apprehensions of the Austrian Ambassador the next day, and the French Foreign Minister discounted the rumours of war, as did an article in the official journal, *Le Moniteur*, the rumours continued to mushroom. Lord Minto was one of the few who seemed to accept Napoleon's reassurances; the Papal Nuncio was not convinced. Sacconi reported to Rome that while the Emperor claimed his aims were peaceful, he could not foresee the eventualities of the next two or three months.[17]

Rome's scepticism was reinforced on 10 January 1859 by Vittorio Emanuele's speech from the throne, indicating that, despite respect for the 1815 treaties, he could not remain immune to the cries of anguish emanating from all parts of Italy. Hudson, the Italophile British representative in Turin, characterized the king's message as nothing less than a rocket falling on the treaties, dashing the hopes of those who wished to preserve the peace. In fact, Cavour confided to friends that things would inevitably go ahead, that there would be no turning back, and he took steps to assure that the established order would collapse. The Apostolic Nuncio at Florence decried the fact that Cavour and his lieutenant, La Farina, aided and encouraged local revolutionaries, and feared for the safety of the Papal States. Furthermore, though Napoleon expressed peaceful intentions, his actions belied his words, as his government continued to arm and prepare for a military campaign.

The march towards war alarmed not only Rome and Vienna, but many in Paris, London and Turin as well. Ollivier questioned the Emperor's aims in his journal, positing that the Emperor's bellicose stance was geared to make the French forget about their lost freedom rather than to provide for Italian liberty. The Ministry and the Salons aligned themselves against the war. Thiers wrote a memorandum against it, which reached Napoleon. In Turin Solaro della Margarita warned of the dire consequences of Cavour's Italian policy and the unfortunate impact on the Pope's temporal power.

In London Lord Malmesbury hoped for an Italian regeneration without violence, perhaps by constraining the King of Naples and the Pope to reform their respective regimes. He deplored Piedmont's bellicose policy which risked both its institutions and its future. Noting he was primarily concerned for neither Austria nor France, Malmesbury confessed that he and Lord Derby would do all within their means to prevent war, which would cost 100,000 lives and desolate one of the most beautiful areas of Europe. He dedicated himself to the preservation of the peace.[18]

The task assumed by Malmesbury proved difficult. The journals noted that Prince Napoleon had ventured to Turin in January and wrote of his impending marriage to Princess Clotilde. Following the prince's arrival in mid-January, a marriage agreement and an offensive–defensive alliance between France and Piedmont were concluded on 18 January 1859, with the marriage occurring at the end of the month. Cavour told Pasolini that all was accomplished, certain that with the marriage Piedmont could count on French support (the marriage having been the necessary preliminary to the war they had planned). On that occasion Vittorio Emanuele gave Cavour a magnificent ring, which Cavour accepted, reminding his king that he had no wife and did not intend to take one. Your bride, responded Vittorio Emanuele, is the *patria*.[19]

The marriage and the alliance caused new consternation in London and Rome. Sacconi warned Cardinal Antonelli that in the light of these actions, one had to conclude that Napoleon had not abandoned his plans for the reorganization of Italy and would seize the opportunity to realize them. In the expectation of French support in the impending war, Cavour procured permission from the Sub-alpine parliament to float a loan of fifty million lire for extraordinary expenditure. While the Prince Consort of England, opposed to Cavour's policies, predicted he would not succeed in raising the money, the loan was in fact oversubscribed, and more than eighty million lire was collected. The war loan, and the news that Cavour had met with Garibaldi, enlisting his services, electrified the country.

When Napoleon opened the French Chambers, on 7 February 1859, he sought to calm Europe and soothe the Austrians. Although Napoleon repeated the declaration of Bordeaux that the Empire meant peace, many doubted his sincerity; some even questioned his ability to control matters. Rome was not reassured, especially since the publication of La Guerronière's pamphlet 'Napoleon III et L'Italie' on

4 February 1859, which reflected the Emperor's sentiments. Pointing to the abnormal condition of Italy in general, and the situation in the Papal States in particular, the pamphlet called for a diminution of the temporal power, conferring upon Pius a type of moral ascendancy that flowed from his presidency over an Italian Confederation. It thus presaged the war in Italy, providing a justification that might even appeal to the English, who opposed the temporal power.

Pope Pius IX, fearing that war was inevitable, worried that the Austrian and French forces which occupied parts of his territory would wage their conflict on his territory. He therefore pressed Antonelli to call for an Austrian and French withdrawal, insisting that the Papal government was sufficiently strong to provide for its own defence. The Secretary of State, aware of the danger cited by the Pope, dreaded the revolutionary agitation and the schemes of Cavour and his allies. Thus he moved cautiously to end the foreign occupation. The only good news received by Rome came from Hubner, the Austrian Ambassador at the Tuileries, who confided to Sacconi, the Papal Nuncio in Paris, that while Vienna was disposed to make some concessions to Napoleon, it would never put pressure upon the Holy See, or any of the Italian states, to grant reforms they did not deem appropriate.[20]

Cavour sought to convince the British that they had to choose between him and Mazzini in Italy. London, however, would have preferred an alternative, and following the Austrian request for mediation, asked Paris and Turin to catalogue their complaints. While Cavour delayed, revealing his disbelief that diplomatic means could resolve the peninsula's problems, the French responded. Walewski, on Napoleon's behalf, indicated the French conditions for relations to return to normal. These included the Austrian abrogation of its protective treaties with the Italian states, the introduction of constitutionalism in these same states and the creation of a separate administration for the Legations. This prompted the extraordinary mission of Lord Cowley, the British Ambassador in Paris, to Vienna, in an attempt to avert a war between France and Austria. In February Lord Cowley was cordially received by the Emperor Franz-Josef.

At this juncture a rift developed between Napoleon, willing to pursue the diplomatic initiative, and Cavour, bent upon waging the war planned at Plombières. The conditions he proposed, including the formation of autonomous regimes for Lombardy and Venetia, and the pontifical provinces east of the Appenines, Cavour knew would not be accepted either by Vienna or Rome. Napoleon, in turn, by means of an article in the *Moniteur* (4 March 1859), proclaimed that he had promised no more than to protect Sardinia if she were menaced by an Austrian attack. Anything beyond this he deemed the exaggerations of the press, lies and folly. The article created a sensation in Europe, distressed Turin and roused the wrath of Cavour.

Prince Napoleon reacted first, resigning his position as Minister in Algeria and denouncing the Emperor for his apparent change of heart. The Piedmontese were angered and remembered the warnings of Hudson, who had predicted that Napoleon would start them dancing and then leave them dangling. His prediction seemed prophetic. However, the Piedmontese pressed ahead and during the Cabinet meeting of 6 March 1859, the king authorized Cavour to call forward the reserves. A few days later the government recalled to active service all soldiers from the class of 1828–32. Then on 17th March, Vittorio Emanuele formally signed the decree nominating Garibaldi commander of the 'Cacciatori delle Alpi'. The bomb had been packed, Cavour told his confidants, and it had to explode; if necessary, he continued, it would explode in the faces of those who had first encouraged and then abandoned the cause.[21]

Fortunately for Turin, Cowley's mission proved inconclusive and he left Vienna on 10th March, convinced that Piedmont would have to disarm before Austria would enter negotiations. Soon after a new danger arose with the Russian suggestion for the calling of a congress of the five major European powers to resolve the differences between Paris and Vienna. Napoleon agreed to participate. The call for the congress was questioned in the capitals, most notably in Turin, London and Vienna. An angry Cavour confided to his friend Massari that while Napoleon, the sovereign of a state of over thirty-five million subjects, could delay and play games, the much smaller Piedmont could only survive by talking frankly and walking straight. He insisted on Piedmontese participation in the projected congress, threatening to resign if it were held without his country. The Papal Nuncio in France surmised that Cavour was determined to force Napoleon's hand.

The British government urged Napoleon to constrain his ally to disarm, and did not favour Piedmontese inclusion in the Congress alongside Britain, France, Russia, Prussia and Austria. The last power not only refused to have Piedmontese participation and insisted on its disarmament, but posed a third condition for the calling of a congress – there would be no discussion of altering the Italian territorial situation. Napoleon did not reject or approve Vienna's conditions, startled by Cavour's outburst of indignation. On 24th March, Cavour was invited to Paris, and word circulated that the Emperor would force his ally to disarm, though it was made clear that she could not expect equal entry to the circle of the major powers. Indeed, on 26th March, Napoleon informed Cavour that Sardinia and the other Italian states would have only a consultative role in the projected congress. Cavour concluded that though his co-conspirator wanted to wage war against Austria in Italy, his foreign minister Walewski opposed it, while the Emperor was perplexed as to the means to effect his desired end. The European Congress threatened to frustrate all of his plans. Cavour thus left Paris with despair in his heart and tears in his eyes.[22]

Nonetheless, once back in Turin, Cavour continued to prepare for war even as the powers sought to preserve the peace. Apparently he had not lost confidence in Napoleon, explaining to those in his inner circle that only the Emperor and Prince Napoleon appreciated the importance of the Italian question. Rome shared his assessment, convinced that Napoleon had not abandoned his liberal and national ideas and sought to reorganize the peninsula. Britain, likewise, fully realized that Piedmontese disarmament could only be attained if Paris insisted on it. The British, therefore, called upon the French to persuade Sardinia to disarm, while they collectively worked to invite Turin to the congress on an equal footing with other powers. On 18th April, the French Foreign Minister informed Cavour that his country accepted the British plan for disarmament. The distraught Cavour prepared to comply, contemplating emigration or perhaps even suicide. He was spared either alternative on 21 April 1859, by the news of an Austrian ultimatum insisting on immediate disarmament. Cavour finally had what he wanted: a clear intention of Austrian aggression and a French commitment to provide assistance. On 26th April, Turin rejected the ultimatum and Vienna declared war. The Machiavellian minister had managed to precipitate the conflict which even his old adversary, Mazzini, deemed a master stroke.

NOTES

1. Michelangelo Castelli, *Il Conte di Cavour, Ricordi di Michelangelo Castelli*, ed. Luigi Chiala (Turin: Roux, 1886), pp. 190–1.
2. Marco Minghetti, *Miei Ricordi* (3rd edn, Turin: Roux, 1888), III, p. 136; *Memoires . . . par le Prince de Metternich*, VIII, p. 394.
3. Costantino Nigra (ed.), *Count Cavour and Madame de Circourt: Some Unpublished Correspondence*, trans: Arthur John Butler (London: Cassell

and Co., 1894), p. 73; Edmondo Mayor (ed.), *Nuove lettere inedite del Conte di Cavour* (Turin: Roux, 1895), p. 356.

4. Minghetti, III, p. 460.
5. Ibid., III, p. 125; Domenico Masse, *Cattolici e Risorgimento* (Rome: Edizione Paoline, 1961), p. 47; Giuseppe Massari, *Il Conte di Cavour. Ricordi biografici* (Turin: Botta, 1873), p. 160.
6. Nigra (ed.), *Count Cavour and Madame de Circourt*, p. 71.
7. Mayor (ed.), *Nuove lettere inedite del Conte di Cavour*, pp. 506–52.
8. *Il Carteggio Cavour–Nigra dal 1858 al 1861* ed. National Commission for the Publication of the Papers of Count Cavour (Bologna: Zanichelli, 1961), I, p. 63.
9. Castelli, *Ricordi*, pp. 79, 196; Massari, *Il Conte di Cavour*, pp. 221, 235.
10. Castelli, Ricordi, pp. 75–7.
11. Mack Walker (ed.), *Plombières: Secret Diplomacy and the Rebirth of Europe* (New York: Oxford University Press, 1968), pp. 27–37.
12. Castelli, *Ricordi*, pp. 75–7; Minghetti, III, p. 219.
13. Giuseppe Massari, *Diario dalle cento voci* (Bologna: Cappelli, 1959), p. 75; Walker, pp. 37–8.
14. Massari, *Diario*, pp. 1, 12, 27, 42, 54; Massari, *Il Conte di Cavour*, p. 239.
15. Massari, *Diario*, pp. 26, 73; Mournier to Filippo Antonelli, 5 June 1858, *Archivio di Stato di Roma, Fondo Famiglia Antonelli, busta 7, fascicolo 6.*
16. Mariano Gabriele, *Il Carteggio Antonelli–Sacconi (1858–1860)* (Rome: Istituto per la Storia del Risorgimento Italiano, 1962), I, pp. 5–7; Walker, pp. 232–4.
17. Massari, *Diario*, pp. 50, 83, 104–6; Gabriele, I, pp. 10–14; Imbert de Saint-Armand, *France and Italy* (New York: Scribner's Sons, 1899), p. 8.
18. Massari, *Diario*, pp. 104–6, 113–15; Gabriele, I, pp. 10–14, 20; Nuncio at Florence to Antonelli, 10 January 1859, *Archivio di Stato di Roma, Miscellanea di Carte Politiche O Riservate, b.* 131, *f.* 4665; Harry Hearder, 'La politica di Lord Malmesbury verso l'Italia nella primavera del 1859,' *Rassegna Storica del Risorgimento*, XLIII, (January–March 1956), p. 40.
19. Massari, *Diario*, p. 128.
20. Gabriele, I, pp. 22–3, 37; Giuseppe Pasolini, *Memorie*, 1815–76, ed. P.D. Pasolini (3rd edn, Turin: Bocca, 1887), p. 226.
21. Massari, *Diario*, p. 118; Gabriele, I, p. 54; Saint-Armand, p. 69.
22. Gabriele, I, pp. 48–9, 60; Massari, *Diario*, p. 166.

CHAPTER SEVEN
Cavour, Garibaldi and Napoleon III in the Wars for the Formation of Italy

In mid-April 1859, the Austrian government revealed its determination to dispatch an ultimatum to Turin, demanding disarmament in three days and threatening to launch an attack if its conditions were not accepted. Metternich commented that the die had been cast.[1] Cavour rejoiced not only because war was inevitable, but since the Piedmontese had been alerted, the prospect of defeat before the arrival of French support was unlikely. On 23rd April, the day the ultimatum was delivered by Count Kellersperg, Cavour convened the Sub-alpine parliament into session, presenting a project placing dictatorial powers in the hands of King Vittorio Emanuele for the duration of the impending conflict. It was approved by a vote of 110 to 24. When Cavour heard that Kellersperg had arrived at the station, he left the Chamber predicting it would be the last of the Piedmontese parliament – the next would be that of the Italian Kingdom.

On 25th April, as the Senate approved Cavour's emergency measure, French forces arrived in Chambèry in trains bearing the slogan, 'Excursion to Italy'. The following day, 26th April, at the appointed hour, Cavour rejected the Austrian ultimatum and awaited events, confident of the future. Relations between Paris and Vienna were now shattered; on 29th April declarations of war were issued by the Vienna and Turin governments. Austria, in her proclamation of war, noted that providence had often relied upon her sword when revolution threatened the continent, and hoped for German, if not European support. The proclamation of Vittorio Emanuele, written by Cavour, blamed Austrian domination and aggression for provoking the war, which Piedmont, in honour, could not avoid. Cavour had Vittorio Emanuele pledge to serve as the first soldier of Italian independence,[2] and welcomed Napoleon to Italy, delighted to see his plans materialize.

On 29 April 1859, the Austrian force finally crossed the Ticino and entered Piedmont. Shortly after, on 3rd May, Napoleon asserted that in attacking his ally, Piedmont, Austria also waged war on France. Napoleon argued that Austrian actions had created a situation whereby the Hapsburgs would either control all of northern Italy, or Italy from the Alps to the Adriatic would be free. To reassure the powers, and above all the British, Napoleon contended that the French had no territorial ambitions, and were seeking only to defend the cause of humanity and Italian independence. Promising to respect the position of all neutrals, Napoleon repeated his promise to protect the Pope.[3] His proclamation publicly reiterated what he had privately assured Pius IX – that during the course of the war in Italy he would uphold the cause of the Holy See and the sovereignty of the Holy Father.[4] The pledge was easier made than kept.

At the outbreak of the war, before hostilities began, national manifestations erupted in Florence, which were echoed in other towns of the duchy, including Pisa, Lucca and Sienna, leading the Grand Duke Leopold II and his family to flee for Mantua. As four coaches spirited the Tuscan Habsburgs back to Austria, the provisional government established in Florence, under the Baron Bettino Ricasoli, offered the Piedmontese king a temporary dictatorship over the duchy, pending a final political solution. Count Cavour orchestrated and funded the rebellion with this prospect in mind, but he and Vittorio Emanuele had to secure the approval of their ally, whose enthusiasm for revolution and upheaval in the peninsula did not match their own. On the French Emperor's suggestion, Vittorio Emanuele refused the dictatorship but secured command of the troops raised in Tuscany, assuming responsibility for the protection of the duchy during the course of the war. Carlo Boncompagni, nominated Sardinian Minister plenipotentiary to Florence, was assigned the dual task of preserving order and Sardinian interests there.

Developments elsewhere in the peninsula followed the course of military events. The Austrian commander, General Ferencz Gyulai, from the first assumed a defensive rather than an aggressive posture, even though his troops outnumbered the Piedmontese and initially outnumbered the combined Franco–Piedmontese forces. (The French dispatched some 128,000 men and the Piedmontese another 70,000, while the Austrians had more than 220,000 soldiers available.) Gyulai did not take advantage of the vulnerability of Turin, the Piedmontese capital, which might have capitulated to a decisive Austrian attack.

The Austrian commander in fact showed little initiative, allowing the French and Piedmontese to link up at Alessandria; Gyulai preferred a war of position rather than of action, assuring that the major battles would be fought in Lombardy and Venetia.

In May the Franco–Piedmontese forces achieved small but strategic moral–building victories at Montebello and Palestro, driving the enemy back across the Ticino. Rumours of an Austrian rout encouraged the peoples of Massa and Carrara, as well as the Duchy of Parma, to appeal to the Piedmontese for assistance against their rulers. Events there, as well as in Modena and the Romagna, would be dictated by the march and fortune of the respective armies, and the attitude assumed by Napoleon III. Pius appealed to Napoleon for protection, deploring the prospect of Catholic Austria and Catholic France waging war in the provinces of the Papal States. For this, among other reasons, the French Emperor urged Cavour and Vittorio Emanuele to exercise caution regarding the Papal States. The Piedmontese king, who wrote to Pius IX imploring absolution from ecclesiastical censure during the course of the conflict, appeared more prone to listen to the Emperor than did Cavour.[5] The Kingdom of the Two Sicilies, at the bottom of the peninsula, declared its neutrality at the outbreak of the war, but the disquieting events in Italy and the death of Ferdinand II on 22 May 1859, rendered its future insecure. The son of 'Bomba', the young and inexperienced Francis II, ascended the Neapolitan throne during the turmoil.

On 4 June 1859 the belligerents waged a three-hour battle at Magenta, on the road to Milan, which the allies won only after the arrival of General Maurice MacMahon leading French reinforcements. Although the Austrian army retreated in good order, Gyulai evacuated Milan. Four days later Napoleon and Vittorio Emanuele triumphantly entered the Lombard capital. Their entry was heralded by a proclamation of 5th June to the people of Milan, urging them to place their trust in Vittorio Emanuele and to enlist in his army.[6] While the proclamation was addressed to the Lombards, its message also aroused the people of Central Italy, whose freedom of action had increased as a result of the withdrawal of the Austrian garrisons from Pavia, Piacenza, Ancona, Bologna and Ferrara, following Magenta.

On 12 June 1859, the Legate in Bologna, Cardinal Giuseppe Milesi Pironi Ferretti, appalled to find his palace surrounded by angry demonstrators no longer restrained by the Austrians, fled to Ferrara. While he entreated respect for the sovereign rights of Pio Nono, the population appealed for the protection of Vittorio Emanuele. In response, the Piedmontese king dispatched 2,000 men, appointing

Massimo D'Azeglio his representative in the Romagna. With the whole of the Romagna on the verge of falling into Piedmontese hands, Catholics in Italy and France wondered how Napoleon could keep his word to the Pope to protect his dominions.[7] When the Austrians withdrew into the security of the Quadrilateral, now under the command of the Emperor Franz-Josef, the upheaval quickly spread to Ravenna and Ferrara.

As the Franco-Piedmontese forces prepared for a confrontation against the Austrians at Solferino on 24th June, Napoleon, fearing the political ramifications in France of the protests of Pio Nono and Cardinal Antonelli, walked a political tightrope. He blocked the Piedmontese absorption of the Romagna, but Antonelli responded by sending the Pope's Swiss troops to retake Perugia which was sacked on 20th June, thus returning the Marches to Papal sovereignty. Meanwhile the diplomacy of the Papal Secretary of State worked to prevent the Piedmontese from moving from the Romagna to the restored provinces of the Marches.

Although the Franco-Piedmontese army triumphed in the bloody Battle of Solferino (24th June), the losses were heavy. The Piedmontese suffered more than 5,000 casualties while their French allies had some 13,000 men wounded or killed – losses greater than their Austrian adversary. Napoleon, no less than Franz-Josef, was shaken by the large number of dead and the miseries of the wounded. To make matters worse, the battle, while important, proved indecisive, for Franz-Josef's forces had retreated in orderly fashion behind the River Mincio, and re-entered the security of the Quadrilateral. The prospect of a quick French victory remained more elusive than ever, and Napoleon worried about the deterioration of his political and military situation. Solferino, like Magenta, had not been an easy victory, and the Emperor faced the prospect of a long siege of the Quadrilateral fortresses, complicated by the possible intervention of Prussia and the German confederation on Austria's behalf. Furthermore, the war was unpopular at home and the plight of the Pope undermined his Catholic support. Finally, his ally, Cavour, seemed lukewarm about the confederation he had accepted at Plombières, and schemed to create a far stronger state than the Emperor had envisioned. For these reasons Napoleon sought negotiations to end the war.

From the outset Napoleon had foreseen the need for a European settlement of the Italian question, and in the light of the difficulties he encountered in Italy and at home, hoped for mediation. Austria, too, was prepared for a negotiated solution, having been disillusioned by

Germany's failure to spring to her defence and the Pope's hesitation to unleash an excommunication against Franco-Piedmontese aggression. (The Habsburgs were, moreover, haunted by the threat of a French-inspired Hungarian revolution.) The suggestions sent to Pio Nono to act as mediator went unanswered, as the Pope could not see on what basis he could propose peace to Austria. Pius perceived that Austria would demand a return to the situation *ante bellum*, but doubted if this would be acceptable to Napoleon.[8] Some hoped that Britain, which had sought to prevent the outbreak of war, could help restore the peace. However, the country's sympathies, the Earl of Derby explained, were neither with France nor Austria, but increasingly in favour of Italy.

On 24th June, the day the Battle of Solferino erupted, the Prince Regent of Prussia requested the support of Britain and Russia in an armed mediation on the basis of the current status quo, and Austrian acceptance of reform in north and central Italy. The offer was rejected by the pro-Italian Cabinet, headed by Palmerston and his Foreign Secretary, Lord John Russell, which in early June had replaced the more conservative Derby Cabinet. The mission of Prince Paul Esterhazy to London in June to persuade the British government to intervene on Austria's behalf likewise proved abortive.

Meanwhile Napoleon telegraphed his ambassador, Persigny, in London, urging the British government to propose an armistice and suggesting as peace terms the creation of an Italian Confederation, under the presidency of the Pope. Napoleon indicated that the Confederation would include an enlarged Piedmont, which would absorb Lombardy and Parma, a new state combining Venice and Modena under an Austrian archduke, the Legations, under the direction of a Piedmontese vicar, while the rest of the Papal States, Tuscany and Naples would be included under their existing regimes. Finally, a European congress would be called to arrange a permanent peace upon these general terms. While Palmerston and Russell, who favoured the formation of a broader Kingdom of Upper Italy, disliked Napoleon's proposals, which fell short of their expectations, Queen Victoria, who was entirely unsympathetic to the Italian cause, indicated that the French initiative should not receive any moral support from Britain.[9]

Napoleon, distressed by the delays in mediation and the pressure from his Foreign Minister, Walewski, for peace, on the evening of 6th July secretly sent General Fleury with a letter to Franz-Josef at Verona, proposing a truce during which they could agree upon peace terms. Napoleon thus violated the provision of his treaty with

Sardinia not to consider any unilateral proposition on the cessation of hostilities. It proved to be neither the first nor the last of Napoleon's displays of bad faith. Franz-Josef, concerned that a long struggle would weaken Austria's power in Germany as well as Italy, accepted immediately, suggesting a meeting at Villafranca to set conditions. On 8th July, the French and Austrian representatives agreed to an armistice until 15th August. Cavour confronted a *fait accompli*. Napoleon called for a meeting of the two emperors at Villafranca, where the two might personally negotiate the preliminaries for the peace treaty. During these discussions Franz-Josef reluctantly renounced the territory the Franco–Piedmontese forces occupied, which included most of Lombardy, apart from the fortresses of Mantua and Peschiera, but would concede no more. Napoleon was free to turn this Lombard territory over to Piedmont, while Venetia would remain in Austrian hands, but join the Italian Confederation presided over by the Pope. The Grand Duke of Tuscany and the Duke of Modena were to return to their states, although they would proclaim a general amnesty, protecting the population which had forced them to flee.

Reaction to Villafranca was immediate and predictable. Russia, whose reformism following the Crimean War required peace and stability, appeared relieved that the conflict which threatened the continent's tranquillity had ended. Britain, whose colonial and maritime ventures likewise called for continental peace, nonetheless found the terms of Villafranca unfortunate, and was distressed by the prospect of an Italian Confederation under the presidency of the Papacy. British ministers were convinced that the projected Austrian participation assured Habsburg domination of Italy. Berlin, which envisioned a role in galvanizing Germany against France, found its efforts truncated and its campaign for German leadership thwarted. Rome was elated, but Pius IX, noting that the enemies of the peace were 'insane and evil' feared that it would not be implemented.[10] Turin, of course, was most disappointed, and the king and his chief minister felt betrayed and cheated.

Cavour, outraged by Napoleon's failure to liberate Italy from the Alps to the Adriatic as promised, pressed Vittorio Emanuele to continue the struggle alone, which the king wisely refused to do. Enraged and frustrated, Cavour resigned on 11th July, and the next day Vittorio Emanuele signed the peace preliminaries, but added before his signature, 'in so far as they concern me'. It was an important reservation, absolving the king and his government from enforcing the unpopular provisions of the peace: the preservation of the integrity of the Papal States, the restoration of the dukes, or even the creation of the Italian Confederation with Austrian participation.

Cavour, acknowledging he had suffered 'a stunning defeat' and no longer issued orders as 'Commander-in-Chief', promised to continue the fight, behind the scenes, 'as a private'. He had no immediate family, he confided to his friend Massari, adding he would do all that he could for the Italian cause.[11] He proved true to his words.

Cavour suggested General La Marmora and Rattazzi to head the successor government that had to confront the implementation of the Villafranca terms. Likewise, Cavour advised the Piedmontese commissioners sent to Central Italy and formally recalled, to remain in an unofficial capacity, directing public opinion against any restoration of the former rulers. They succeeded, as Pio Nono complained to Napoleon that Piedmont still fomented anarchy in Central Italy, preventing the restoration of the 'legitimate' order. Finally Cavour's outburst of indignation against the Villafranca agreement placed Napoleon on the defensive and made it difficult for him to claim either Nice or Savoy according to the Plombières pact. The distraught Cavour bristled that, having failed to keep his part of the bargain, Napoleon should not expect the Piedmontese to fulfil theirs.

In August 1859 Cavour, writing from abroad, explained that the pain of Villafranca was mitigated by the admirable conduct of central Italy, which prevented the return of the dukes and the Papal regime, and therefore owed its independence not to foreign arms but its own efforts. Cavour played no small part in this development, leading Massari to conclude that he remained the real prime minister of Italy. Word reached Turin that Lord John Russell and Palmerston supported Cavour's central Italian policy, reminding the Piedmontese that God helps those who help themselves. The Liberal government disagreed with the Conservative non-interventionist course, and was prepared to play a more active role to achieve an Italian settlement. The British representative to Turin, Sir James Hudson, advised the Piedmontese to establish a Regency over central Italy. Meanwhile conservative Catholics who questioned Cavour's policies *vis-à-vis* Rome, acknowledged his popularity in Piedmont and abroad.

The actions in Tuscany, Emilia and the Romagna in favour of union with Piedmont created a dilemma for Napoleon. The Emperor was torn between his desire to fulfil his pledge to the Pope while honouring his commitment to Austria at Villafranca, and his national programme and the promises he had made to Cavour. The double game played by Napoleon led Lord Cowley to quip during the

summer of 1859, that he never knew any man to talk so little and te
so many lies. It was a sentiment shared by Pius IX, who refused to
consider Napoleon's plan for a vice-realm for the Romagna under
Piedmontese protection, and provided only vague assurances as
regards the French demand for Papal reforms. Disregarding Napoleon's call for compromise and concessions, early in October the
Piedmontese Minister to Rome was handed his passport and hustled
out of Rome.[12]

The November Treaty of Zurich confirmed the terms of Villafranca. Proclaiming the rights of the legitimate rulers in central Italy,
no provision was made for their return. To make matters worse from
Rome's perspective, Article 18 stipulated that the two signatory
parties concurred in their efforts to assure that the Holy Father would
make necessary reforms in the administration of his state. The final
Italian settlement would be determined at a European congress to be
convened in Paris on 19 January 1861.

Napoleon's stance at the projected congress was revealed in the
pages of a pamphlet entitled 'Le Pape et Le Congrès', supposedly
written by La Guéronnière, but widely believed to have been inspired
by the Emperor himself. The work acknowledged that France could
not permit the forceful restoration of the deposed rulers against the
popular will, while calling for the separation of the Romagna from
the Papal States. It thus made the participation of Rome and Vienna
in the congress impossible, effectively scuttling it in the process.
Finally, it paved the way for Cavour's return to power, as the sole
figure capable of dealing with the inscrutable French Emperor.
Cavour returned to Turin on 20 January 1860, amid scenes of public
celebrations and excitement, during which illuminations also lit up
the streets of Bologna.[13]

Britain was delighted to have Cavour at the helm again. Lord John
Russell preferred his common sense and extraordinary ability to the
'nonentities' who had governed in his stead. France was also pleased,
now that Walewski had resigned, and Napoleon schemed to have
Cavour cede the provinces of Nice and Savoy to the French. Cavour,
in turn, considered this cession the price he had to pay to the man
who held the keys to central Italy, for the absorption of Tuscany, the
Duchies and the Legations. Knowing that the exchange had to be
justified before the courts of Europe, Cavour instructed his agents in
central Italy to conduct plebiscites to demonstrate that the people of
these provinces supported the decisions of their assemblies which
favoured union with Piedmont. The French concurred as the new
Foreign Minister, Thouvenel, did not mince words in warning Rome

that the restoration of the dynasties to the duchies or the Legations to the Holy See was unlikely. He also hinted that if central Italy were absorbed by Piedmont, France would have to be compensated by the acquisition of Nice and Savoy.[14]

The British, favouring a strong kingdom in northern Italy, were prepared to recognize Piedmontese acquisitions there, but deplored the French designs on Nice and Savoy. Early in February Lord Cowley transmitted an English project to solve the Italian question, prohibiting either France or Austria from intervening without the consent of the great powers. Cavour was alarmed to receive reports that Paris and London had reached an agreement to give them only Parma, Modena and the Legations, with the latter remaining under the nominal sovereignty of the Pope. Tuscany would have a Piedmontese prince rather than become a Piedmontese province. Cavour complained that the proposed arrangement was acceptable neither to the Piedmontese nor the people of central Italy. He confided to La Farina, who headed the National Society, that they could not rely on diplomacy alone to achieve their objectives, and that they would have to present the courts of Europe with actions.[15]

Rome resented the sequence of events and French Catholics lamented the persecution of the Church. Catholics in Turin marvelled at the radical shift in public opinion that led even moderates to make proposals concerning the Pope and the Papal States that had been unthinkable earlier. The winds of change did not reach the Curia, however. Pius IX and Antonelli protested that they would never willingly surrender the Legations to the Piedmontese. Their solution called for the complete evacuation of the Romagna by the Piedmontese and its restoration to the Holy Father. Pio Nono branded Vittorio Emanuele's suggestion that he transfer the Romagna to him as neither wise nor worthy of a Catholic king of the House of Savoy.[16]

Turin and Paris were deterred neither by the opposition of the Pope, nor the threat of ecclesiastical fulminations. Early in March, Cavour's agent in Bologna, Luigi Carlo Farini, announced a plebiscite to determine the future of the area. Napoleon, in turn, sent Count Vincent Benedetti, chief of the political bureau of the French Ministry of Foreign Affairs, to Turin with the agreement whereby central Italy would go to Piedmont and the latter would transfer Nice and Savoy to France. Once again Napoleon and Cavour had become co-conspirators. The vote in the Romagna, the Duchies, and Nice and Savoy, confirmed what the French and the Piedmontese had predetermined. Cavour warned Agostino Depretis, the Piedmontese agent in

Brescia, that the moment the results of the plebiscite were announced they could expect an excommunication from Rome, alerting him to take steps to preserve tranquillity.[17] Garibaldi, like Pio Nono, was scandalized by Cavour's schemes.

Garibaldi, denied a key role during the campaign of 1859, was angry with Cavour's ministry, which he saw as responsible for the slight, and wounded by the 'betrayal' of Napoleon at Villafranca. His sense of outrage was compounded because Mazzini and others on the extreme left had predicted that Cavour and Napoleon could not be trusted and would conspire to exploit him. In Turin, Giorgio Asproni of the parliamentary left deplored the vacillations of Cavour, denouncing him as vain, mendacious, autocratic, superficial, overbearing, inconsiderate and unscrupulous. Garibaldi concurred with Asproni's assessment as the drama of Nice and Savoy unfolded.

There had been rumours, which Cavour continued to deny, that Napoleon coveted Nice and Savoy. Nevertheless, on 12th March, he signed the secret agreement providing for their cession to France, and two weeks later, on 24th March, Napoleon demanded that this transfer be made public, informed his people the next day of the pending acquisition. In April, Garibaldi, who was elected to the enlarged Piedmontese parliament, cross-examined Cavour on the 'deal' which led him to abandon Nice to the 'executioner' of the Roman Republic of 1849 and threatened to make him a foreigner in his own land. Though Garibaldi questioned the morality as well as the constitutionality of the transfer, he was overruled by the majority which concurred with Cavour that the loss, however unfortunate, was politically necessary.

Garibaldi vowed never to forget the bartering of his home province to the French, and never forgave Cavour for negotiating the arrangement. Nonetheless, the rapid course of events in the peninsula did not allow Garibaldi the leisure to sulk over his loss. For some time republican stalwarts had been planning an expedition to the South, not only to overturn the illiberal Neapolitan government, but also to provide a popular initiative for the Italian movement that would contest the role of Cavour and the monarchical party in the unification movement. Crispi implored Garibaldi to lead such an expedition, but he reacted cautiously. On 15 March 1860, he promised Crispi he was prepared to risk his life to combat the enemies of his country and champion its cause. In an obvious reference to the policies of Cavour, Garibaldi lamented that the country was guided by empirical politicians who relied on diplomacy to achieve their objectives and blinded the people by the prospect of success. The revolutionary movement had to await the failure of the diplomatic and pragmatic course presently in vogue.[18]

By early April two factors led Garibaldi to re-evaluate his stance, prompted by his outrage at the cession of Nice, made public after 25th March, and the outbreak of rebellion in Palermo on 5th April. Garibaldi still hesitated assuming command of the planned expedition, but decided to assess the attitude of the Turin government, whose help would be crucial. Apparently Cavour, and his Minister of the Interior, Farini, responded that while they could not offer any public support, they would not attempt to prohibit the venture. Privately they assured financial and military assistance, for Garibaldi returned to Genoa determined to lead the expedition. Indeed he confided to potential recruits that Vittorio Emanuele and the Piedmontese government secretly incited him to undertake the enterprise against the Neapolitan government.[19]

For years the left had envisioned a drive to topple the Neapolitan government, with Mazzini proposing a Sicilian coup to Garibaldi in 1854, and inspiring the ill-fated Pisacane expedition to Sapri in 1857. Mazzini did not lose hope, although in the later 1850s the Sicilian Francesco Crispi emerged as the leading advocate of action against Sicily. When Sicilian revolutionaries, encouraged by Crispi, invoked his assistance in the fall of 1859, Garibaldi spoke of the need to act under the banner of 'Vittorio Emanuele and Italy'. Both Garibaldi and the Sicilians were encouraged by the assurances provided by La Farina, President of the Italian National Society, and Cavour's unofficial spokesman. They learned that Cavour's Piedmont, which was accountable to the international community, could not intervene on behalf of the Sicilians against their Neapolitan king, but promised that if they liberated themselves, the king's government would act to prevent their reconquest. Encouragement also came from Britain where Lord John Russell provided moral support, concluding it was meritorious to overturn a tyrannical government.[20]

Although the Turin government claimed to oppose Garibaldi's manoeuvres, it nevertheless allowed him and his volunteers to embark from Quarto, near Genoa, on 6th May, with arms from the government depot. Admiral Persano's Sardinian fleet, which might have blocked the passage south, received no instructions to do so. Rome, Naples, as well as Paris, all suspected Piedmontese complicity, but Cavour was most concerned about the irritation and exasperation of Napoleon. Cavour explained that he had no choice but to allow the expedition to depart for Sicily, pleading that any attempt to block this crusade would create grave problems for the Sub-alpine government and threaten his ministry's popularity and parliamentary support.[21]

On the night of 5 May 1860, Garibaldi's volunteers boarded two ships the *Piemonte* and the *Lombardo*, owned by the Rubattino Shipping Company of Genoa, and set out for Talamone in Tuscany. Once at sea, Garibaldi caused some consternation among the republicans on board, when he announced that their programme was to unite Italy under the House of Savoy, unfolding the banner of 'Italy and Vittorio Emanuele'. Garibaldi, seeking to undermine the Papal States as well as the Kingdom of the Two Sicilies, left a small force under Callimico Zambianchi behind with the mission of crossing into the Papal States and initiating a revolution. Zambianchi did not find the population of what remained of the Papal States restive, while their 'corrupt' army proved both loyal and efficient. The small band of *Garibaldini* was easily repulsed by the Papal troops, forcing the invaders back across the border into Tuscany.

The main band of the 'thousand' fared better, landing virtually unopposed at Marsala, Sicily, on 11th May. When Cavour, who was prepared to reap the advantages offered by Garibaldi, should he succeed, but to disavow him in case of failure, heard of the landing he hastened to provide additional assistance. Cavour allowed Garibaldi's followers in Piedmont to collect money, men and supplies for the venture, and a number of the 'volunteers' were secretly armed, outfitted and paid by the Turin government. Cavour, who had thought of annexing Southern Italy but attended to matters in northern and central Italy first, immediately grasped the opportunity provided by Garibaldi. The prospect of unification of the entire peninsula rose before Cavour, and despite the dangers which it entailed, it was an opportunity he was not prepared to let pass.

Cavour had to move cautiously, lest his complicity be exposed before the international community. The fact that Garibaldi fought under the Italian Tricolour adorned with the seal of Savoy, and that at Marsala he proclaimed a dictatorship in the name of Vittorio Emanuele, roused suspicion in Rome, Naples and Paris. Even the American Minister to Turin recognized that Cavour's Sardinia had covertly waged war against the Kingdom of Naples. Meanwhile the *Garibaldini* victory over the Neapolitans at Calatafimi, on the way to Palermo, convinced the islanders of his invincibility, bringing him additional volunteers. Both the charisma of Garibaldi and the incompetence of the Neapolitan viceroy, Ferdinando Lanza, contributed to the Neapolitan evacuation of Palermo early in June, to the surprise of all of Europe. In Rome a startled Pius IX exclaimed that the success of the expedition, which stunned contemporaries, would undoubtedly mystify succeeding generations.

Cavour may have been jolted, but immediately regained his balance, taking steps to secure Turin's position in Sicily. On 7th June, the very day that the Neapolitan forces evacuated Palermo, Cavour's agent, La Farina, landed in the Sicilian capital, to begin the campaign to bring the island under the aegis of Piedmont. Placards calling for annexation were distributed by La Farina, to the disgust of republicans and Mazzinians. Meanwhile Cavour's agents cautioned the aid committees working for Garibaldi in Turin and Genoa to keep an eye on the charismatic and popular military leader. Agostino Depretis, a friend of Garibaldi's, was advised to venture to Sicily to monitor the general's actions. While these men recognized that Garibaldi was the arm of the operation, they insisted that the popular hero needed guidance and direction.[22]

Turin's blatant attempts to profit from Garibaldi's actions, which it publicly condemned, both confused and roused the anger of the general. While La Farina and his master in Turin seemed content to absorb Sicily, Garibaldi had broader ambitions, convinced that the rest of Italy had to be incorporated. Distressed by the intrigues and interference of La Farina and his National Society, Garibaldi expelled him from the island early in July. Cavour, dreading the triumph of republicanism and the international complications resulting from Garibaldi's threat to occupy Naples and then Rome, termed the expulsion 'a savage act'. He retaliated by prohibiting Garibaldi's agents in Genoa from transmitting any further men or supplies to reinforce the general. However, pragmatism prevailed over pique, and realizing that Garibaldi could be of further service, Cavour countermanded the embargo, so the flow of arms and money from Piedmont to Sicily continued.

Cavour continued to condemn the expedition, denying all complicity and territorial ambitions. Indeed, his government encouraged the Neapolitans to believe that an alliance might be concluded between Turin and Rome. But, despite his public protestations, Cavour privately contemplated Piedmontese absorption of a good part of their dominion and the creation of a Kingdom of Italy spanning the entire peninsula. Nonetheless, republicans in Garibaldi's camp and royalists in Naples believed that Cavour seriously considered a strategic alliance between Piedmont and Naples. While the former feared the consequences of such an arrangement, and sought to frustrate it, Francesco in Naples thought that the establishment of constitutionalism in his state would facilitate such an agreement.[23]

Both were fooled by Cavour, who acknowledged a certain duplicity on his part, justifying his conduct on the basis that it served the Italian cause rather than his own personal profit.

In order to reassure Paris and Rome, Vittorio Emanuele ordered Garibaldi to refrain from his plan to march first on Naples and then on Rome. Garibaldi refused to obey the king's request and proceeded with his plans. In Naples, Francesco, perturbed by Garibaldi's threats, called upon Pius IX to pray for him. One day in June, stricken by a particularly severe panic attack, the young Neapolitan King telegraphed for the Pope's blessing on five different occasions.[24]

The Pope, suspicious of Garibaldi and his Piedmontese paymasters, did not share Francesco's apprehensions. He realized that Garibaldi considered him and Antonelli traitors for provoking the intervention of the Catholic powers against the Roman Republic in 1849, and had named his ugliest donkeys on the island of Caprera 'Pio Nono' and 'Antonelli'. Nonetheless, he remained calm in Rome, awaiting the dramatic outcome of events undermining the status quo. The Pope, confident of divine providence and the diplomacy of Antonelli, refused to budge from Rome.[25]

Neither Napoleon nor Cavour shared the Pope's calm. The Emperor was troubled by Garibaldi's proposed programme: the annexation of Naples, Rome, Venice and afterwards Nice, to be followed by a revolution in southern France against the tyranny of the Empire. Paris was alarmed by Garibaldi's open expression of hatred against the Empire. From Vienna Franz-Josef, still suspicious of Napoleon's schemes, was scandalized by the audacity of the revolutionary spirit that triumphed in Italy and threatened both thrones and altar. Cavour, who many considered the sole figure capable of piloting the ship of state in these perilous and uncharted waters, was likewise troubled. He compared himself to a sailor in a storm, who in the midst of the wind and waves vowed never to expose himself again to the perils of the deep.[26]

Cavour, aware that his king clandestinely encouraged Garibaldi, sought to re-establish his own bond with the general, which had originally been disrupted by the news of the cession of Nice and Savoy. At the same time the 'Piedmontese Machiavelli' secretly sent men, money, arms and advice to Naples, with the aim of provoking a revolution, hoping that once his revolutionary committee triumphed in the capital it would call for Piedmontese intervention. Neither scheme materialized as Cavour proved unable either to win over Garibaldi or to initiate a revolution in the Neapolitan capital. Nonetheless, he did not despair, and sought to consolidate his position in Sicily. He alerted Depretis in late August that since Garibaldi had crossed the straits and taken Reggio, and would soon be in Naples, a plebiscite should be held on the island, proposing union with Piedmont.[27]

Cavour's schemes and suggestions aroused suspicion in Sicily as well as on the mainland. There was resistance to his public attempts to frustrate Garibaldi's advance, as well as word of a new bargain with Napoleon, once again on the basis of sacrificing Italian soil. Rumours abounded that the French Emperor might allow the Piedmontese to absorb additional Italian territory, but only on condition that Cavour relinquish the Liguria and the Island of Sardinia to France. Cavour appreciated that Garibaldi had been angered by the cession of Nice and Savoy, but countered that it had served as a powerful stimulus. He confided to friends that without that cession, Garibaldi would most likely still be on the island of Caprera rather than completing the work assigned to him by providence for Italy.

In August 1860, while publicly preserving his pose of opposition to Garibaldi's conquest of southern Italy, Cavour privately confided that without Piedmontese assistance the general's mission would have ended in failure. Garibaldi, he argued, would not have had the men to fight the Neapolitan government, the ships to transport the expedition to the south, the arms to fight the Bourbon soldiers, not to mention the diplomatic skills which prevented outside intervention. For reasons of public security Cavour insisted this information would have to remain confidential. Finally, he confessed that whatever arrangements he made to assure the success of Garibaldi's mission and the completion of Italian unity, it did not include the further transfer of any Italian territory. He would rather see his two hands cut off, he pledged, than cede one more inch of Italian territory whether on the continent or on the island of Sardinia.[28]

Although Cavour publicly criticized Garibaldi's intention to march to Rome, then on to Venice and Nice, he immediately proceeded to use the threat to his advantage. Cavour insisted that Garibaldi's antagonism towards the French government, as well as his other indiscretions, constrained the Piedmontese government to take energetic measures regarding the Marches and Umbria. To further frighten the French, he sought to stimulate revolutionary agitation in the Papal States, and then present the spectre of a revolutionary upheaval undermining not only the stability of Italy but the whole of Europe. In August, Cavour proposed his solution to exorcize this spectre, knowing that Napoleon found it inconsistent to strike against the Italian nationalism he had inspired and would not permit Austrian intervention in Italy. Piedmont would have to enter and take possession of Umbria and the Marches to crush the revolutionary agitation and block Garibaldi's march north.

In late August Napoleon met in Savoy with the Italian Minister of War, Farini, and General Cialdini, who convinced him of the dire consequences of Garibaldi's northward advance. The Emperor posed no objection to Cavour's proposal to annex the bulk of what remained of the Papal States, so long as the Pope was left in possession of Rome and its immediate environs. Indeed the Emperor's parting words to his Italian visitors supposedly were 'Good luck, and act quickly'. To those around him, the Emperor added, that if Piedmont believed this intervention in the Papal States was needed to save herself, Italy and Europe from grave danger, she should do so – but she alone would have to shoulder the risk and responsibility.[29]

Napoleon was particularly concerned about the reaction of Rome and French Catholics, who had hitherto supported him. Rome did not doubt that Cavour and the Turin government were behind the Garibaldi enterprise, pulling all the strings. Pius and Antonelli suspected that the Piedmontese lusted after all the Papal provinces. The Emperor assured the Cardinal Secretary of State, Antonelli, that his government would oppose an unprovoked Piedmontese intervention upon Papal territory. 'Your Majesty knows I am devoted to the cause of Italian independence', the French Emperor wrote to Vittorio Emanuele on 9 September 1860, 'but if your troops, without legitimate reason, enter the states of the Pope, I will be forced to oppose the venture.'[30] Word of the French threat to break diplomatic relations with Turin was simultaneously sent to the Papal government, both to reassure it and convince French Catholics that the Emperor had kept his promise to the Pope and Antonelli. Cavour, who was privy to the Emperor's real intentions and knew he had warned Vienna not to violate Villafranca by an intervention in central Italy, was not deterred.

Cavour provided precise instructions to General Fanti, poised on the border of the remaining Papal territory, alerting him that his mission was as much political as military. The moment the disturbances which Cavour had plotted and prepared erupted, Fanti was to warn the commanders of the Papal forces to desist from any repression or attempt to stifle these 'national manifestations'. Should the Papal Commander refuse to follow these 'humane considerations', Fanti and his Piedmontese forces were to occupy the areas to spare the population violence and bloodshed. In so doing, Cavour cautioned

Fanti, his actions had to be justified before the twin tribunals of diplomacy and public opinion.[31]

Although Napoleon had promised to protect the Pope against 'unprovoked aggression', Cavour sensed that, given the proper pretext and the subterfuge of popular revolution, Napoleon would not molest the Piedmontese, so long as they avoided French-held positions in Rome and the surrounding region. His assessment proved accurate, for while Napoleon withdrew his ambassador from Turin following the Piedmontese occupation of the Marches, he did nothing militarily, and little else diplomatically, to prevent the Piedmontese from absorbing the bulk of the Papal States and imposing their laws and tariffs. Cavour reassured General Fanti that while the French press condemned their actions and the French Emperor continued to insist on the rights of the Pope, Paris would place no real obstacles in their way.[32] 'Italy is in a very critical position', Cavour wrote in September 1860, 'On the one side diplomacy, on the other Garibaldi – that is not exactly comfortable.'[33] In fact, Cavour managed to achieve his Italian objectives precisely because he knew how to play one off against the other.

Early in September, as Garibaldi approached Naples, Francesco and the royal family abandoned the capital for the fortress of Gaeta in the north. Cavour dispatched half the Sardinian army, more than 30,000 men, into the Papal States to occupy the area and block any Garibaldian venture against the French, who protected the Pope in Rome. 'Please keep in mind, General', Vittorio Emanuele wrote to his Commander Fanti, 'that Garibaldi is not to cross the frontier of the Kingdom of Naples into the Papal States; I promised Napoleon he would not.'[34] In his public proclamation, inspired by Cavour, the king insisted that his entry into the Pope's territory was governed neither by greed nor ambition. His mission was humane and pacific, seeking to introduce liberty in Italy while freeing Europe from the scourge of war and revolution. When a revolutionary movement erupted in the Neapolitan province of Abruzzi, and the provisional government implored Vittorio Emanuele to enter that kingdom, Cavour had a pretext for intervention.

Early in October, while the parliament convened in Turin, Garibaldi, in the battle of the Volturno, frustrated the Neapolitan attempt to reopen the road to Naples. Since the Neapolitan army of 50,000 men remained entrenched in the fortresses of Capua and Gaeta, they could easily resume their offensive. Thus Francesco's Neapolitans, more than Napoleon's French forces or Cavour's Piedmontese troops, prevented Garibaldi from advancing to Rome. Recognizing that his volunteers lacked the strength, equipment and discipline to besiege the fortresses, Garibaldi urged Vittorio Emanuele to lead his army into the southern kingdom. In mid-October the king complied, meeting Garibaldi's forces near Teano, north of Capua. Meanwhile the people of the kingdom had voted overwhelmingly for inclusion in a united Italy under the constitutional rule of Vittorio Emanuele.

By the end of October 1860, the Kingdom of Italy had been made if not yet promulgated. In mid-March 1861, the Italian parliament unanimously proclaimed Vittorio Emanuele II King of Italy. The state formed in 1861 included Piedmont, Lombardy, the Duchies of Central Italy, most of the Papal States and the Kingdom of the Two Sicilies. Two major areas remained outside: Venice and Rome, and Cavour believed these would be incorporated when the issue of German unification arose.

NOTES

1. *Mémoires, Documents et Ecrits Divers laissés par le Prince de Metternich*, ed. M.A. Klinkowstroem (Paris: Plon et C., 1884) VIII, 629.
2. War Proclamation of Vittorio Emanuele II, 29 April 1859, *Archivio Centrale dello Stato, Archivio Depretis, serie* I, *busta* 1, *fascicolo* 6.
3. 'Proclamation L'Empereur au Peuple Français', *Le Moniteur Universel. Journal Officiel de L'Empire Français*, 3 May, 1859.
4. Napoleon III to Pius IX, 1 May 1859, *Archivio Segreto del Vaticano, Archivio Particolare Pio IX, Sovrani, Francia*, no. 42.
5. Vittorio Emanuele II to Pius IX, 25 May 1859 and 29 May 1859, *ASV, Archivio Particolare Pio IX, Sovrani, Sardegna*, No. 52.
6. Proclamation to the Citizens of Milan, 5 June 1859, *ASV, Segreteria di Stato Esteri*, 1860, *rubrica* 165, *fascicolo* 79.
7. Mariano Gabriele (ed.), *Il Carteggio Antonelli – Sacconi (1858–1860)* (Rome: Istituto per la Storia del Risorgimento Italiano, 1862), I, p. 136; Federigo Sclopis di Salerano, *Diario Segreto (1859–1878)*, ed. Pietro P. Pirri (Turin: Deputazione subalpina di storia patria, 1959), p. 134.
8. *Il Carteggio Antonelli – Sacconi*, I, p. 158; Pietro P. Pirri, (ed.), *La Questione Romana* (Rome: Pontifica Università Gregoriana, 1951), II, p. 80.
9. *The Letters of Queen Victoria*, first series, ed. Arthur C. Benson and Viscount Esher (London: John Murray, 1907), III, pp. 337, 352–3.
10. Antonio Monti, *Pio IX nel Risorgimento Italiano con Documenti Inediti* (Bari: Laterza, 1928), p. 146.
11. Giuseppe Massari, *Diario dalle cento voci* (Bologna: Capelli, 1959), p. 308.
12. Ibid. p. 345; *Archivio di Stato di Roma, Miscellanea di Carte Politiche o Riservate, busta* 132.
13. *ASV, Segreteria di Stato Esteri*, 1860, *rubrica* 165, *fascicolo* 79.

14. *Posthumous Papers of Jesse White Mario: the Birth of Modern Italy*, ed. Duke Litta-Visconti-Arese (New York: Scribners, 1909), pp. 294–5; L. Thouvenel (ed.), *Le Secret de L'Empereur. Correspondance confidentielle et inédite échangée entre M. Thouvenel, Le Duc de Gramont et Le Général Compte de Flahaut 1860–1863* (Paris: Calmann-Levy, 1889), I, pp. 8–10.

15. Cavour to Manfredo Fanti, 18 February 1860, *Archivio Centrale dello Stato. Archivio Fanti, scatola 1*.

16. Pius to Vittorio Emanuele II, 14 February 1860, *ASV, Archivio Particolare Pio IX, Sovrani, Sardegna*, no. 57; Pirri (ed.), *La Questione Romana*, II, p. 160.

17. Plebiscite in Bologna in March 1860, *ASV, Segreteria di Stato Esteri, 1860, rubrica 165, fascicolo 79*; Cavour to Depretis, 14 March 1860, *Archivio Centrale dello Stato, Archivio Depretis, serie I, busta 3, fascicolo 9, sottofascicolo 9*.

18 *The Memoirs of Francesco Crispi*, ed. Thomas Palamenghi-Crispi, trans. Mary Prichard Agnetti (New York: Hodder and Stoughton, 1912), I, pp. 134, 308.

19. Gaetano Tortonellogo to Cardinal Giacomo Antonelli, *ASV, Segreteria di Stato Esteri, 1860, rubrica 165, fascicolo 71, sottofascicoli 57–8*.

20. Lord John Russell to Queen Victoria, 30 April 1860, *The Letters of Queen Victoria*, III, p. 398.

21. Ettore Passerin D'Entreves, 'Appunti sull' impostazione delle ultime trattative del governo cavouriano colla S. Sede per una soluzione della questione romana (novembre 1860–marzo 1861', in *Chiesa e stato nell'Ottocento. Mischellanea in onore di Pietro Pirri*, ed. R. Aubert, A.M. Ghisalberti and E. Passerin D'Entreves (Padua: Editrice Antinore, 1962), II, p. 568.

22. The Garibaldi Aid Society to Depretis, 20 June 1860, *Archivio Centrale dello Stato, Archivio Depretis, busta 2, fascicolo 8, sottofascicolo 2, no. 8*.

23. Sovereign Act by which Francis of Naples concedes Constitutional Government, 25 June 1860, *Archivio di Stato di Roma, Miscellanea di Carte Politiche o Riservate, busta 134, fascicolo 4870*.

24. Harold Acton, *The Last Bourbons of Naples (1825–1861)* (New York: St Martin's Press, 1961), pp. 448–9.

25. Pius IX to Archduke Ferdinand Maximilian, 7 August 1860, *ASV, Archivio Particolare Pio IX, Sovrani, Austria*, no. 33.

26. Franz-Josef to Pius IX, 27 August 1860, *ASV, Archivio Particolare Pio IX, Sovrani, Austria*, no. 35; Cavour to Madame de Circourt, 16 July 1860, *Count Cavour and Madame de Circourt: some Unpublished Correspondence*, ed. Costantino Nigra, trans. Arthur John Butler (London: Cassell and Co., 1894), p. 86.

27. Cavour to Depretis, 27 August 1860, *Archivio Centrale dello Stato, Archivio Depretis, serie I, busta 3, fascicolo 9, sottofascicolo 9*.

28. Cavour to Cabella, August, 1860, *Archivio di Stato di Roma, Miscellanea di Carte Politiche o Riservate, busta 134, fascicolo 4862*.

29. Thouvenel (ed.), *Le Secret de L'Empereur*, I, pp. 185–6, 252.

30. French Minister of Foreign Affairs to French Minister at Rome, 11 September 1860, *Archivio di Stato di Roma, busta 1*.

31. Cavour to General Fanti, 7 September 1860, *Archivio Centrale dello Stato, Archivio Fanti, scatola 1*.

32. Cavour to General Fanti, 11 September 1860, *Archivio Centrale dello Stato, Archivio Fanti, busta* 1.
33. *Count Cavour and Madame de Circourt*, p. 89.
34. Vittorio Emanuele II to General Fanti, *Archivio Centrale dello Stato, Archivio Fanti, busta* 1.

CHAPTER EIGHT

Origins and Consequences of the Third War of Italian Independence

During Garibaldi's southern campaign, which provided the pretext for Piedmontese intervention and absorption of the greater part of the Papal States, Rome was by-passed. Its future depended on the ambitions of the Italians, the attitude of the Powers, the policies of Pio Nono and Cardinal Antonelli, and the ability of Napoleon to juggle his confusing and contradictory commitments. On the one hand the French Emperor promised Antonelli and the Catholics he would preserve the Eternal City for the Pope, while on the other, he resented Papal and Austrian opposition to the completion of Italian unity, pledging to overcome their resistance.[1] Mazzini no less than Pius, questioned the motives and ambitions of Napoleon, denouncing his duplicity.

As a united Italy miraculously emerged, the Papal police in Rome preserved order, preventing any demonstration of sympathy and support.[2] They suspected that Turin coveted Rome, and their assumption proved correct. Prior to the proclamation of Italy, Cavour determined that it be parliamentary and eventually include both Venice and Rome. The new kingdom, which covered some 248,692 square kilometres and 21,894,925 inhabitants did not incorporate either Lazio, which remained under Papal control, or Venice, still subject to the Habsburgs. The Chamber of Deputies elected in March 1860 no longer represented the extended state, so at the end of January 1861 new elections were called. On 18 February 1861, Deputies throughout the peninsula, save the Veneto and Rome, convened in Turin. Opening as the eighth session of the Sardinian parliament, it closed as the first of the new Italy. Championed by some, the Kingdom of Italy was denounced by others.

While all patriots agreed that unification had to be completed, they differed sharply as to the means to achieve this objective. The Mazzinians, having little faith either in the desire or the ability of the monarchy to fulfil the task, attacked the institutions of the new state and looked to establish a republic. Invoking popular initiative, they sought insurrection to topple the kingdom and acquire Venice and Rome. The Party of Action, which had broader support, under the leadership of Garibaldi, likewise demanded immediate liberation of Rome and Venice, even at the cost of waging war against France and Austria. The moderate party, under Cavour, burdened with the responsibility of power, recognized the need to consolidate the state before attempting to resolve these thorny issues.

Cavour, Bettino Ricasoli, Marco Minghetti, Luigi Carlo Farini and others of the moderate camp, appreciated the importance of extending the geographical boundaries of the kingdom, but understood that considerable political and diplomatic groundwork was necessary to accomplish the goal. Cavour preached caution, lest they endanger everything they had accomplished. Contending that the revolutionary element had already made its contribution, he insisted those who governed be allowed to select the time and means of acquiring Rome and Venice. Above all, Cavour contended that these provinces had to be absorbed with the approval of Napoleonic France and the European powers. The moderate party realized that Italy could not 'do it alone'. It lacked the wherewithal to wage war against Austria for Venice, and could ill afford to antagonize Napoleon, the ally who had made possible the consolidation achieved to date, over the question of Rome.

Mazzini, from his exile, found both the structure and the boundaries of the unitary state, wanting. He complained to Garibaldi, who had conquered the south, that neither Cavour nor Vittorio Emanuele could be trusted to complete the national edifice. Both, he maintained, were too timid to initiate an assault on the Veneto or publicly call upon Napoleon to withdraw his troops from Rome.[3] Mazzini insinuated that once again direct and popular action was needed, and looked to Garibaldi to unsheath his sword to finish the work he had started. The guerrilla chieftain shared many of his ideological mentor's concerns, like him distrusting the two who had bartered away his birthplace. The actions and statements of both Cavour and Napoleon roused his ire. The French Emperor remained as elusive and enigmatic as ever, asserting that while he could not oppose Italian unification, he predicted it would not succeed.[4]

On 17 March 1861, the Chamber proclaimed Vittorio Emanuele II, by the Grace of God and the will of the nation, King of Italy. A week later Cavour, selected by his Monarch as the country's first prime minister, had the Chamber approve the Boncompagni bill, which made Rome, still garrisoned by French forces for the Pope, capital of Italy. This stop provided Pius with additional justification to withhold recognition and preclude any negotiation with the 'Piedmontese faction.' The Pope denounced the call for pacification and negotiation as unlikely as a pact between Christ and the devil.[5] Pius persevered in his prohibition until his death in 1878, when his successors assumed his intransigent stance.

Rome's refusal to disavow the temporal power and recognize the Kingdom of Italy created problems for Paris, Turin, Vienna, and the other capitals. Thus Napoleon found himself on the horns of a dilemma concerning the completion of Italian unity, caught as he was between his national aspirations and Catholic supporters. A compromise solution either with Austria for Venice or with the Papacy concerning Rome, appealed to the Emperor, as did the thought of shifting the burden of the solution to the shoulders of a European congress. Neither prospect materialized, so that Napoleon was constrained to await the course of events. At the end of 1860 a brochure by the banker M. Isaac Pereire, but probably inspired by Napoleon, proposed that Austria sell Venetia to Italy, and purchase Bosnia-Herzegovina from Turkey by way of compensation. The suggestion was not well received in Vienna.

The Roman imbroglio and the Italian question, which disrupted the Empire's internal quiet and weakened its international position, distressed Napoleon, who sought to extricate himself from the labyrinth. His anger was compounded by Rome's decision to provide a haven for Francis II and his family, disgruntled Legitimists, and French Republicans, who challenged his authority. Early in 1861 he reproached Pius for permitting Rome to become the centre of a conspiracy against his person and government. The Emperor lamented that his efforts, made at great cost and carrying grave consequences, were little appreciated by the Curia. Protesting his fidelity to preserve what remained of the temporal power, he confessed that events in the peninsula had taken a turn he had neither foreseen nor favoured. Pius responded that he did not shelter or encourage the Emperor's enemies.[6]

Cavour recognized the need for the support of much of Europe in his quest for Venice, and even more so in that for Rome, relying on diplomatic and moral means to achieve his ends. Soon after his parliamentary declaration, in the autumn of 1860, that Rome must serve as the capital of the kingdom, he sought to open negotiations with the Papacy. His hopes for a peaceful solution were dashed by the expulsion of his agent, Diomede Pantaleoni, from Rome, and then by the Papal Allocution of 18 March 1861, denouncing the notion of a conciliation between the Holy See and the new kingdom. A week later Cavour was questioned in parliament about the means by which he proposed to acquire Rome. In his response of 27 March 1861 Cavour reaffirmed his earlier resolution that Rome serve as capital of Italy. Promising the Papacy broad liberty, he aimed to resolve both the Roman question and Church–state relations by the formula of 'a free Church in a free state'. Rome rebuffed the offer. The temporal power was not simply a national issue, the Cardinal Secretary of State, countered, but a Catholic and international one whose resolution required the input of the Catholic world.[7]

Neither Mazzini nor Garibaldi appreciated the difficulties confronted by Cavour. Indeed, in March of 1861 Britain was one of the few nations to recognize the new Italy. However, not one government, Catholic or non–Catholic, deemed it legitimate to deprive the Papacy of its temporal power by taking Rome. Perhaps Protestant England proved the most sympathetic, as Palmerston recognized that so long as Venice and Rome remained outside the Italian union, it would remain beholden to France. The larger and stronger the new state became, he advised Queen Victoria, the more resistant it would be to French coercion. His solution was to have the French Emperor and Italian king accept Pio Nono's sovereignty during his lifetime, but refuse to recognize the temporal power of subsequent Popes.[8]

Palmerston's pragmatic proposal did not satisfy the impatient Garibaldi, who was elected to represent the first district in Naples in the Italian parliament. He ventured to Turin in April 1861 not only to chastise Cavour's government for its treatment of his volunteers, but to call for the creation of a potent new military force to complete Italian unification. Sporting his symbolic red shirt, Garibaldi denounced Cavour for provoking a civil war, and for his subservience to Napoleon III. Asserting that Italy could only resolve its difficulties by arming, arming and again arming, he proposed the creation of a large force under his supervision, which would be ready to tackle the difficult problems facing the nation. Cavour made it clear that the Ministry deemed it inopportune to provoke a war at the moment, and therefore refused to accept Garibaldi's modified proposal calling for a force of 25,000–30,000 volunteers. Neither Vienna nor Paris would tolerate such a military build-up without taking counter-measures jeopardizing the kingdom's position.

Cavour recognized that the acquisition of Venice would have to await the impending question of German unification and the outbreak of an Austro-Prussian War. In January 1861 he sent General La Marmora to Berlin to congratulate William I on his accession to the throne, and this prompted the Prussian king to send a military mission to Turin. Regarding Rome, Napoleon proposed an agreement whereby he would withdraw his garrison from the Eternal City within the next few months, in return for an Italian guarantee of the truncated Papal State. Cavour considered this the best he could expect from Napoleon; since the Italians did not have to defend the Papal regime against any internal opposition, it provided him with the pretext for a revolutionary upheaval, once the French abandoned the city.

Negotiations for a Franco-Italian agreement began, but Cavour's illness in the summer of 1861 prevented its conclusion. Until the last minute, and indeed on his deathbed, Cavour reflected that though weary, he had two more things to do – acquire Venice and Rome.[9] He confessed that he, no less than his critic Garibaldi, wanted to go to Venice and Rome, but insisted that time was needed. Unfortunately his time ran out on 6 June 1861. The disappearance of the chief architect of the Italian state deprived Italy of her greatest statesman, certainly the one best qualified to continue the unification process. Even the writers of the *Osservatore Romano* wondered what would happen in the peninsula now that Cavour's sure hand had gone.[10]

Two figures prominently tipped as successors to Cavour were the Tuscan nobleman, Bettino Ricasoli, and the Piedmontese barrister, Urbano Rattazzi. The king chose the former, who belonged to the Destra (or Party of the Right), rather than the pliant Rattazzi of the centre-left, who had close ties with the Party of Action. In mid-June the French Foreign Minister, Thouvenel, transmitted a dispatch finally recognizing the existence of the Kingdom of Italy, but making it clear that his government neither approved of the means employed in its creation, nor guaranteed its existence. Furthermore, French troops would remain in Rome until Catholic France was certain that the Pope's position was secure. Ricasoli, like Cavour, was haunted by the question of Rome which occupied his thoughts throughout the remainder of 1861.

Before his death, Cavour had stressed the advisability of acquiring Rome before Venice, a priority his successor Ricasoli preserved. Early in September 1861 the 'Iron Baron' sent a long letter to Pius IX and Antonelli, seeking a solution of the Roman Question on the basis of Cavour's 'Free Church in a Free state'. The overture was not opposed by Paris, which urged the Cardinal Secretary of State to reach some accommodation with the new state. However, neither the promptings from Turin nor Paris persuaded the Pope, who remained little disposed to reach any sort of agreement which compromised the temporal power. Indeed Father Lavigerie, auditor of the Rota, warned the French Foreign Minister that Pius was not prepared to renounce even an inch of his territory and would not consider negotiations so long as the Italians controlled one village of the former Papal States.

Lavigerie's assessment was confirmed by the tone of the *Gazzetta di Roma* which brushed aside Ricasoli's proposal as 'ridiculous' and indicative of 'the cupidity and greed' of the Turin government. Neither the Pope nor his chief minister were moved by the petition of the Italian clergy, pressing the Pope to reach an accord with the Kingdom of Italy, and were angered and aroused by the address to Vittorio Emanuele invoking his intervention in Rome. The Italian bishops, almost to a man, supported the Pope's position.[11]

Ricasoli understood that France would not tolerate any Italian-inspired insurrection against the Papal Regime, warning the Party of Action to abandon any thought of an armed incursion. The British, while sympathetic to Italian national interests, were determined to preserve the peace and protect Central Europe from revolutionary upheaval. Ricasoli made it clear that he would apply the full force of the law against those who undermined Italy's diplomatic stance by attempting a popular move against Rome or Venice. His position was publicly supported by Vittorio Emanuele, who assured the British government – one of the few to have immediately granted Italy recognition – that the policy of his Cabinet was temperate, discouraging any violent or venturesome enterprise to complete unification. Like Cavour, he promised recourse to moral and diplomatic means.

The Italians considered the compromise suggested by Lord John Russell to Napoleon. The English Minister proposed that the French occupation be restricted to the Vatican and Civitavecchia, leaving the remaining Roman land to the Italians. The Pope would preserve his temporal power by controlling a truncated territory, but retaining the full exercise of his spiritual authority. While Turin showed interest, Paris did not, as the French Emperor flatly rejected the Italian request to make Rome their capital. Antonelli maintained his intransigent stance, indicating that Pius would reject any proposition until his entire state had been restored. Ricasoli's failure to resolve the Roman question, the bristling of Vittorio Emanuele at the restrictions and restraints imposed by the haughty Tuscan on the Crown's activity, and the intrigues of Rattazzi, all contributed to the Iron Baron's fall in February 1862.

The replacement of the rigid 'Grand Seigneur', Ricasoli, by the pliant and intriguing Piedmontese, Rattazzi, which was orchestrated by the king, delighted the Party of Action. Garibaldi, who was allowed to preside over a meeting of the radical left in the City of Genoa, appeared gratified and vindicated. He was further pleased when the new ministry encouraged him to visit the major cities of northern Italy to institute the *Tiro Nazionale*, or Rifle Association, which would hopefully provide the basis of a permanent volunteer force. Meanwhile rumour was rife about a possible Garibaldi mission to Greece or to the Danubian provinces to strike the Habsburg Empire in the rear, so forcing it to disgorge Venice in the west. There was even talk of a volunteer incursion into the South Tyrol or the Trentino, creating concern in Vienna, Paris and London. As Turin received pointed enquiries about plots hatched in its territory, Rattazzi suddenly awoke to the perils of this policy. Confronted with the possible diplomatic consequences of condoning if not aiding and abetting Garibaldi's manoeuvres, a number of his volunteers were arrested in Sarnico in Lombardy. The Party of Action felt betrayed, but both the king and Rattazzi secretly met with Garibaldi to explain the apparent *volte face*. Garibaldi then returned to Caprera for the time being.

Frustrated in his Venetian enterprise in the North, Garibaldi now turned to the South and Rome, denouncing Napoleon for preventing the Italian acquisition of the Eternal City. The French Emperor, for his part, reiterated his support for legitimate Italian national interests, warning the Italians not to make unreasonable demands, and the Papacy to reach some reasonable accommodation with the kingdom. He proposed that Pius should be satisfied with the territory he retained, and that the Italians should renounce their claim to Rome in return for Papal recognition. Since neither Turin nor Rome accepted his premise, Napoleon believed that the European powers would have to intervene to assure the Pope's possession of Rome and the recognition of Italy.[12] In May 1862 Napoleon replaced the pro-Papal General de Goyon as French Commander in Rome with the Count de Montebello, who was less sympathetic to Papal pretensions for a full restoration. The alteration may have influenced Garibaldi, if not Rattazzi, to focus on the Roman Question.

In June Garibaldi sailed for Sicily without hindrance from the Italian naval forces and officials, who remained convinced that the general again moved at the behest of secret royal orders. Arriving in Palermo at the end of June, he announced that Napoleon, the assassin of the Roman Republic and executioner of French liberty, had to be pushed out of Rome, invoking the assistance of the 'people of the vespers'. In mid-July at Marsala, when someone shouted 'Either Rome or Death!' Garibaldi adopted this as his rallying cry and prepared for action. Early in August Garibaldi assumed command of some 3,000 volunteers determined to liberate Rome, while the government in Turin watched and waited. The king, in a proclamation of 3rd August, warned hotheads against attacking Italy's closest ally, arguing that at an appropriate time he would lead the movement to complete unification. However, many in and out of the peninsula regarded the king's words as mere rhetoric, convinced that Vittorio Emanuele and Rattazzi secretly supported Garibaldi. The fact that the general and his volunteers were allowed to commandeer two merchant ships and sail to Calabria served to confirm their suspicions.

At first Rattazzi intimated that Garibaldi could only be stopped if the Italian government occupied Rome, but neither France nor Austria accepted his logic, demanding that the Italian government move against the volunteers. Reluctantly the government had to declare martial law, and General La Marmora then Prefect in Naples and Commander-in-Chief of the army in the south, reinforced the troops in Calabria. In turn, General Cialdini ordered Colonel Emilio Pallavicini to 'crush the movement' and force Garibaldi to accept 'unconditional surrender'. On the heights of Aspromonte, on 29 August 1862, the royal army fired on the *Garibaldini*, wounding Garibaldi in his ankle, and imprisoning him and a number of his followers. Though soon amnestied, Garibaldi was disgusted with the conduct of the Rattazzi government, which resigned in December 1862. In Paris, Napoleon, irritated by Piedmontese schemes and Garibaldi's aggressive actions, replaced his pro-Italian Foreign Minister, Thouvenel, with Drouyn de Lhuys, who championed the maintenance of the status quo in Italy.[13]

During the short-lived ministry of Luigi Carlo Farini, followed by that of Marco Minghetti, Vittorio Emanuele continued his conspiracies for Rome and Venice, shifting his priority to the latter. The king, like his former minister and co-conspirator Rattazzi, was convinced that Italian unification would last, and therefore did not shy from expedients that others feared threatened its existence.[14] Napoleon did not share his enthusiasm for such adventures, and harped upon the need for a European congress to resolve the thorny issues of Rome and Venice. The treaties of 1815 no longer existed, the Emperor proclaimed in his speech from the throne in November, inviting the powers to participate in a proposed European congress to adjust borders and preserve the peace.

London, Rome and Vienna did not share Napoleon's optimism. In a courteous but firm response, Lord John Russell made it clear that under the prevailing situation the English government did not believe such a congress would be productive. He observed that in general, congresses such as the French proposed followed long and exhausting wars when the parties were prepared to compromise. At present neither Austria nor Russia, which were called upon to make concessions, were under such constraints. Russell's analysis proved accurate. Austria opposed the idea of a congress, fearing that the French would attempt to press them to abandon Venice, a step they were not prepared to take. Pius IX, for his part, wrote to Napoleon that his attempt to establish peace in Europe through the mechanism of a congress was admirable, but stressed that he would not compromise on the question of temporal power. The Cardinal Secretary of State likewise did not expect anything positive to come from Napoleon's suggested European congress.[15]

When the congress failed to materialize, Vittorio Emanuele resumed his conspiratorial efforts directed mainly for the acquisition of Venice, while his minister Minghetti commenced direct negotiations with Napoleon for the evacuation of Rome. Apparently the two were working independently of each other. While Vittorio Emanuele sought to create internal dissension within the Habsburg Empire, forcing her to concentrate on the planned insurrection in Galicia or Hungary, Venice could be snatched from her grasp. As before, the king looked to the Party of Action for assistance, and counted upon the leadership and charisma of Garibaldi. The latter, however, had left Caprera for a triumphal tour of England, so that Vittorio Emanuele for the moment lacked the charismatic figure who could galvanize the masses. This did not prevent the king from opening talks with the republican Mazzini and sending messengers to Garibaldi in London inviting him back home to lead the proposed expedition. The king's conspiracy was exposed by an article in one of the radical journals, which momentarily put the Venetian question on ice.[16]

Minghetti and his Foreign Minister, Visconti Venosta, on the other hand, opened secret talks with Napoleon for a French withdrawal from Rome on the basis of the convention earlier planned with Cavour. However, Napoleon added two elements not present in the earlier proposal. The first provided for a staged withdrawal over a two-year period, and the second called for some indication that the Italians would respect the Pope's position in Rome. Eventually the parties agreed that the transfer of the Italian capital from Turin to another city, which Minghetti deemed essential in any case, would be sufficient to calm French apprehensions about the future of Papal Rome. The conclusion and subsequent publication of the Convention in mid-September led to riots in Turin and the collapse of the Minghetti government. It encouraged Pio Nono in Rome to publish the encyclical *Quanta cura*, to which was attached the 'Syllabus of Errors', condemning many developments and ideologies of the contemporary age.

The Italian attempt to acquire Venice proved no easier than the drive for Rome, since the reluctance of Austria to cede Venice equalled that of the Pope to abandon Rome. One major difference was that Napoleon, who blocked the Italian acquisition of Rome, favoured their absorption of Venice. Nonetheless, he was not prepared to wage a war against Austria to acquire Venice for Italy. Instead he hoped that Vienna could be persuaded either by diplomacy or by a congress to cede the province, in return for territorial compensation in the Balkans. The Emperor also envisioned some monetary compensation for the Austrians. Finally, Napoleon, like Cavour earlier on, recognized that the Austrian–Prussian rivalry in Germany could work to Italy's advantage, forcing the Austrian government to mend its fences in Italy as it prepared to confront Prussia in Germany.

The Italians understood that Prussia nourished German ambitions thwarted by Austria, and Bismarck believed that only a military confrontation could resolve the rivalry. The government, which had transferred to Florence in the spring of 1865, was therefore distressed to see the two German powers cooperate in the war with Denmark over Schleswig-Holstein. Napoleon did not share the concern, reassuring the Italians that this cooperation was temporary and would inevitably lead to a later clash of arms, providing them with the opportunity to seize Venice. For the moment this prediction seemed far-fetched. The Italians, who hoped for a Franco-Prussian *rapprochement*, were disappointed by Bismarck's visit to Biarritz in the autumn of 1864. Subsequently, the Emperor, diffident towards Bismarck's overtures, noted sarcastically that the Prussian Minister had offered him all sorts of things that were not his to give. Bismarck, in turn, branded Napoleon, the 'unknown incompetent'. Indeed, Napoleon now cautioned the Italians to disarm, predicting that would lead to an Austrian recognition of the kingdom – a necessary prerequisite to its cession of Venetia, once offered adequate compensation. General La Marmora, who had succeeded Minghetti, observed that the public would perceive disarmament as a renunciation of Venice, and could not follow the French counsel.[17]

Meanwhile relations between Vienna and Berlin deteriorated. Bismarck expressed his determination to incorporate the duchies into Prussia's military, postal and commercial system and in the face of Austrian opposition, settle matters by war. He prepared the groundwork by seeking the neutrality of France and the active assistance of the Italians. In August 1865 Count Usedom travelled to Florence, to enquire of La Marmora whether Italy would join Prussia in a war against Austria. The Italian Minister, pleased by the proposal, responded cautiously, unwilling to make any commitment before knowing the sentiments of Napoleon. The latter responded enigmatically to queries from Florence, making it clear that while Paris would not encourage war, it would not block it, asserting Italy's liberty to act as it saw fit. La Marmora, suspicious of Bismarck's intrigues, dispatched Count Malguzzi to Vienna to purchase Venice for 100,000,000 lire, but the offer was flatly rejected. The Italians concluded that Austria would cede Venice only under threat of war; thus they reconsidered the Prussian proposal.

In early October 1865 Bismarck again ventured to Biarritz to confer with Napoleon and his advisers. Debate still exists concerning the exact content of the conversations on the terrace of Eugénie's villa by the sea, and later in Paris. Apparently the Prussian Minister revealed his intention of incorporating the German areas of Schleswig-Holstein, ceding the Danish territory to Denmark, and creating a North German Confederation under Prussian leadership. Knowing Napoleon's penchant for the Venetian Question, Bismarck indicated that Austria would be constrained to cede Venice to the Italians in return for compensation in the Balkans. France, in turn, could annex Belgium or Luxemburg, and Bismarck also dangled further prospects before the startled Emperor. Napoleon did not know whether to conclude that the Prussian Minister was crazy or crafty, but was much more impressed by his person and policies than during their earlier encounter. Neither Napoleon nor Bismarck chose to make concrete their agreement in a formal accord, preferring to retain their freedom of action.

The French ruler, who perceived the advantages his Empire might accrue as a result of an Austrian–Prussian War, believed in the military superiority of Austria over Prussia. Consequently, he readily supported the formation of a countervailing Italian–Prussian Alliance, which was the main object of Bismarck's visit to Biarritz. Bismarck understood that Vittorio Emanuele and the Italians would not join an alliance without Napoleon's approval, and obtained it at Biarritz. In his talks with Nigra in Paris, on his way back to Berlin, Bismarck confided his conviction that a war against Austria was inevitable, thus revealing his desire to have Italy fight alongside Prussia. He suggested that if Italy had not existed, Prussia would have had to invent her.[18]

Napoleon sent mixed signals to Florence. On the one hand he offered his approval for the formation of an Italian–Prussian bloc against Austria, while on the other, he proposed that the Italians seek a *rapprochement* with Vienna. La Marmora was confused, but conscious of the difficulties in improving relations with Austria and the continuing reluctance of Vienna to cede Venice. To further frustrate the Italians, the Austrian Emperor, Franz-Josef, supported the person and policies of Pius IX, championing both the interests of the Church and the preservation of the temporal power of the Papacy.[19] Under the circumstances, La Marmora did not foresee the prospect of an accord with Austria.

Relations between Florence and Berlin, on the other hand, became increasingly cordial. Following Biarritz, early in 1866 the Prussians negotiated the formation of a commercial agreement between Italy and the *Zollverein*, while William I conferred the Order of the Black Eagle on Vittorio Emanuele. The commercial agreement was ratified on 12th March, followed by the recognition of the kingdom of Italy on the part of all the members of the German Tariff League. Meanwhile, Berlin proposed that the Italian government dispatch a general to Prussia, to explore their respective positions, should war erupt. The Italians momentarily hesitated, seeking an alternative to war as a means of acquiring Venice.

In February 1866 Prince Couza of Romania was deposed, the throne fell vacant and the Italians explored the prospect that Vienna would trade Venice for Romania. The Italians, who sought the assistance of Napoleon in effecting the exchange, responded that the Austrians would probably reject the suggestion, but promised to float the proposal in London. However, he was pessimistic concerning its prospect and urged the Italians not to abandon talks with Berlin. Consequently La Marmora sent General Giuseppe Govone to Berlin, and the Italian emissary had his first meeting with Bismarck on 14th March. Since both La Marmora and Govone still hoped for the Romanian–Venetian transfer, they both saw the Italo-Prussian talks as another means of pressuring the Austrians to accept the exchange. The Italians suspected that the Prussians were doing more or less the same, using the talks as a means of frightening the Austrians into forcing Vienna to accept their absorption of the duchies. By 17th March the Italians had learned that Britain, Russia and Austria all opposed the Venetian–Romanian agreement, and so began serious negotiations with the Prussians.

The Italians wished to bind Prussia to a definite time-table for the impending war, while Bismarck, concerned about the attitude of William I and Napoleon III, sought to preserve his freedom of action.[20] At the end of March a six-point compromise was ironed out. Among other things Italy was bound to join the war against Austria, once Prussia had opened the conflict. The agreement would only be implemented if Prussia initiated hostilities against Austria within three months following ratification of the treaty. Any armistice or peace concluded with the enemy had to be by mutual consent of the signatories, and would become operative when Austria was prepared to cede Venice to Italy and an equally populated territory to Prussia. La Marmora, whose nightmare was to be left in the lurch by Bismarck, found these terms acceptable, as did Napoleon. While the latter encouraged the Italians to formally sign the accord with Prussia on 8 April 1866, he assumed no responsibility or obligation of any sort. Napoleon, in Nigra's opinion, expected to exploit the crisis and possibly the war to push the French frontier to the Rhine.

As La Marmora ordered the mobilization of the Italian army on 26th April, and early in May Bismarck placed the Prussian forces in a state of readiness, French public opinion, not privy to the scheming of the Emperor, was alarmed at the prospect of a war which strengthened Prussia and Italy. On 3rd May Adolphe Thiers, rejecting the notion of German unification, called upon Napoleon to take steps to prevent Prussian aggrandizement. The Emperor was already weighing that possibility as Austria, finally awakened to the nightmare of a two-front war, offered to cede Venice to Italy if France and Italy would remain neutral in the coming war, and would allow the Habsburgs to seek compensation at Prussia's expense.

On 4th May, Napoleon transmitted the Austrian offer to the Italians who pondered the proposal. The obvious advantage was that Italy would gain Venice without cost or bloodshed, if Austria won and received compensation from Prussia. The Florentine government quickly perceived the disadvantages. What if Prussia won? How could the Italians explain their inactivity and failure to take advantage of the opportunity to acquire Venice? It might well lead the radicals to initiate their own campaign to the detriment of the monarchy and public order. Furthermore, a victorious Austria that had scored a major triumph in Germany could not be trusted to cede Venice, and even if she did, the balance of power would remain tilted in Vienna's favour. Since the transfer of Venice was to be effected via France, this would increase Gallic influence in Italian affairs. Finally, Italy needed a popular war to help cement unity and strengthen the still fragile state. For all these reasons, but specifically citing loyalty and keeping one's word to Prussia, La Marmora telegraphed to Napoleon that Italy could not accept the Austrian proposal.[21]

In his speech of 6 May 1866, Napoleon returned to one of his earlier schemes: the calling of a European Congress to settle the affairs of Schleswig-Holstein, Venice, and the organization of the German Confederation. Confronted with the threat of war in Central Europe, Britain and Russia accepted the French offer. Italy and Prussia agreed informally to the Congress, the latter much more reluctantly than the former, and it was believed that Vienna would accept the invitation which was sent out on 24th May. Napoleon and Bismarck were astounded by the Austrian assent which was conditional and tantamount to a rejection. Count Mensdorf insisted on the exclusion from the agenda of any matter leading to the territorial extension or increase in power of any participating state. Furthermore, he insisted that the Pope be invited to take part in the discussion and resolution of the Italian question.[22] The Austrian response killed the Congress and, in Bismarck's words, made war inevitable.

Napoleon was convinced that Austria would emerge victorious from a war with Prussia, and therefore opened negotiations with Vienna to influence the ensuing peace. The Duke de Gramont ventured to Vienna on 4th June, and on 9th June, signed an accord. By its terms the French government promised a strict neutrality in the impending war, while assuming the obligation to persuade the Italian government to do likewise. Austria, in turn, pledged to respect the existing situation in Italy, to cede Venice no matter what the outcome of the conflict, to renounce any attempt to achieve hegemony in Germany, and further promised not to introduce any territorial changes, without French permission, that might undermine the European equilibrium. When Napoleon transferred Venice to Italy, he was to obtain an Italian agreement to respect what remained of the temporal power of the Pope, securing a recognition from the Florentine government of the Austrian–Italian frontier, renouncing all claims to the Italian Tyrol and Trieste.

Napoleon also received verbal assurances from the Prussians that whatever the outcome of the war, matters which concerned France would not be settled without her consent. The Emperor, for his part, pledged that he did not seek Gallic aggrandizement from the civil war in Germany, unless the map of Europe was changed to benefit one great power, or some provinces freely sought union with France.

Although he adhered to the letter of his 9th June agreement with Austria, by passing word of the cession of Venice and suggesting that Italy might wish to avoid war with Austria, the prospect of the civil war in Germany pleased him. The transfer of Venice to the Italians, the guarantee of the truncated Papal States, the restriction of Prussia north of the Main border, and the substitution of French for Austrian influence in south Germany were all possible consequences. Finally, there was the lure of territorial revision as the Emperor in turn considered the acquisition of the frontier of 1814 or a buffer state on the Rhine.

On 10 June 1866 the Prussians presented their outline for a reorganization of Germany, which excluded Austria, leading to a suspension of diplomatic relations between Vienna and Berlin and the mobilization of the forces of the German Confederation. On 15th June, the Prussian army went on the offensive, declaring war the following day. Austria, because of her procrastination, proved unable to dislodge Italy from her Prussian alliance; thus she faced the difficult prospect of waging a war on two fronts. Franz-Josef decided to employ the Archduke Albrecht, the best commander in the Habsburg ranks, in the Italian theatre, where he proved his mettle. Field Marshal Ludwig von Benedek, whose military career had been in Italy, was transferred to preside over the northern campaign.

In Italy, the outbreak of the Austrian–Prussian War on 16 June 1866, was followed by General La Marmora's move to the front, and Bettino Ricasoli's assumption as head of the government. On 19th June, the Italians declared war on Austria and prepared for the campaign. The Italians enjoyed a number of advantages. Firstly, the Austrian willingness to transfer Venice to France to hand over to the Italians, assured that they would not assume the offensive on the southern front and would limit their action to a defence of their positions. Secondly, the regular Italian forces outnumbered the Austrians by two to one. Garibaldi, as in 1859, led his volunteers, and while only some 15,000 were expected to enrol, more than double that figure rushed to fight under his banner. Finally, since Austrian rule in Venice was deemed unpopular, some expected the Venetians to rise in rebellion as they had in 1848 during the course of the First War of Liberation. The course of events proved otherwise.

The Prussians suggested that the Italians skirt the Quadrilateral and penetrate the Dalmatian coast, possibly using Garibaldi to rouse the population against the Austrians, and then drive on to Vienna. The proposal was seconded by Garibaldi, but rejected by La Marmora, whose strategy was more restricted and less audacious. Indeed, La

Marmora decided to implement the plan prepared by the French and Sardinian general staff in 1859, before the war had been closed by Villafranca. The Italian forces were divided, with La Marmora and the main army of some 120,000 men on the Mincio, General Cialdini's 80,000 troops on the lower Po, which was to act as a diversion, and Garibaldi's volunteers directed against the Austrian position in the Tridentine mountains assigned the dual task of closing the valley of the Adige and capturing Trento.

La Marmora, assuming that the Austrians would be focused on Cialdini's manoeuvring on the Po, believed his actions on the Mincio would not be seriously contested. Unfortunately, while the Italian commander had little information on the plans and activities of the Archduke Albrecht, the latter was well informed of the movements and intentions of the three major Italian forces. On 23rd June the bulk of La Marmora's forces bivouacked on the left, or Venetian side, of the Mincio, advancing on the 24th with the intention of gaining control of the heights between Peschiera and Verona, which unbeknown to the Italians was already garrisoned by the Austrians. When the two armies met, the Austrians had the advantage of surprise and control of the high terrain. Although Italian and Austrian losses during the second battle of Custozza were about equal (the Italians endured some 720 fatalities and 3,112 wounded, while the Austrian casualties were respectively 960 and 3,690), the Italians panicked and withdrew.[23]

The command of the regular Italian Army left much to be desired. Although La Marmora resigned as Commander-in-Chief, following the second battle of Custozza, confusion still prevailed. It was hoped that the Italian navy would perform better. At sea, as on land, the Italians had the numerical advantage, possessing a fleet of thirty-three vessels, which included twelve ironclads, to Austria's fleet of twenty-seven, of which only seven were ironclad. However, the commander of the Italian fleet, Count Carlo di Persano, lacked the ability and confidence possessed by the Danish commander of the Austrian fleet, Wilhelm von Tegethoff. The disparity in ability and preparation was manifest during the battle of Lissa, fought on 20th July, during the course of which the Italian fleet lost three vessels, including the flagship, the *Re d'Italia*, with the loss of almost a thousand lives, while the Austrians emerged virtually unscathed.

The poor performance of the Italian armed forces was highlighted by the spectacular victory achieved by the Prussians at Sadowa on 3rd July. The progress made by General Cialdini in Venice, once Archduke Albrecht and the bulk of his troops were recalled to the German theatre, and Garibaldi's tentative advances in the valley of the Trento, proved small compensation. While the Italians were discouraged, the French were alarmed at the prospect of a total Austrian collapse and a Prussian reorganization of Germany. Both Napoleon's belief in an Austrian victory or in a long war which would permit French intervention were shattered. The only positive developments were Vienna's decision to immediately transfer Venice to France and its call for French mediation for an armistice. The prospect of a French diplomatic intervention which might turn to a military one prompted Bismarck to come to terms with Austria quickly. On 25th July, Prussia signed the preliminaries of a peace with Vienna without consulting her Italian ally. As in the war of 1859 the Italians had been left in the lurch; once again they realized the impossibility of continuing the conflict without their ally. Prevented by Napoleon from militarily seizing Venice, now under French control, and receiving no support from either Berlin or Paris for their claim to the Italian Tyrol, the Italians reluctantly agreed to an armistice on 12th August.

By the peace of 3 October 1866, the Italians finally acquired formal recognition from Austria as well as Venice, which was transferred to Italy by France. The vote in the plebiscite, overwhelmingly in favour of union, supposedly 642,000 for and only sixty-nine against, did not seem to reflect the sentiment of the population. Not one Venetian city had risen during the course of the war of 1866, and few Venetians had flocked to Garibaldi's standard. Furthermore, while Venice had finally been attained, Rome still remained outside the kingdom. Thus, when the results of the plebiscite were presented to Vittorio Emanuele, who claimed it was the greatest day of his life, referring to Rome, he noted that while Italy was made, it was as yet incomplete.[24]

NOTES

1. Text of Napoleon's speech to his troops, 1860, *Archivio di Stato di Roma*, *Miscellanea di Carte Politiche O Riservate*, busta 137, *fascicolo* 4913.
2. Police Report of 1860, *ASR*, *Miscellanea di Carte Politiche O Riservate*, busta 134, *fascicolo* 4815.
3. Giuseppe Leti, *Roma e lo Stato Pontificio dal 1849 al 1870. Note di storia politica* (2nd edn, Ascoli Piceno, 1911), II, pp. 212–15; Francesco Crispi, *The Memoirs of Francesco Crispi*, ed. Thomas Palamenghi-Crispi (New York: Hodder and Stoughton, 1912), I, pp. 271–2.

4. William E. Echard, *Napoleon III and the Concert of Europe* (Baton Rouge: Louisiana State University, 1983), p. 142.
5. 'La Confederazione Italiana e l'Unità piemontese', *Civiltà Cattolica*, Series IV, X, 529–55.
6. Pius IX to Napoleon III, 14 February 1861. *Archivio Segreto del Vaticano, Archivio Particolare Pio IX, Sovrani, Francia*, no. 56.
7. *I Documenti Diplomatici Italiani*, I, 79.
8. *The Letters of Queen Victoria*, first series, ed. Arthur C. Benson and Viscount Esher (London: John Murray, 1907), III, pp. 428, 441.
9. *Count Cavour and Madame de Circourt: some Unpublished Correspondence*, ed. Costantino Nigra, trans. Arthur John Butler (London: Cassell and Co., Ltd., 1894), p. 15.
10. *L'Osservatore Romano*, 4 July 1861.
11. *The Roman Journals of Ferdinand Gregorovius, 1852–1874*, ed. Friedrich Althaus, trans. Mrs Gustavus Hamilton (London: George Bell and Sons, 1907), p. 152.
12. L. Thouvenel (ed.), *Le Secret de L'Empereur. Correspondance confidentielle et inédite échangée entre M. Thouvenel, Le Duke de Gramont et Le Général Comte de Flahaut 1860–1863* (Paris: Calmann-Levy, 1889), I, pp. 8–10.
13. De Corcelles to Pius IX, 1 November 1862, *ASV, Archivio Particolare Pio IX, Francia, Particolari*, no. 155.
14. Emile Ollivier, *Journal*, ed. Theodore Zeldin and Anne Troisier de Diaz (Paris: Julliard, 1961), II, p. 71.
15. Pius IX to Napoleon III, 4 November 1863, *ASV, Archivio Particolare Pio IX, Sovrani, Francia*, no. 65.
16. *Il Diritto*, 10 July 1864.
17. Costantino Bulle, *Storia del Secondo Impero e del Regno d'Italia* (Milan: Società Editrice Libraria, 1909), II, pp. 375–8.
18. Alfonso La Marmora, *Un po di luce* (Mangonza, 1873), p. 57.
19. Franz-Josef to Pius IX, 22 October 1865, *ASV, Archivio Particolare Pio IX, Sovrani, Austria*, no. 52.
20. Otto Pflanze, *Bismarck and the Development of the German Empire: The Period of Unification, 1815–1871*, (Princeton: Princeton University Press, 1963), p. 287.
21. Bulle, pp. 383–90.
22. Echard, p. 234.
23. Countess Evelyn Martinengo Cesaresco, *The Liberation of Italy, 1815–1870* (Freeport, New York: Books for Libraries Press, 1972), pp. 365–9.
24. Ibid., p. 380.

CHAPTER NINE

Italy, the Powers and the 'Fourth War of Italian Liberation': 1866–71

Vittorio Emanuele's comment to the Venetian deputation that Italy was made but incomplete revealed his, as well as the national, obsession for Rome. It found expression in subsequent developments. During the Ministry of Alfonso La Marmora from September 1864 to June 1866, the diplomacy of the Third War of Liberation, and then the waging of the war, dominated events. In the aftermath of the conflict, following the transfer of Venice to Italy, the Roman question again loomed large. However, the Italians, plagued by domestic problems and pressed by the French to respect the remaining temporal power, proved unable to acquire Rome. The incursion and insurrection in Palermo in September 1866 revealed both the southern distrust of the northern government and the fragility of unification. Only the dispatch of troops from the mainland restored order, solving neither the pressing problems of Sicily nor bridging the gaping division between North and South.

At the end of the year, in December 1866, the last French troops departed from Rome under the terms of the September Convention. The French withdrawal was widely expected to return the Roman question to the forefront. Lord Stanley, the British Foreign Minister, warned Odo Russell, the special British representative to the Vatican, that they could expect not only a reopening of the issue, but material changes in the relations between the Pope and the Italian government. Her Majesty's Government, the Foreign Minister continued, sought to avoid involvement in a matter which concerned Italy and the Roman Catholic Church, but did not impinge on English vital interests. Still, Lord Stanley worried that the open wound might disturb the tranquillity of Europe.[1]

Pius IX, fearing the worst, predicted that the French departure would encourage the revolution to storm the gates of Rome. He lamented that Napoleon sustained him only indirectly by ineffective means, questioning the Emperor's will to keep his promise to uphold what remained of the temporal power. To the assurances that Napoleon was there, an irritated Pope retorted that he was here, and everyone knew that Paris was far from Rome. The Pope foresaw that the great distance, both physical and psychological, undermined the effectiveness of Napoleon's commitment. He bitterly resented Napoleon's failure to respond promptly to Vittorio Emanuele's comment that Italy was made but not complete, revealing intentions that did not bode well for the future.[2]

Some feared that the imminent danger might encourage Pius to abandon his capital, provoking foreign intervention and plunging Italy into chaos. Among those concerned was the Comte de Chambord, the legitimist claimant to the French throne, who offered his sword to Pius, charging that Napoleon had abandoned the Pontiff to the revolution.[3] The offer antagonized the Emperor without providing the Pope with the protection he required. Pius, for his part, complained of the machinations against him and his government, finding solace in that sovereign who was not only potent, but omnipotent. In fact while 'volunteers' threatened the integrity of his state and hovered on his borders, the Pope remained absorbed in religious affairs, announcing his decision to call an Ecumenical Council in Rome.[4]

In Florence Bettino Ricasoli, who had replaced La Marmora as prime minister in June of 1866, sought to resolve the Roman question by moral means, following the peace with Austria. His efforts proved abortive as Antonelli followed Pio Nono's intransigent instructions. Meanwhile the Italian Chamber showed itself unwilling to approve the Baron's legislation regulating Church–state relations in the kingdom, and the new Chamber, elected in March 1867, proved equally recalcitrant. In April the disappointed Baron resigned, and on 11 April 1867, Urbano Rattazzi assumed power. The Party of Action preferred Rattazzi to Ricasoli, who was disinclined to tolerate, much less sanction, private efforts to wrest Rome from Papal control.

While the Party of Action awaited some movement on the part of the Rattazzi government, Garibaldi invoked immediate action and initiated matters during the spring of 1867. The impetuous general, who despised Napoleon for toppling the Roman Republic in 1849, murdering the Second French Republic in 1851, abandoning Venice to Austria at Villafranca and stealing Nice and Savoy in the process, resented his interference in the Roman question. Forgetful of the disastrous consequences of the First War of Italian Liberation, when the Italians failed to resolve matters while working alone, the charismatic Garibaldi called for unilateral action to make Rome the capital of Italy. Critical of Cavour's cautious approach during the tumultuous events of 1859–60, Garibaldi never appreciated his agile manoeuvring between Paris and the Redshirts, which secured a reluctant French acceptance of the absorption of central and southern Italy. The absence of Cavour in 1867 belatedly revealed the magnitude of his achievement.

Garibaldi and the government in Florence, seeking to duplicate Cavour's *realpolitik*, hoped that a revolution in Rome would provide the pretext for intervention. Indeed, early in April, a pamphlet circulated in the Eternal City, calling upon its occupants to throw off the yoke of their priestly oppressors, and promising assistance in their struggle for liberation. Garibaldi was hailed as the leader of the insurrection in the remaining Papal province which contained slightly more than half a million inhabitants. Neither the Pope nor Antonelli were reassured by Napoleon's criticism of the government in Florence or the antics of the volunteers. Nonetheless the Emperor pledged that if there were an invasion, French forces would reoccupy Rome.[5] In the early summer of 1867, as Garibaldi both in words and actions showed his disdain for the temporal power of the Papacy, while discounting the French assurances to the same, the Italian government did little to restrain him. On the other hand, Rattazzi hastened to condemn the French for allowing one of their generals to inspect the Légion d'Antibes, which served Papal Rome, maintaining that this action violated the 'spirit' of the September Convention.

At this juncture the Italians dared to displease the French, who were preoccupied by developments on the Rhine and frightened by the prospect of German unification. Article 2 of the Peace of Nikolsburg of July 1866, stipulated that Germany would be divided into two spheres, with the South as well as the North permitted to federate. Even this German settlement generated fear and frustration in Paris, and to calm national sentiment Napoleon pressed for French territorial compensation. Originally asking for the frontiers of 1814, the Emperor's emissaries escalated their demands by also seeking Mainz and the Bavarian Palatinate. In the face of Prussian reluctance to cede any German territory, Napoleon sought Bismarck's diplomatic support for his acquisition of Belgium and Luxemburg – to no avail. After 1867 relations between Berlin and Paris deteriorated and a Franco-German war seemed inevitable.

Convinced that Paris was busy on the Rhine, Rattazzi believed he had some leeway on the Tiber. Thus, during the summer of 1867, when Garibaldi's volunteers were preparing for an incursion into Papal territory, they were aided and abetted by Italian officials with the apparent blessing of the Italian government. General Genova di Revel, the Minister of War, condemned the inactivity of his government and its flagrant failure to live up to the commitment undertaken in the September Convention. His protest found scant support in the Italian capital, but was loudly seconded by the French government. France, humiliated by Prussia's rapid victory in 1866, the reorganization of Germany and the creation of the North German Confederation, and humbled in Mexico, which French troops abandoned early in 1867, could not tolerate humiliation at the hands of the Italians.

After allowing Garibaldi to make speeches and issue manifestos against the temporal power for more than a month, Rattazzi suddenly shifted his course. Under pressure from his Minister of War, and also Napoleon, Rattazzi precipitously, if reluctantly, ordered Garibaldi's arrest at Sinalunga on 23 September 1867. Although the hero of Sicily was shipped back to his island of Caprera, where he was granted complete liberty, a number of his volunteers slipped across the border into the Papal States. Restricted to Caprera, which was guarded by nine royal ships, Garibaldi managed to evade their blockade and reached the island of Madalena by canoe in mid–October. From Madalena he ventured to Sardinia, from which he sailed for the Tuscan coast, reaching Florence on 20 October 1867. In Rome the Papal Secretary of State, Cardinal Antonelli, complained that if the Italian government did not openly aid Garibaldi and the volunteers who threatened the Papal States, all the available evidence exposed its encouragement of him.[6] The French concurred with this observation.

The Italian government revealed its complicity by refusing to rearrest Garibaldi and take the field against his volunteers, who had already penetrated the Papal States, where they made little headway. Genova di Revel, the Minister of War, resigned in disgust. When Paris called upon Rattazzi to take steps to fulfil the September Convention and the French Council of Ministers threatened intervention if the Convention were not honoured, Rattazzi resigned. Thus when Garibaldi arrived in Florence and publicly called for an invasion of Rome, there was no government in place, and little inclination to block the march on Rome. Antonelli, watching these developments, labelled it a prearranged comedy whose plot was predictable. Napoleon hoped that Vittorio Emanuele and the Italians would come to their senses, and from 18th to 26th October he agonized as to whether to dispatch to Rome the troops gathered at Toulon.

On 26 October 1867, Napoleon ordered French forces back to Rome. Belatedly, Vittorio Emanuele appointed General Menabrea as prime minister. General Manabrea shared Di Revel's conviction that the Italian government had to move against the volunteers to preserve its credibility. It was too late, however, Garibaldi had left Florence for Terni and rejoined his volunteers, and the French fleet was on its way to Civitavecchia. Events now proceeded apace. On 26th October, Garibaldi occupied Monte Rotondo, one of the strategic heights overlooking Rome, and word spread in the Eternal City that he was at the gates. Garibaldi, and even more so Vittorio Emanuele and Rattazzi, hoped that the volunteers' daring would inspire a revolution in Rome, thus legitimizing Italian intervention and precluding a French intervention. The desired revolution never materialized, however, while in the countryside the population proved unreceptive to Garibaldi's overtures.

Meanwhile word of the French landing at Civitavecchia and Menabrea's condemnation of the volunteers led many of the latter to desert. The Papal forces, on the other hand, remained committed to Pio Nono's cause. In Rome, Gregorovius, consistently hostile to the Papal position, ironically noted that it was easier for Garibaldi to overturn the rotten throne of Naples than to defeat the army of the Pope. The latter had remained loyal without one single case of desertion.[7] The two forces met at Mentana on 3rd November, where they were joined shortly after by the French, who first made use of their new guns, the rapid firing *chassepots*. Pius, who applauded the performance of his troops, recognized that the volunteers, aided in a thousand ways by the Florence government and its 'pathetic' king, might have succeeded in their plot against him, but for French assistance.[8] In the words of General de Failly, the '*chassepots* had done wonders'.[9] Garibaldi was arrested and returned to Caprera. In December, when the Roman question was discussed in the Corps Legislatif, the French prime minister, Eugène Rouher, emphatically declared that France would never permit the Italians to take Rome. At the same time, the Archbishop of Paris wrote to Pius on Christmas day, reassuring him of Napoleon's determination to preserve the integrity of what remained of the temporal power.[10]

The return of French forces to Rome, and the public opposition of the Paris government to the Italian acquisition of the Eternal City, undermined Italo-French relations at a time when Napoleon frantically sought allies in the expected war against Prussia. Once again Napoleon sought to resolve the Roman question by a European congress, but his proposal at the end of 1867 generated little enthusiasm outside Spain and the minor powers. Benedetti failed to persuade William of Prussia to participate. The Habsburgs agreed to attend, but displayed little interest, in the expectation that the idea would be dropped. Russia, likewise, proved lukewarm to the congress, agreeing to it in principle, but accepting only conditionally, which was tantamount to a courteous diplomatic refusal. England, in calling for a solution that would satisfy both the Pope and the Italians, was proposing an impossible programme, given the continuing enmity between Florence and Rome.

Costantino Nigra, the Italian representative at Paris, demanded a Franco–Italian understanding prior to the opening of the congress and a commitment from Paris that during its deliberations nothing would be approved that was detrimental to Italy. Rome continued to insist on the restoration of all its territory as a necessary precondition for any negotiation. Pius steadfastly refused to refer to Italy, continuing to speak of Piedmont. He deemed the people of the latter state good, deploring the fact that they were corrupted by evil leaders, who were responsible for the unfortunate condition of the peninsula.[11] The contradictory and irreconcilable positions assumed by Rome and Florence rendered the congress abortive in 1868. Vittorio Emanuele's attempts throughout the year to secure a *modus vivendi* with Rome, via French mediation, proved equally abortive.[12]

The year 1868 proved largely uneventful in the Italian peninsula, apart from the marriage of Prince Umberto to his cousin Margherita of Savoy, and Pio Nono's setting of the opening date for his projected Ecumenical Council. While the latter event frightened Italians, especially as word leaked out of the Pope's intention of having the doctrine of Papal Infallibility proclaimed, the behaviour of the Archbishop of Turin during the marriage, roused the anger of Pio Nono. In Archbishop Riccardi's address to the clergy and people of Turin, on the occasion of the marriage of Umberto and Margherita, he called upon Italians to rejoice and share in the happiness of the couple, hoping that the Italian family, so long divided, might become one under this dynasty.[13]

The Archbishop's conciliatory words were little appreciated by Pius, who refused to grant the plenary indulgence on the occasion of the tridium to celebrate the marriage. The Pope proceeded to criticize the Archbishop's public speeches during the festivities, deeming them inappropriate. He expected such 'drivel' from a revolutionary bishop, but not from one such as Riccardi who was true and loyal. How could the Archbishop urge Catholics in the peninsula to rejoice, when millions of them were burdened by the unfortunate policies of the usurpers? The Pope then proceeded to catalogue the grievances of the Church and the Papacy against the Piedmontese. He concluded that in light of the war being waged against the Church, the Papacy, religion, and God, Italians should be stricken by tears of sorrow rather than those of joy.[14] He transmitted more or less the same message to Vittorio Emanuele, insisting that in light of the iniquities committed against the Church and religion, he could not regularize relations with his government.[15]

While Italian developments reached an impasse during the course of 1868, dramatic changes exploded elsewhere in Europe. The deterioration in relations between Paris and Berlin continued, while a rebellion in Spain in the autumn of 1868 led to the flight of Queen Isabella and the vacancy of the Spanish throne. Eventually the two events were to precipitate the Franco-Prussian War, by leading to the prospect of a Hohenzollern on the throne of Spain and the virtual French veto of this candidacy. The threat of a struggle prompted Napoleon to seek allies, and to open talks with both the Austrians and the Italians for the formation of a triple alliance against Prussia. The Tuileries began negotiations with Vienna about a possible anti-Prussian alliance as early as July 1868, when the Austrians were advised by the French to secure some commitment from Prussia not to pass the Main line. Vienna, in turn, suggested that Paris secure from Berlin the necessary assurances regarding the Peace of Prague.

France encountered graver problems in its negotiations with the Italians, who had given a warm reception to Prince Frederick William when he attended the wedding of Umberto to Margherita. The cordiality reflected the anti-French sentiment following the French return to Rome, and the growing conviction that they could only get into the Eternal City by aligning themselves with Prussia against their former ally. No less a figure than Mazzini communicated with Bismarck, through Count Usedom, the Prussian Minister in Florence, on the need to prevent a Franco-Italian alliance against Prussia. He denounced a Franco-Italian accord against the Prussians as a grave crime which would besmirch the banner of the new Italian state.[16] During the course of 1868, when discussions for a Franco-Italian alliance had been conducted informally and secretly, only Vittorio Emanuele and those in his strictest confidence were aware of their content. However, during the course of 1869, when a concrete alliance was contemplated, the Italian Ministry necessarily became embroiled in negotiations.

The Italian prime minister, General Luigi Menabrea, who had denounced the adventurism of Garibaldi, remained equally firm in his insistence that Rome serve as the Italian capital. When the Italian parliament reopened in Florence in December 1867, he reported that the desire to see the Roman question resolved was not restricted to the revolutionary groups, but was broadly based in the peninsula. The truncated Papal State divided the kingdom physically as well as psychologically, thus aggravating the new kingdom's southern problem. Furthermore, the Papal State served as a centre of conspiracy against the unitary Italian state, so undermining the existence of the latter. Small wonder then that the Party of Action capitalized on this real grievance, creating difficulties not only for Italy but for the whole of Europe. The agitation of the Garibaldian Party in Florence alarmed both Rome and Paris.

During the course of 1869, when Menabrea learned of the French desire to secure Italy as an ally in her impending war against Prussia, he immediately posed as a precondition the need to resolve the Roman question. Italy could not subscribe to the proposed Triple Alliance until the Roman issue had been resolved. Austria supported the Italian contention, but France did not. Napoleon promised to seek a diplomatic solution to the Roman question at the appropriate time, but for the moment could not, and would not, make any unilateral concession on the matter. Disappointed, Menabrea predicted that one day Napoleon might regret not having accepted the 400,000 Italian bayonets that would have been at his disposal, had he given his support on the Roman issue. In the face of the ministerial hostility to an accord without an understanding on the issue of Rome, Napoleon suggested a general agreement among the French, Austrian and Italian rulers regarding their common aims, while pledging general reciprocal support. There followed an exchange of letters in September 1869 along these lines. If Napoleon conceived of this as a concrete commitment for assistance, neither Vienna nor Florence shared his interpretation. Furthermore, Pio Nono continued to show himself ill-disposed towards any compromise with the Italians.[17]

There were those who suggested that during the course of the inevitable Franco-Prussian conflict, the Italians should wage a 'fourth war of liberation' to seize Rome. This was neither diplomatically nor financially an easy undertaking. The three previous wars of liberation – in 1848–49, in 1859, and most recently in 1866 – had contributed to the vast Italian debt. The prospect of a future Franco-Prussian War, into which the kingdom was likely to be drawn, provided the rationale for massive increases in the budgets of the army and navy. The kingdom could not keep spending more than it raised without grave risk to its credit.

Menabrea's Ministry, deeply disturbed by the impending Vatican Council and its consequences for Italy, introduced a series of remedies for the country's fiscal problems.[18] Essentially his government proposed to reduce the deficit by increasing the already high tax rate on consumer goods, while imposing a grist tax on the grinding of grain. The latter tax, first proposed by Quintino Sella who was Minister of Finance in 1865, was promulgated by Luigi Cambray-Digny, Menabrea's Finance Minister, in July 1868. When it went into effect in January 1869, riots erupted throughout the peninsula, and in their wake hundreds of lives were lost.[19] Criticized for both the riots and the repression, and accused of profiting from the privatization of the tobacco monopoly, Menabrea was forced to resign in November 1869.

Internal and international affairs, many of them centring on the still unresolved Roman question, combined to render the choice of a successor difficult. Vittorio Emanuele had found it difficult to part with Menabrea, not only because of his proven loyalty, but also because he appreciated that the king had assumed obligations with Napoleon regarding the projected Franco-Prussian conflict. Both the king and Menabrea clung to the conviction that they could persuade the French Emperor to let them go to Rome, in return for their participation in the Triple Alliance against Prussia. Giovanni Lanza and Quintino Sella, mentioned as probable successors, did not share Vittorio Emanuele's optimism. The king's worst fears materialized when Lanza presented his conditions for the formation of a Ministry: the dismissal of three favourites of the Crown (including Menabrea) from their court positions, and fiscal cuts in the military appropriations.

Vittorio Emanuele reluctantly agreed to sacrifice his favourites, but balked at slashing the military, which he claimed endangered national security during a period of European crisis. His views were seconded by General Cialdini, who was given the task of forming a government but did not succeed in doing so. The king, who threatened abdication, opened talks with Sella, paving the way for a reconciliation with Lanza. On 14th December, Lanza was made prime minister, while also exercising control over the Ministry of the Interior, and Sella assumed the Ministries of the Treasury and Finance. While Lanza called for economies in the military in order to placate the left, which provided this ministry with considerable support, as well as the right, which appreciated the need to balance the budget, Sella perceived other advantages in the retrenchment. Aware of the king's desire to honour his personal commitment to Napoleon, Sella considered

Italy's lack of military preparedness a good pretext for keeping Italy out of the Triple Alliance and the war with Prussia.

Sella, who was aware of the military potential of Germany, concurred with the left, the Party of Action and the Mazzinians that Italy should not bind itself to the French Empire. He convinced Lanza that Napoleon would not open Rome to the Italians in return for their participation in the Triple Alliance, citing that even the new liberal Ollivier Ministry in Paris, was disinclined to compromise on the issue of Rome. In mid-July 1870, when the Vatican Council was on the verge of proclaiming the doctrine of Papal Infallibility, Vittorio Emanuele was shocked to hear of the outbreak of the Franco-Prussian War. He anxiously telegraphed Lanza, reminding him that the Crown had assumed obligations *vis-à-vis* Napoleon. Lanza and Sella remained noncommital. On 23 July 1870, the *Gazzetta Ufficiale* proclaimed Italian neutrality.

In Rome Pio Nono, who celebrated the fiftieth anniversary of his elevation to the priesthood, and Cardinal Giacomo Antonelli, who executed Papal directives, recognized the danger that a Franco-Prussian war posed for the Vatican, and sought to mediate peace.[20] Napoleon responded that the precipitous course of events had rendered impossible the Papal peace efforts.[21] Meanwhile discussions were opened between the French and Italians, with the French government announcing its intention of withdrawing its troops from Rome in return for the Italian government's recognition of the September Convention of 1864. Assured of Italian compliance, the French withdrawal began at the end of July and was completed on 19th August. Even the Austrians realized that this was hardly sufficient to satisfy the Italians, specifying that to bring them into the Triple Alliance it was necessary to provide Franco-Austrian approval for their march into Rome. In July and early August Paris still proved unwilling to compromise, claiming that it could not defend its honour on the Rhine while sacrificing and shaming it on the Tiber.

By mid-August, following the evacuation of the remaining French forces from Civitavecchia, the unfortunate course of the war for France finally led Napoleon to alter his position. On 19 August 1870, Napoleon dispatched Prince Napoleon on a special mission to Florence to secure Italian assistance in the form of an expeditionary force of 70,000 men. In return, the Italians could ask what they liked, with the prince indicating that Napoleon had signed a blank cheque. Thus France belatedly provided the Italian government with its consent to march into Rome.[22] But the consent had arrived too late. If such an agreement might have brought Italy into an alliance earlier on, at this juncture the prospect of entering a losing war seemed counterproductive, if not ludicrous. Whereas France had previously been in a position to exercise a prohibition on an Italian entry into Rome, she no longer exercised that option, unable to defend her own territory. Still Lanza and Sella moved cautiously regarding Rome. They saw the advantage of subsidizing rebellion in the Papal territory, to provide a pretext for intervention, but recognized the need to reassure conservative Europe by keeping the volunteers out of action. Finally, Lanza and Sella saw the importance of moving against Rome with the approval of the major courts of the continent.

The Italians, determined to complete the edifice of unity by taking Rome, began their preparations. An army corps for central Italy was formed by the Minister of War, Govone, and entrusted to General Raffaele Cadorna. Its instructions, for the moment, were to prevent penetration of the Papal States from Italian soil. To counter the complications that might result from revolutionary agitation, Mazzini was arrested in Palermo in August and Garibaldi confined to the island of Caprera. By this time even the king concurred that the military preparations undertaken to date, and the recall to arms of two categories of enlisted men on 10th August, should be directed to secure a solution of the Roman question. Parliament was called into session on 16th August, and asked to vote an additional forty million lire for the army. The left desired some statement that the monies appropriated would be used for the occupation of Rome, but the government avoided any direct statement or commitment beyond its cautious promise to safeguard national interests *vis-à-vis* Rome.

Methodically and carefully, the ministry made public its determination to move into Rome. At the end of August the Italians informed the French of the volatile situation of the peninsula, citing the need to protect the Papacy from revolutionary upheaval and the peninsula itself from chaos. On 29 August 1870, the Foreign Minister, Emilio Visconti-Venosta, alerted the other Powers of his government's decision to intervene in Rome. He met little opposition. However, the majority of the Italian Cabinet, with the exception of Sella, still hesitated. The French disaster at Sedan on 2nd September, the capture of the Emperor and the collapse of the Empire shortly afterwards allayed their fears, while providing the justification for action. The September Convention, which had been signed with Napoleon, was clearly nullified and Italian freedom of action restored.

On 5th September, the Lanza Cabinet unanimously resolved to move immediately against Rome, assuring the Powers that the Papacy's spiritual authority would be respected and protected. Count

Ponza di San Martino was to be dispatched to Rome as a special envoy of the king, revealing the reasons that induced the Italians to move into the remaining Papal territory. To reassure the public that the government was finally acting, news of the mission was published in the official gazette. On the evening of 9th September, the Italian envoy departed with Alessandro Guccioli for Rome. Shortly after his arrival, he had a long meeting with Cardinal Antonelli, transmitting to the Cardinal Secretary of State a letter written by Giovanni Lanza along with a ten-point programme for the resolution of the Roman question.[24]

The next morning, 10th September, Count Ponza di San Martino who had been lulled by the cordiality and amiability of the Secretary of State, confronted an angry Pius IX. Setting aside diplomatic niceties, the Pope muttered that while the king claimed to write with the affection of a son and the faith of a Catholic, he had imposed an ultimatum. Furthermore, the king's contentions that the Pope faced disorder and revolution requiring outside intervention was contradicted by the calm which prevailed in the territory. Not surprisingly the enraged Pope categorically refused both the king's request to have his forces enter the capital and his government's proposed solution to the Roman question. As the embarrassed and confused Count San Martino scurried out of the Pope's presence – initially heading for a window rather than the door – the Pope formalized his opposition in a letter to Vittorio Emanuele, in which he made plain his rejection both of the king's premises and his request to enter the Eternal City.[25]

On 11th September – the day of the Pope's formal rejection of Vittorio Emanuele's ultimatum – Italian forces crossed the frontier, preceded by a proclamation signed by General Cadorna but written by Visconti-Venosta. The Italian army, it proclaimed, entered the Papal territory to ensure tranquillity while respecting the independence of the Holy See. Its double function, acknowledged Visconti, was to mitigate any internal resistance, while reassuring the international community. As more than 50,000 Italian troops menaced Rome, the prospect that they could be stopped by General Kanzler's men, numbering less than 15,000, was slim. The Pope, who continued to adhere to his calendar of events, despite Rome's encirclement, believed in miracles and predicted that the Italians would not enter his capital.

By mid-September the Italian occupation of Città Castellana, Viterbo and Civitavecchia paved the way for the Italian occupation of Rome. Cadorna asked Kanzler not to resist the Italian entry into the capital, in order to avoid unnecessary bloodshed, but his suggestion was spurned. Von Arnim, the Prussian Minister to Rome, urged Cadorna to give him time to plead personally with the Pope to reconsider his determination to resist the Italians, but his effort likewise proved futile. On 18th September, Lanza telegraphed Cadorna, that all peaceful efforts to enter Rome having failed, his troops were to storm its walls. The time and means were left to Cadorna, but Lanza advised promptness and prudence.

Pius had earlier outlined his course of action in contending with a forced Italian entry into Rome. He concurred with Antonelli that the diplomatic situation had changed dramatically since 1848, and therefore did not seriously ponder flight, as he had during the course of the First War of Italian Liberation. Furthermore, Pius considered it crucial that the Catholic world and the international community be cognizant of the fact that the thief entered violently, without any complicity on the part of the Papal government. For these reasons, and to preserve the honour of the men who so loyally and valiantly defended his cause, the Pope insisted that the invasion be resisted. He wrote to General Hermann Kanzler on 19th September that the duration of the defence be limited to the simple act of contesting the violence and nothing more. Thus he proposed that the moment the walls of Rome were breached, negotiations for surrender should begin.

Early in the morning of 20th September, Italian batteries began pounding the walls of the Eternal City. During the course of the bombardment, between six o'clock and six-thirty, a frightened diplomatic corps flowed into the Vatican, where Pio Nono celebrated Mass without interruption. Following Mass, the Pope received the diplomats in his library, protesting against the invasion. After nine o'clock, when Pius heard the walls had been breached at Porta Pia and an Italian entry was imminent, he informed the diplomats that he had issued an executive order to capitulate. Pius, deeply distressed, while seeking to avoid needless bloodshed, insisted that the world should know that the Italians had entered Rome violently, by breaking the doors down, rather than being admitted.[26] They finally entered at eleven o'clock that morning.

Although Cardinal Manning, in the solemnity of Westminster Cathedral, denounced Vittorio Emanuele as a second Pontius Pilate, while in Dublin Cardinal Cullen predicted a disastrous end for the Italian king, and the Comte de Chambord deplored the Italian seizure,[27] the only diplomat to protest against the Italian entry was Garcia Moreno of Ecuador. There were those who hoped that Prussia, in the process of defeating France and creating the German Empire, might provide some protection to the Pope, but that proved illusory. Visconti-Venosta realized that whatever sympathy Prussia had for the person of the Pope was tempered by Berlin's desire for cordial relations with Italy. Nonetheless, the Italian Cabinet hastened to reassure the Powers of their intention of guaranteeing the spiritual independence of the Pontiff.

The capitulation, signed at the Villa Albani on 20 September 1870, left all of Rome, save the Leonine City, in the hands of the Italian troops. It also provided for the disbanding of the Papal forces, and this latter provision encouraged demonstrations and disturbances which frightened Pio Nono. The Pope and Antonelli, haunted by the memory of being besieged in the Quirinale Palace during the upheaval of 1848, determined to avoid a similar nightmare. They asked Cadorna to occupy the Leonine City, thereby assuming responsibility for the personal safety of the Pope and the security of the Vatican. Perhaps the two also wished to demonstrate the utter dependency of the Papacy, possibly sparking some movement for foreign intervention. At any rate, both Antonelli and Pio Nono saw all sorts of problems with the Italian proposal to leave the Pope the Leonine City. Above all, to accept this small piece of land in a corner of Rome signified the Papacy's acceptance of the loss of the rest of the temporal dominion.

The Italians, for their part, appreciated the need to legitimize what Antonelli denounced as blatant aggression. The seizure and forced entry into the Quirinale Palace, early in October, roused the Pope who denounced the 'Piedmontese' treachery. To counter their stream of complaints, Lanza called for a plebiscite on 2 October 1870, barely two weeks after the collapse of the Pope's temporal power. Despite the apathy the Romans had shown to all Italian initiatives for revolution, and their genuine loyalty to the Pope, if not the Papal regime, the vote was overwhelmingly in favour of union with the Kingdom of Italy. Out of 167,548 eligible votes 133,681 voted for union, with a mere 1,507 against.[28] By the royal decree of 9 October 1870 (No. 5903), Rome and its surrounding territory were annexed. Assurances were given to the Pope of his inviolability and personal sovereignty.

Outraged by the Italian annexation of the Holy City, Pius was not to be placated. However, he denounced the vote, and the electoral violence and chicanery employed to secure it, and resisted the call to abandon Rome. He refused to accept the *fait accompli*, responding in his encyclical of 1st November, 'Respicientes', which launched a mass excommunication of the invaders. Condemning the intrigues and aggression of the House of Savoy and the Piedmontese against his temporal sovereignty, Pius claimed that they jeopardized the spiritual authority of the Papacy and the Church. Before God and the Catholic world, the Pope lamented, he found himself in a virtual prison, unable to expeditiously and freely exercise his supreme pastoral authority.[29] The tone of his encyclical, and his diplomatic efforts to secure an end to the Franco-Prussian War,[30] led the Italians to conclude that Pius and Antonelli were scheming to provoke foreign intervention.

The Italian fears were not groundless. Even the English spoke of the need for an international conference to regularize the position of the Papacy – a prospect attractive neither to the Italians nor Antonelli. Officials in the peninsula feared that once the Franco-Prussian War ended and peace was restored, there would be international interference in the conflict between the Italians and the Pope, which might undermine their belated acquisition of the Eternal City. To preclude the possibility of such diplomatic meddling, the Italian parliament sought to calm the apprehensions of the international community and the Catholic powers by guaranteeing the Pope's personal immunity and complete liberty in the exercise of his spiritual power.

On 9 December 1870, the President of the Council, Lanza, presented a law project to stabilize and regularize the Italian possession of Rome by assuring the international and Catholic community that they would respect and protect the dignity and independence of the Supreme Pontiff. While in committee in the Chamber of Deputies in mid-January 1871, the governmental proposal was modified to specify that the Pope's sovereignty was spiritual rather than temporal, and he exercised political authority over no portion of the Italian peninsula. The Law of Guarantees thus did not function as a treaty, which would have required the Pope to have some temporal authority, but simply as a law of the Italian state. It was discussed in the Chamber from 23 January to 21 March 1871, and approved by a vote of 185 for and 106 against. In the Senate, where it was examined and debated from 20 April to 26 April 1871, the vote was 105 for and twenty against. It received royal sanction, was published, and went into effect on 13 May 1871.

The Law of Papal Guarantees, which declared the Pope's person sacred and inviolable also guaranteed his full freedom as head of the Catholic Church, including freedom of communication with the Church worldwide. Likewise, provision was made for the Pope's complete diplomatic liberty. To implement these assurances, the law provided for the extraterritoriality of the Vatican and other apostolic palaces and buildings, and accorded the Pope an annual grant of 3,225,000 lire free of taxation. The second half of the law, which regulated relations between Church and state in Italy, represented a modified version of Cavour's doctrine of a 'free Church in a free state'.

The measure which provided full and free diplomatic access of the diplomatic corps to the person of the Pope satisfied the international and Catholic community that the personal sovereignty of the Pope and the freedom of the Church had been preserved. All the major powers eventually recognized the Italian acquisition of Rome, and while they maintained representatives at the Vatican, sent their diplomats to the Quirinale, which became the official residence of the king. Pope Pius, however, refused to accept the Law of Papal Guarantees, which he denounced as a monument of barbarous ignorance.[31] Both the Pope and Antonelli feared that without any temporal power, the Papacy would be subject to the Italian government, whose good faith alone assured it freedom. The Law of Guarantees which satisfied the international community did not satisfy the Papacy, which refused to recognize its validity or come to terms with liberal Italy. Thus the 'Fourth war of Italian Liberation', fought and won in September 1870, did not witness a formal peace treaty until the Lateran Accords of 1929.

NOTES

1. Kenneth Bourne, 'The British Government and the Proposed Roman Conference of 1867', *Rassegna Storica del Risorgimento, anno* XLIII (October–December 1956), IV, 761.
2. Pius IX to Cardinal Bonnechose, 10 November 1866, *Archivio Segreto del Vaticano, Archivio Particolare Pio IX, Francia, Particolari*, No. 183.
3. Comte de Chambord to Pius IX, 12 December 1866, *ASV, Archivio Particolare Pio IX, Francia, Sovrani*.
4. Antonio Monti, *Pio IX nel Risorgimento Italiano con documenti inediti* (Bari: Laterza, 1928), p. 269; Eugenio Cecconi, *Storia del Concilio Ecumenico Vaticano scritta sui documenti originali* (Rome: Tipografia Vaticana, 1872), I, pp. 57–63.
5. Cardinal Bonnechose to Pius IX, 28 July 1867, *ASV, Archivio Particolare Pio IX, Francia, Particolari*, no. 188.
6. Giulio Andreotti, *La sciarada di Papa Mastai* (Milan: Rizzoli, 1967), p. 59.
7. *The Roman Journals of Ferdinand Gregorovius, 1852–1874*, ed. Friedrich Althaus, trans. Mrs Gustavus Hamilton (London: George Bell and Sons, 1907), pp. 297–301.

8. Pius IX to Monsignor Luciano Bonaparte, 8 November 1867, *ASV, Archivio Particolare Pio IX, Stato Pontificio*, no. 163A.
9. *Le Moniteur Universel*, 10 November 1867.
10. Archbishop of Paris to Pius IX, 25 December 1867, *ASV, Archivio Particolare Pio IX, Francia, Particolari*, no. 191.
11. Pius IX to Archbishop of Turin, 31 January 1868, *ASV, Archivio Particolare Pio IX, Sardegna, Particolari*, no. 30.
12. Vittorio Emanuele II to Pius IX, 21 July 1868, *ASV, Archivio Particolare Pio IX, Sardegna, Sovrani*, no. 72.
13. Archbishop of Turin's Address and Homily on Occasion of Marriage of Prince Umberto to Margherita of Savoy, 22 April 1868, *ASV, Archivio Particolare Pio IX, Sardegna, Sovrani*.
14. Pius IX to Archbishop Riccardi of Turin, 14 May 1868, *ASV, Archivio Particolare Pio IX, Sardegna, Particolari*, no. 33.
15. Pius to Vittorio Emanuele II, 7 June 1868, *ASV, Archivio Particolare Pio IX, Sardegna, Sovrani*, no. 71.
16. Giuseppe Mazzini, *Venezia e Roma* (Rome: Castelli, 1875), p. 59.
17. Pius to Vittorio Emanuele II, 10 December 1869, *ASV, Archivio Particolare Pio IX, Sardegna, Sovrani*, no. 79.
18. Count Alessandro Adorni to Cardinal Giacomo Antonelli, 20 May 1869, *ASV, Segreteria di Stato Esteri, 1869, rubrica 284, fascicolo 1.*
19. Count Alessandro Adorni to Cardinal Giacomo Antonelli, 6 January 1869, ibid.
20. Pius IX to Napoleon III, July 1870, *ASV, Archivio Particolare Pio IX, Francia, Sovrani*, no. 85.
21. Napoleon III to Pius IX, 27 July 1870, *ASV, Archivio Particolare Pio IX, Francia, Sovrani*, no. 86.
22. Andreotti, p. 72.
23. *Gazzetta Ufficiale*, 10 September 1870.
24. An English translation of the draft agreement will be found in my study *Cardinal Giacomo Antonelli and Papal Politics in European Affairs* (Albany: State University of New York Press, 1990), pp. 158–9.
25. Pius IX to Vittorio Emanuele II, 11 September 1870, *ASV, Archivio Particolare Pio IX, Sardegna, Sovrani*, no. 83.
26. Paolo Dalla Torre, *Pio IX e Vittorio Emanuele II. Dal Loro Carteggio privato negli anni deliceramento* (1861–78) (Rome: Istituto di Studi Romani Editori, 1972), pp. 157–60.
27. Comte de Chambord to Pius IX, 3 October 1870, *ASV, Archivio Particolare Pio IX, Francia, Sovrani*, no. 87.
28. Andreotti, p. 114.
29. Monti, p. 199.
30. Pius IX to Archbishop of Tours, 12 November 1870; Archbishop of Tours to French government of National Defence, 29 November 1870; Archbishop of Tours to King of Prussia, 19 December 1870, *ASV, Archivio Particolare Pio IX, Francia, Particolari*.
31. Monti, pp. 203–4.

CHAPTER TEN
Conclusion

The Wars of Italian Liberation, including the first war of 1848–49, the second of 1859–60, the third of 1866, and the campaign for Rome of 1870 (sometimes dubbed the 'fourth war of Italian Liberation') were waged by the moderate and monarchist Piedmontese party on the one hand, and the republicans and democrats of the Party of Action, on the other. While the Piedmontese party supplied the 'blood and iron', and perhaps more importantly the diplomatic expertise to win the wars, the Party of Action provided a broader degree of popular support, transforming the movement from a dynastic to a national one. Neither the moderates nor the republicans were truly popular, for both failed to appeal to the broad mass of workers and had little peasant support. Nonetheless they differed in their programmes, memberships and temperaments. The two camps also disagreed on the means of planning, waging and winning the wars, as well as having divergent visions of the final outcome. However, they needed each other to overcome Austria and her allies in the peninsula, and this assured some degree of cooperation.

The tone of the wars was set during the course of the First War of Italian Liberation (1848–49), when Carlo Alberto's Piedmont chose as its slogan, 'Italia farà da se', predicting that the Italians would be able to liberate the peninsula without foreign assistance. In practice the secretive Piedmontese ruler and his suspicious ministers relied almost exclusively on the kingdom's regular army to oust the Austrians. During the course of this conflict, the conservative Savoyard monarchy seemed more bent on Piedmontese expansion than Italian union, revealing a distrust of the other Italian states as well as the rural masses. Carlo Alberto's campaign, marred by indecisiveness, incompetence and parochialism, and betraying dynastic more than national ambitions, led to the disasters of Custozza and Novara. The dreams of 1848 disintegrated in the dust of the restoration of 1849.

The mutual rivalry and suspicion of the Italian princes, coupled with the Piedmontese reluctance to invoke outside intervention or encourage internal upheaval by rousing the masses, meant that the little state of Piedmont had to confront the powerful Austrian empire alone. Its population of less than five million proved unequal to the task in the struggle against an empire having more than six times that number. Consequently, Piedmont, which waged war against Austria in 1848 and then in 1849, was twice defeated.

The period following the restoration of 1849 proved to be one of preparation for reopening the conflict and waging the Second War of Liberation, with the Piedmontese state acting as the motor for unification. In the decade from this restoration to the outbreak of this Second War in 1859, the moderates were aided by a number of factors. For one thing the European powers protected Piedmontese independence and territorial integrity, assuring the Savoyards the freedom of action to launch another attempt to dislodge the Habsburgs from the peninsula. Secondly, the overly cautious members of the Piedmontese party were superseded by a more daring leadership, personified by Count Camillo di Cavour. Cavour recognized that Italy could not achieve unification alone, and that outside assistance would be necessary to challenge Austria, which at that time possessed one of the strongest armies. Thus Cavour looked to London, and even more so to Paris, well aware that tiny Piedmont did not enjoy the international autonomy to act unilaterally. His national strategy called for the collaboration of the Second French Empire. Nonetheless, he concluded after the Congress of Paris of 1856 that some degree of national support was essential to legitimize Piedmontese ambitions, providing at once both a popular and Italian element to the Second War of Liberation.

Mazzini's Party of Action likewise reconsidered its position in the decade from the Second Restoration to the outbreak of the Second War of Liberation, but the master himself, who had long championed the notion of unification, proved unwilling and unable to compromise his goals or reconsider his ideology. Mazzini refused to abandon his dream of religious regeneration and his nebulous philosophical doctrines, little understood or appreciated by the illiterate masses. Thus while the 'soul of Italian unification' pleaded for the involvement of the Italian people in the unification process, he did not know how to translate this goal into reality. Although the prophet had faith in popular initiative and enthusiasm, he consistently failed to rouse either. Mazzini proved incapable of offering the peasants a concrete programme of economic transformation and land reform that might have galvanized them into action.[1] Furthermore, Mazzini even more than Garibaldi and the Party of Action, distrusted Napoleon and shunned French involvement in Italian affairs.

Cavour, beholden to the propertied classes on the one hand, and dependent upon the goodwill of the courts of Europe, who feared revolution and communism, on the other, had neither the inclination nor the leeway to involve the peasants, preferring to let 'sleeping dogs lie'. Determined to preserve social stability as much as to achieve unification, the aristocratic Cavour relied first and foremost on the regular army, diplomacy and the bureaucracy to fulfil his ambitions. Popular movements, carefully controlled and guided, might supplement but not replace his strict reliance on the organs of state. On the war issue, he continued Carlo Alberto's cautious policy. The rural masses were not encouraged to take part in the campaign of 1848–49, and in that fateful year, the countryside often sided with General Radetzky against the Piedmontese. Later, too, the peasants failed to rise, and during the ensuing campaigns often stripped and robbed the fallen soldiers on both sides, in every battlefield.[2]

In the competition between the Piedmontese Party and the Party of Action, led respectively by Cavour and Mazzini, most of the advantages rested with the Machiavellian minister rather than the idealistic philosopher. Cavour, recognizing that a measure of broad support was required in the reorganization of the peninsula, under the auspices of the Piedmontese state, knew how to win adherents for his war of position. He proved able to drag the greater part of the bourgeoisie and aristocracy into his national bloc, while neutralizing the ultra-conservative and Catholic forces. Mazzini, championing a popular war, could not rouse the masses. Small wonder that substantial numbers from the left abandoned his cause and reorganized under the banner of the National Society, founded in 1857, committing themselves to cooperation with Cavour and the Piedmontese. The fact that an increasing contingent from the Party of Action joined Cavour's coalition affected not only the future of Mazzinianism, but the nature of the state which emerged from unification.

Among the first republicans to question the dogmas of Mazzini was the wealthy Lombard aristocrat, the Marchese Giorgio Pallavicino Trivulzio, who had transferred to Turin. Implicated in the revolutionary upheaval of 1821, and a 'martyr' of the Spielberg, his nationalist credentials and reputation were impeccable. Early in 1849, he hinted that republicanism might have to be sacrificed for independence. Since Piedmont preserved the Albertine Constitution of 1848, and had soldiers and cannon, he proclaimed himself 'Piedmontese'. He explained to Massimo D'Azeglio that there were two wings in the republican camp, one led by Mazzini and the second by Manin. Trivulzio predicted that the latter would support the Piedmontese monarchy if it committed itself to the holy goal of independence.[3] The prediction materialized following the formation of the National Society in 1857.

The failure of Mazzinianism and Cavour's Alliance with the National Society substantiated Vittorio Emanuele's observation that they had the Party of Action in their pocket.[4] It meant that the left had to await the initiative of the moderates, and that the wars which made Italy would not involve the broad masses. Thus it is not surprising that Italian casualties in the various conflicts for Italian Liberation were light. It is estimated that some 3,000 perished in the first (1848–49) and second wars (1859–60). Only fourteen were killed in battle during the Crimean War of 1855, while another thousand perished on land and sea during the third war.[5] The *Garibaldini* suffered more than 600 deaths at Mentana (1867), while the Italian Regulars had only twenty-four deaths during the campaign of September 1870.[6]

Thus it is estimated that the total casualties of the regular and volunteer forces between 1848 and 1870 were about 6,000 dead and some 20,000 wounded.[7] In fact more died in the post-unification pacification, branded 'brigandage' by the national government, than perished in all the Wars of Liberation. This led Piero Marconi first, and Italian imperialists later, to denounce the Risorgimento as a small story, not sufficiently irrigated by blood.[8]

While the Piedmontese picked up the Italian standard from the dust of Novara by the diplomacy of Cavour and the army of Vittorio Emanuele, playing a major role in provoking and waging the Second War of Liberation of 1859–60, they did not do it alone. In addition to French military assistance, and eventual British diplomatic support, they also secured internal allies. From 1857 to 1862 the Italian National Society published a newspaper, first a weekly and then a daily, with a national circulation, which popularized the national goal while prodding the Piedmontese to action. The society drafted volunteers into the campaign against Austria in 1859, its committees orchestrated the revolutions in the towns of central Italy when the Papal and Austrian forces withdrew, and it played a key role in the plebiscites which sanctioned Piedmontese action. In 1860 the society was implicated both in Garibaldi's invasion of the Kingdom of Naples and

Cavour's incursion into the Papal States, thus ensuring that the kingdom of 1861 would be national rather than northern.[9]

The burden of funding the wars of liberation fell primarily upon the Piedmontese kingdom, and the Italian kingdom which succeeded in 1861. It proved heavy. Calculations reveal that the war of 1848–49 cost some 200 million lire, with an additional 50 million spent for the Crimean War of 1855. The Second War of Liberation cost nearly 400 million lire with 89 million going for the Piedmontese campaign, another 60 million to cover the expenses of their French ally, 100 million lire to provide for that portion of the Lombard debt assumed by the French, and another 145 million to cover the remaining Lombardo-Venetian debt. The total expenditures for the Third War of Liberation have been estimated as high as 800 million lire.[10]

The onerous cost of waging the Wars of Liberation affected first Piedmont's and then Italy's social, political, military, diplomatic and fiscal policies. Thus, during the course of the First War of Liberation, paper money became more common throughout the peninsula, and above all in Piedmont, where the government virtually 'forced' the population to accept its treasury notes as legal tender. The drain of the second War of Liberation (1859), followed by the high cost of waging the third war (1866), brought the deficit to a peak of 740 million lire after the war for Venice. To cope with this grave financial situation, and the spectre of ruin, the Italian government in May 1866 decreed the inconvertibility of banknotes, introducing the '*corso forzoso*'.[11]

The Kingdom of Piedmont–Sardinia, in placing her diplomatic and military efforts at the service of Italian unification, incurred grave financial burdens which compromised the process of modernization which Cavour had begun in the 1850s. The diplomatic pretensions of the new Italian kingdom, and the need to create a modern infrastructure of roads, bridges and railroads, to 'stitch the peninsula together' only aggravated the problem.[12] To be sure, there were compensations for Piedmont which sacrificed itself to absorb Italy. By setting the tone and directing the Wars of Liberation, the moderate Piedmontese party imposed its stamp on the society and state which resulted. Despite the fact that the Party of Action was more nationalist in attitude and outlook, and its leaders such as Mazzini and Garibaldi shared international reputations, their influence on the unitary state proved marginal in comparison to that of Cavour and his allies.

The liberal historian Adolfo Omodeo in a series of works

applauded the contribution of the patriotic minority which forged Italy at great cost. Likewise the philosopher and historian Benedetto Croce's *Storia d'Italia* provided a positive evaluation of the efforts and edifice created by the liberal directing class in the Risorgimento era. Not all shared this vision, however. In his *Rivoluzione liberale*, Piero Gobetti branded the Risorgimento a 'failed revolution', conducted by men who proved unwilling and unable to involve the Italian masses in the project, thereby failing to create a modern state structure. The latter assessment influenced Antonio Gramsci's thoughts on the Risorgimento.

The debate on the manner in which Italy was transformed from a 'geographical expression' into a 'political entity' began early. 'Italy is made, now we must make the Italians' observed Massimo D'Azeglio. Mazzini and Pio Nono feared that the Italians would be made in the Piedmontese image. The 'soul of Italian unification' who died alone and dissatisfied with the state forged by the Piedmontese, proved almost as critical of the unitary kingdom as did Pio Nono, the 'Cross' of Liberals and Nationalists alike. Following the proclamation of unification, Mazzini complained that the Italians had been led astray, accepting material in place of moral unity. He warned that any system not inspired by God would perforce have to resort to blind and brutal force.[13] Pio Nono, for once, found himself in total agreement with Mazzini, denouncing the 'so-called' Risorgimento as a moral, civil and religious oppression.[14] God alone, he insisted, could provide true guidance and consolation.[15] Indeed, the Pontiff suspected that he, Garibaldi and Mazzini were the only men who got nothing out of the Risorgimento.[16]

In his December 1870 speech from the throne, Vittorio Emanuele proclaimed that since Italy was 'free and united' the task was now to make her 'great and happy'. The post-Risorgimento had begun, and some found the prose of consolidation considerably less exciting than the poetry of liberation. The new state, divided into fifty-nine provinces in 1861 and sixty-nine after the acquisition of Venice and Rome, possessed a population of approximately twenty-seven million; thus it ranked as the sixth greatest European power after Russia, Germany, France, Austria–Hungary and Britain. Nonetheless, the patriotic poet Carducci derided this little Italy as 'Italietta', while others despaired that Trent and Trieste had not been included. Thus irredentism emerged as an important movement, eventually propelling Italian entry into the First World War, which some have dubbed Italy's fifth and final War of Liberation.

NOTES

1. Antonio Gramsci, *Sul Risorgimento*, ed. Elsa Fubini (Rome: Editori Riuniti, 1967), pp. 108–14.
2. Denis Mack Smith, *Italy: a Modern History* (Ann Arbor: University of Michigan Press, 1959), p. 39.
3. Raymond Grew, *A Sterner Plan for Italian Unity: the Italian National Society in the Risorgimento* (Princeton: Princeton University Press, 1963), pp. 9–11.
4. Gramsci, p. 120.
5. Mack Smith, *Italy*, p. 79; Mack Smith, *Cavour* (New York: Knopf, 1985), p. 83.
6. Costantino Bulle, *Storia del Secondo Impero e del Regno d'Italia* (Milan: Società Editrice Libraria, 1911), pp. 719, 1023.
7. Christopher Seton-Watson, *Italy from Liberalism to Fascism, 1870–1925* (London: Methuen and Co., 1967), p. 3.
8. Gramsci, p. 49.
9. Grew, pp. ix–xii.
10. Shepard B. Clough, *The Economic History of Modern Italy* (New York: Columbia University Press, 1964), pp. 34, 42; Mack Smith, *Italy*, p. 85.
11. Clough, pp. 22, 53.
12. Countess Evelyn Martinengo-Cesaresco, *The Liberation of Italy 1815–1870* (Freeport, New York: Books for Libraries Press, 1972), p. 403.
13. Frank J. Coppa, 'The Religious Basis of Giuseppe Mazzini's Political Thought', *Journal of Church and State*, XII (Spring, 1970), 253.
14. Antonio Monti, *Pio IX nel Risorgimento Italiano con documenti inediti* (Bari: Laterza, 1928), p. 171.
15. Pius IX to Louis Napoleon, 5 July 1871, *Archivio Segreto del Vaticano, Archivio Particolare Pio IX, Sovrani, Francia*, no. 96.
16. Glorney Bolton, *Roman Century: A Portrait of Rome as Capital of Italy, 1870–1970* (New York: The Viking Press, 1970), p. 63.

Bibliography

I ARCHIVAL SOURCES

(1) *L'Archivio di Stato di Roma*

This is a rich source for the study of Piedmont, the Papacy, and the Italian states during the turbulent years of the *Risorgimento*. This archive, and especially the *Fondo Famiglia Antonelli*, is the repository of the private and family papers of Cardinal Antonelli, and includes some of his public papers as well. Also useful are the *Carte Miscellanea Politiche O Riservate*, which are arranged chronologically and contain a diverse selection of political papers and diplomatic documents. The papers of the *Fondo Repubblica Romana* is invaluable for an understanding of the course of events in Rome in 1849. The papers of the *Consiglio di Stato* and the *Consulta di Stato* place particular emphasis on the politics and policies of the Papal States during the First War of Italian Liberation. The correspondence between Antonelli and the Nuncio at Paris, Carlo Sacconi, found in the *Archivio di Stato di Roma* was edited by Mariano Gabriele and published as *Il Carteggio Antonelli–Sacconi (1850–60)* (Rome: Istituto per la Storia del Risorgimento Italiano, 1962).

(2) *L'Archivio Segreto del Vaticano*

The papers of the Pontificate of Pius IX in the Vatican Archives were opened to scholars in 1967. Within this vast repository a number of collections are particularly useful for a study of Papal Rome and the other states of the peninsula during the age of the Wars of the Risorgimento. Considerable information can be gleaned about papal foreign policy during the Risorgimento and Counter-Risorgimento from the *Archivio della Segreteria di Stato Esteri* and the *Archivii delle Nunziature*, especially the *Fondo Archivio della Nunziatura di Firenze*, the *Fondo Archivio della Nunziatura di Parigi*, and the *Fondo Archivio della Nunziatura di Vienna*. The rich mine of material found in the *Archivio della Segreteria di Stato* traces developments during the revolutionary period 1848–49, for which the *Corrispondenza de Gaeta a Portici* is invaluable. Foreign affairs and Church matters were supervised by Antonelli in the years following the restoration, and the record of his supervision can be traced in the papers of the *Segreteria di Stato* for the entire period. Additional light on the Vatican's *modus operandi* is shed by the papers of the *Stato Pontificio*, those of the *Miscellanea Corpo Diplomatico* and those collected in the *Nunziature e Delegazioni Apostoliche* all found in the Secret Vatican Archives.

Since the opening of the *Archivio Segreto del Vaticano* for the Pontificate of Pio Nono, some of the papers have been published including the correspondence between Antonelli and the Nuncio at Madrid, Monsignor Lorenzo Barili, which is drawn primarily from the *Archivio della Segreteria di Stato Esteri* and the *Archivio della Nunziatura di Madrid*. This correspondence has been edited by Carla Meneguzzi Rostangi under the title *Il Carteggio Antonelli–Barili, 1859–1861* (Rome: Istituto per la Storia del Risorgimento Italiano, 1973). Some of the papers drawn from the *Segreteria di Stato Esteri* and the *Nunziatura di Vienna* have been edited by Lajos Lukacs and published as *The Vatican and Hungary, 1846–1878: Reports and correspondence on Hungary of the Apostolic Nuncios in Vienna* (Budapest: Akademiai Kiado, 1981).

(3) *Fondi Archivistici del Museo Centrale del Risorgimento*

These archives provide a wide variety of sources for an examination of the Risorgimento, Counter-Risorgimento, and the Wars of Liberation. Included are the papers of Nicola Roncalli and his *Cronaca di Roma*, some fifty-one bound volumes, providing a chronicle of events in the Papal States from 1844 to 1870. This newsletter, based on what the author saw, read or heard about events in the capital and the provinces offers a wide range of information about developments during these years. The archives of the *Museo Centrale del Risorgimento* also contains part of the correspondence of Michelangelo Caetani, Duke of Semoneta, Garibaldi, Callimaco Zambianchi, Luigi Carlo Farini and others. The miscellaneous volumes (114) on the *Stato Pontificio* contain a number of apostolic letters, encyclicals and circulars regarding the Roman State from the Congress of Vienna to the collapse of the temporal power. *Busta* 11 of the *Archivio Amat* is useful, as are the bound manuscript volumes and especially the *Notizie politiche della Provincia Pontificia, 1833–1846* and the *Bollettini Politici di Roma*.

(4) *L'Archivio Centrale dello Stato, EUR*

This central archive of the Italian State contains the papers of the various ministries of unitary Italy and contains a number of archives that are useful for the earlier period, as well as the years 1861–78. Among the most useful papers for this particular study are some of the documents of the *Archivio Agostino Depretis*, those of the *Famiglia Benso di Cavour* and those of the *Archivio Fanti*.

(5) *L'Archivio Storico del Ministero degli Affari Esteri*

This archive contains diplomatic sources of the Italian State proclaimed in 1861 as well as considerable papers of the various states which were merged into the new kingdom.

II DIPLOMATIC DISPATCHES AND CORRESPONDENCE

Bianchi, Nicomede. *Storia documentata della diplomazia in Italia dall' anno 1814 all' anno 1861.* 8 vols, Turin: Unione Tipografico, 1872.

Blakiston, Noel (ed.). *The Roman Question: Extracts from the Despatches of Odo Russell from Rome, 1858–1870.* London: Chapman and Hall, Ltd., 1962.

Confederate States of America. *The Messages and Papers of Jefferson Davis and the Confederacy Including Diplomatic Correspondence 1861–1865.* Introduction by Allan Nevins and compiled by James D. Richardson. New York: Chelsea House, Robert Hector Publishers, 1966.

Costa, Emilio (ed.) *Il Regno di Sardegna nel 1848–49 nei Carteggi di Domenico. Buffa Vol. III: 20 febbraio 1848–29.* Rome: Istituto per la Storia del Risorgimento Italiano, 1970.

Cummings, Raymond L. 'Come la Nunziatura di Napoli informava Roma nel 1859–1860'. *Rassegna Storica del Risorgimento*, **67** (1980, n. 2), 154–76.

Dalla Torre, Paolo. *Pio IX e Vittorio Emanuele II. Dal Loro Carteggio privato negli anni del dilaceramento (1865–1878).* Rome: Istituto di Studi Romani Editori, 1972.

Elliot, Sir Henry. *Some Revolutions and other Diplomatic Experience.* London: John Murray, 1922.

Gabriele, Mariano (ed.). *Il Carteggio Antonelli–Sacconi (1850–1860).* Rome: Istituto per la Storia del Risorgimento, 1962.

Great Britain. *British and Foreign State Papers*, xxxvi (1847–48); xxxvii (1948–49); lxv (1873–74).

Il Carteggio Cavour–Nigra dal 1858 al 1861. Ed. National Commission for the Publication of the Papers of Count Cavour. Bologna: Zanichelli, 1961.

Italia. Commissione per la pubblicazione dei Documenti diplomatici. *I Documenti Diplomatici Italiani. Prima serie (1861–1870).* Rome: La Libreria dello Stato, 1952.

La diplomazia del Regno di Sardegna durante la prima guerra d'indipendenza. ii: *Relazioni con lo Stato Pontificio (Marzo 1848–luglio 1849).* Ed. Carlo Baudi di Vesme. Turin: Istituto per la Storia del. Risorgimento Italiano, 1951.

Le relazioni diplomatiche fra il governo provvisorio siciliano e la Gran Bretagna. III serie: 1848–1860. Vol. unico (14 aprile 1848–10 aprile 1849). Ed. Federico Curato. Rome: Istituto storico italiano per l'età moderna e contemporanea, 1971.

Le relazioni diplomatiche fra L'Austria e il Granducato di Toscano. III serie: 1848–1860. Volume III: 10 maggio 1851–30 dicembre 1852. Ed. Angelo Filipuzzi. Rome: Istituto storico italiano per l'età moderna e contemporanea, 1968. *Volume V: 19 maggio 1856–12 maggio 1859.* Rome, 1969.

Le relazioni diplomatice fra L'Austria e il Regno di Sardegna e la guerra del 1848–49. III serie: 1848–1860. Vol. I: 24 marzo 1848–11 aprile 1849. Ed. Angelo Filipuzzi. Rome: Istituto storico italiano per l'età moderna e contemporanea, 1961.

Le relazioni diplomatiche fra L'Austria e lo Stato Pontificio. III serie: 1848–1860. I: 28 novembre 1848–28 dicembre 1849. Ed. Richard Blaas. Rome: Istituto storico italiano per età moderna e contemporanea, 1973.

Le relazioni diplomatiche fra la Gran Bretagna e il Regno di Sardegna. III serie: 1848–1860. Vol. IV: gennaio 1852–10 gennaio 1855. Ed. Federico Curato. Rome: Istituto per l'eta' moderna e contemporanea, 1968.

Le relazioni diplomatiche fra lo Stato Pontificio e la Francia. III serie: 1848–1860. Vol. I: 4 gennaio 1848–18 febbraio 1849. Ed. Michele Fatica. Rome: Istituto storico italiano per la età moderna e contemporanea, 1971.

Le relazioni diplomatiche fra lo Stato Pontificio e la Francia. III series:

1848–1860. Vol. II: 19 febbraio 1849–15 aprile 1850. Rome: Istituto storico italiano per la eta' moderna e contemporanea, 1972.

Lukacs, Lajos. *The Vatican and Hungary 1846–1878: Reports and Correspondence on Hungary of the Apostolic Nuncios in Vienna*. Trans. Zsofia Karmos, Budapest: Akademiai Kiado, 1981.

L'Unificazione italiana vista dai diplomatici statiunitinesi. Vol. IV: 1861–1866. Ed. Howard Marraro. Istituto per la storia del Risorgimento Italiano, 1971.

Marraro, Howard R. (ed.), *Diplomatic Relations between the United States and the Kingdom of the Two Sicilies*. 2 vols, New York: S.F. Vanni, 1952.

Martina, Giacomo. *Pio IX e Leopoldo II*. Rome: Pontifica Università Gregorian, 1967.

Meneguzzi Rostagni, Carla (ed.). *Il Carteggio Antonelli–Barili (1859–1861)*. Rome: Istituto per la Storia del Risorgimento Italiano, 1973.

Olszmowska-Skowronska. *La correspondence des Papes et des Empereurs de Russie (1814–1878) selon les documents authentiques*. Rome: Pontifica Università Gregoriana, 1970.

Pirri, Pietro. *Pio IX e Vittorio Emanuele II dal loro carteggio privato. I: La laicizzazione dello Stato Sardo, 1848–1856*. Rome: Universita' Gregoriana, 1944. *Pio IX e Vittorio Emanuele II dal loro carteggio privato. II: La questione romana, 1856–1864. Parte I: Testo, Parte II: Documenti*. Rome: Università Gregoriana, 1951.

Stock, Leo Francis (ed.). *Consular Relations between the United States and the Papal States: Instructions and Despatches*. Washington, DC, American Catholic Historical Association, 1945; *United States Ministers to the Papal States: Instructions and Despatches, 1848–1868*. Washington, DC, American Catholic Historical Association, 1933.

Zanichelli, Nicola (ed.). *Cavour e L'Inghilterra: Carteggio con V.E. D'Azeglio*. Bologna: Commissione Reale Editrice, 1933.

Zanichelli, Nicola (ed.). *La questione romana negli anni 1860–61. Carteggio del Conte di Cavour con D. Pantaleoni, C. Passaglia. O. Vimercati*. Bologna: Commissione Reale Editrice, 1933.

III ROLE OF OTHER STATES DURING ITALIAN WARS OF LIBERATION

Aubry, Octave. *Eugénie: Empress of the French*. Trans. F.M. Atkinson. Philadelphia: Lippincott, 1931.

Barker, Nicholas. *Distaff Diplomacy: the Empress Eugénie and the Foreign Policy of the Second Empire*. Austin: University of Texas, 1967.

Barrie, Ottavio. *L'Inghilterra e il problema italiano nel 1848–49*. Milan: Giuffrè, 1965.

Beust, Comte de. *Trois-quarts de siècle. Memoires du Comte de Beust*. Paris: L. Westhausser, 1888.

Bismarck, Otto von. *Reflections and Reminiscences*. Ed. Theodore S. Hamerow. New York: Harper and Row, 1968.

Blakiston, Noel. 'Con Odo Russell a Roma nel 1860'. *Rassegna Storica del Risorgimento, anno* XLVII (January–March, 1960), 61–8.

Brazao, E. *L'Unificazione italiana vista dai diplomatici portoghesi*. Rome: Istituto per la Storia del Risorgimento Italiano, 1962.

Brodsky, Alyn. *Imperial Charade*. New York: Bobbs-Merrill, 1978.

Craven, A. *Lord Palmerston, sa correspondance intime pour servir l'historie diplomatique de l'Europe de 1830 à 1865*. Paris: Didier, 1879.

Fleury, Comte. *Memoirs of the Empress Eugénie*. New York: Appleton and Co., 1920.

Giusti, Renato. 'Il Problema Politico Italiano nella *Revue des Deux Mondes*, II'. *Archivio Storico Italiano* **142** (1984, n. 1), 77–146.

Hollyday, F.M. (ed.). *Bismarck*. Englewood Cliffs, New Jersey: Prentice-Hall, 1970.

Hubner, Count Joseph. *Neuf ans de souvenirs d'un ambassadeur d'Autriche à Paris sous le Second Empire, 1851–59*. Paris: Plon, 1904.

Jenks, William A. *Francis Joseph and the Italians, 1848–1859*. Charlottesville: University Press of Virginia, 1978.

Leonardis, Massimo de. *L'Inghilterra e la questione Romana 1859–1870*. Milan: Universita' Cattolica del Sacro Cuore, 1980.

Liverani, Francesco. *Il Papato, L'Impero, e il Regno d'Italia*. Florence: Barbera, 1861.

McIntire, C.T. *England Against the Papacy, 1858–1861: Tories, Liberals and the Overthrow of Papal Temporal Power during the Italian Risorgimento*. Cambridge: Cambridge University Press, 1983.

Mémoires du Comte Horace De Viel Castel sur le Regne de Napoleon III. 2nd edn. Paris: Tous les Libraries, 1884.

Metternich, Klemens von. *Mémoires, documents et écrits divers laissés par le Prince de Metternich*. ed. Prince Richard Metternich, papers clasified by M.A. de Klinkowstroem. 8 vols, Paris: 1880–84.

Monti, Antonio. *La politica degli Stati Italiani durante il Risorgimento*. Milan: Casa Editrice Francesco Vallardi, 1948.

Morley, John. *The Life of William E. Gladstone*. New York: Macmillan, 1904.

Ollivier, Emile. *Journal, 1861–1869.* Ed. Theodore Zeldin and Anne Troisier de Diaz. Paris: Julliard, 1961.

Redlich, Joseph. *Emperor Francis Joseph of Austria.* New York: Macmillan, 1929.

Saint-Armand, Imbert de. *France and Italy.* Trans. Elizabeth Gilbert Martin. New York: Scribner's, 1899.

Sauvigny, G. de Bertier de. *Metternich and his Times.* Trans. Peter Ryde. London: Darton, Longman and Todd, 1962.

Thompson, J.M. *Louis Napoleon and the Second Empire.* New York: Norton and Co., 1955.

Urban, Miriam. *British Opinion and Policy on the Unification of Italy 1856–1861.* Scottsdale. PA: Mennonite Press, 1938.

Wellesley, F.A. (ed.). *Secrets of the Second Empire: Private Letters from the Paris Embassy, Selections from the Papers of Henry Richard Charles Wellesley, 1st Earl Cowley, Ambassador at Paris 1852–1867.* New York: Harper and Brothers Publishers, 1929.

IV   THE FIRST WAR OF ITALIAN LIBERATION

Anzilotti, Antonio. *Gioberti.* Florence: Valecchi, 1922.

Berkeley, George F. and J. Berkeley. *Italy in the Making, 1815–1848.* 3 vols Cambridge: University Press, 1932–40.

Berra, Luigi Francesco. 'La fuga di Pio IX a Gaeta e il racconto del suo scalco segreto.' *Studi Romani, anno* v (1957), 672–86.

Biaggini, Carlo Alberto. *Il pensiero politico di Pellegrino Rossi di fronte ai problemi del Risorgimento Italiano.* Rome: Vittoriano, 1937.

Biagini, Antonello and F. Maurizio. 'La riorganizzazione dell' esercito pontificio e gli arruolamenti in Umbria tra il 1815 e il 1848–49'. *Rassegna Storica del Risorgimento, anno* LXI (April–June 1974), 214–25.

Boero, Giuseppe. *La rivoluzione romana al guidizio degli imparziali.* Florence, 1850.

Boyer, Ferdinand. 'Pie IX a Gaete et Amiral Baudin'. *Rassegna Storica del Risorgimento, anno* XLIII (April–June 1856), 244–51.

Cecchini, Ezio. 'Le campagne di Garibaldi: 1849'. *Rivista Militare* **105** (1982, no. 2), 197–205.

Colonna, Gustavo Brigante. 'Mazzini al Quirinale'. In *Strenna dei Romanisti*, ed. Giuseppe Romani. Rome: Standerini Editore, 1947.

Coppa, Frank J. 'Papal Rome in 1848: from Reform to Revolution'.

Proceedings of the Consortium on Revolutionary Europe, 1979, pp. 92–103.

Coppa, Frank J. 'Rome and Revolution: from Pius VI to Pius IX'. *Proceedings of the Consortium on Revolutionary Europe*, 1984, 268–76.

Cordie, Carlo. 'Il 1847 negli scritti e nell' epistolario del Cavour'. *Pensiero Politico* **13** (1980, n. 1), 88–98.

D'Arlincourt, Viscount. *L'Italia rossa o storia della rivoluzioni dall' elezione di Pio IX al di lui ritorno in sua capitale*. Trans. Francesco Giuntini. Florence, 1851.

Della missione a Roma di Antonio Rosmini negli anni 1848–1849. Turin: Paravia, 1881.

Demarco, Domenico. *Pio IX e la rivoluzione romana del 1848. Saggio di storia economico–sociale*. Modena Tipografia Modenese, 1947.

Demarco, Domenico. *Una rivoluzione sociale. La Repubblica romana del 1849*. Naples: M. Fiorentino, 1944.

Falzone, Gaetano. *La Sicilia nella politica mediterranea delle grandi potenze*. Palermo: S.F. Fracconio, 1979.

Gajani, Gugliemo. *The Roman Exile*. Boston: J.B. Jewett and Co., 1856.

Ghisalberti, A.M. *Roma da Mazzini a Pio IX, Ricerche sulla Restaurazione Papale del 1849–1850*. Milan: Giuffrè, 1958.

Ginsborg, Paul. *Daniele Manin and the Venetian Revolution of 1848–49*. Cambridge: Cambridge University Press, 1979.

Gouraud, Carlo. *L'Italia: Sue ultime rivoluzione e suo stato presente*. Florence: Carletti, 1852.

Hobrook, Francis X. and John Nikol. 'Reporting the Sicilian Revolution of 1848–1849'. *American Neptune* **43** (1983, n. 3), 165–76.

Johnston, R.M. *The Roman Theocracy and the Republic, 1846--1849*. London: Macmillan, 1901.

Leroy-Beaulieu, Antale. *Un Empereur, Un Roi, Un Pape, Une Restauration*. Paris: Charpentier, 1879.

Malvezzi, Nino. 'Pellegrino Rossi, Marco Minghetti, e Carlo de Mazade'. *Nuova Antologia, anno* LXI (October 1926), 437–53.

Menabrea, Luigi Federico. *Memorie*. Florence: Giunta-Berbera, 1971.

Minocci, Carlo. *Pietro Sterbini e la rivoluzione romana (1846–1849)*. Naples: Edizioni La Diana, 1967.

Moos, Carlo. 'Intorno ai Volontari Lombardi del 1848'. *Risorgimento* **36** (1984, n. 2), 113–60.

Omodeo, Adolfo. *La legenda di Carlo Alberto*, 1941.

Pivano, Lilio. 'Mazzini Dittatore (1849)'. *Nuova Antologia, anno* LXI (February 1926), 265–9.

Robertson, Priscilla. *Revolutions of 1848: a Social History*. New York: Harper, 1960.

Rodolico, Niccolo. *Carlo Alberto*. 3 vols, Florence: Le Monnier, 1936–48.

Rota, Ettore (ed.). *Il 1848 nella storia italiana ed europea*. Milan: Villardi, 1948.

Senior, Nassau William. *Journals Kept in France and Italy from 1848 to 1852*. London, 1871.

Sked, Alan. *The Survival of the Habsburg Empire: Radetsky, the Imperial Army and the Class War, 1848*. Harlow: Longman, 1979.

Stefanutti, J.A. *La lega italiana promossa da Pio IX*. Tarcento: Grafiche Stefanutti, 1951.

Taylor, A.J.P. *The Italian Problem in European Diplomacy, 1847–1849*. Manchester: Manchester University Press, 1934.

Thayer, William Roscoe. *The Dawn of Italian Independence and Rebirth of Italy*. 2 vols. Boston: Houghton-Mifflin, 1892.

Trevelyan, George Macaulay. *Garibaldi's Defence of the Roman Republic 1848–49*. London: Longmans, Green, 1914.

Trevelyan, George Macaulay. *Manin and the Venetian Revolution of 1848*. London: Longmans, Green, 1923.

V THE SECOND WAR OF ITALIAN LIBERATION

Acton, Harold. *The Last Bourbons of Naples (1825–1861)*. New York: St Martin's Press, 1961,

Beales, Derek. *England and Italy, 1859–1860*. London: Nelson, 1961.

Berkeley, G.F.H. and J. Berkeley. *The Irish Battalion in the Papal Army of 1860*. Dublin: Talbot Press, 1929.

Bersezio, V. *Il Regno di Vittorio Emanuele II. Trent anni di vita italiana*. 8 vols Turin: Roux e Favale, 1878.

Bianchi, Nicomede (ed.). *Il Conte Camillo di Cavour. Documenti editi e inediti*. Turin: Unione Tipografico, 1863.

Bianchi, Nicomede (ed.). *La politica di Massimo D'Azeglio dal 1848 al 1859*. Documenti. Turin: Roux e Favale, 1884.

Blumberg, Arnold. *A Carefully Planned Accident: the Italian War of 1859*. Cranberry, New Jersey: Susquehanna University Press, 1989.

Commission for Publication of Correspondence of Cavour (ed.). *Carteggio di Camillo Cavour. La Liberazione del Mezzogiorno e la Formazione del Regno D'Italia*. 5 vols. Bologna: Zanichelli, 1949–54.

Cummings, Raymond L. 'Come La Nunziatura di Napoli informava Roma nel 1859–1860'. *Rassegna Storica del Risorgimento* **67** (1980, n. 2), 154–76.

Delzell, Charles (ed.). *The Unification of Italy, 1859–1861: Cavour, Mazzini, or Garibaldi?* New York: Holt, Rinehart, Winston, 1965.

Di Nolfo, Ennio. *Storia del Risorgimento e dell' Unita' d'Italia*. Milan: Rizzoli, 1965.

Galasso, Giuseppe. 'Garibaldi, il Mezzogiorno e L'Unificazione italiana'. *Veltro* **26** (1982, nn. 5–6), 345–59.

Hearder, Harry. 'La politica di Lord Malmesbury verso L'Italia nella primavera del 1859'. *Rassegna Storica del Risorgimento, anno* XLIII (January–March 1956), 35–58.

Isastia, Anna Maria. *Roma nel 1859*. Rome: Istituto per la Storia del Risorgimento Italiano, 1978.

Jenks, William A. *Francis Joseph and the Italians, 1849–1859*. Charlottesville: University Press of Virginia, 1978.

Lezzani, Mario. 'Noterelle epistolari di un Romano dei Mille'. *Rassegna Storica del Risorgimento, anno* XXII (December 1935), 928–31.

Mack Smith, Denis. *Cavour and Garibaldi, 1860: A Study in Political Conflict*. Cambridge: Cambridge University Press, 1954.

Mack Smith, Denis. *The Making of Italy, 1796–1870*. New York: Harper, 1968.

Marchetti, Leopoldo. 'Ottaviano Vimercati'. *Risorgimento* **14** (1962), 22–37.

Martin, George. *The Red Shirt and the Cross of Savoy*. New York: Dodd, Mead and Co., 1969.

Pallavicino, Giorgio. *Memorie di Giorgio Pallavicino Pubblicate per cura dei figli*. Turin: Roux, Frassati and Co., 1895.

Trevelyan, George Macaulay. *Garibaldi and the Making of Italy* (June–November 1860). New York: Longmans, Green, 1948.

Ugolini, Romano. *Cavour e Napoleone III nell' Italia Centrale*. Rome: Istituto per la Storia del Risorgimento Italiano, 1973.

Urban, Miriam B. *British Opinion and Policy on the Unification of Italy, 1856–1861*. Scottdale, PA: Mennonite Press, 1938.

Walker, Mack (ed.). *Plombières: Secret Diplomacy and the Rebirth of Italy*. New York: Oxford University Press, 1968.

Whyte, Arthur J. *The Political Life and Letters of Cavour, 1848–1861*. London: Oxford University Press, 1930.

VI THIRD WAR OF LIBERATION AND ACQUISITION OF VENICE

Balan, Pietro. *La Politica italiana dal 1863 al 1870, secondo gli ultimi documenti.* Rome, 1880.

Beust, Comte de. *Trois-quarts de siècle. Mémoires du Comte de Beust.* Paris: L. Weshausser, 1888.

Bismarck, Otto von. *Reflections and Reminiscences.* Ed. Theodore D. Hamerow. New York: Harper and Row, 1968.

Bush, John W. *Venetia Redeemed: Franco-Italian Relations, 1864–1866.* Syracuse: Syracuse University Press, 1967.

Caccani, Domenico. 'L'Italia, la questione del Veneto e i principati danubiani'. *Storia e Politica* **19** (1980, n. 3), 435–56.

Cappelletti, Licurgo. *Storia di Vittorio Emanuele II.* 3 vols, Rome: Voghera, 1892–93.

Cilibrizzi, Saverio. *Storia parlamentare politica e diplomatica d'Italia da Novara a Vittorio Veneto.* 8 vols. Vols 1–6, Naples: STE, 1939–43.

Clark, Chester Wells. *Franz Joseph and Bismarck: the Diplomacy of Austria Before the War of 1866,* Cambridge: Cambridge University Press, 1934.

Debidour, Antonin. *Histoire diplomatique de l'Europe, 1814–1878.* 2 vols. Paris: Alcan, 1891.

Echard, William E. 'Conference Diplomacy in the German Policy of Napoleon III, 1868–1869'. *French Historical Studies,* IV (1966), 239–64.

Echard, William E. *Napoleon III and the Concert of Europe.* Baton Rouge, LA: Louisiana State University Press, 1983.

Ghiron, Isaia (ed.), *Annali d'Italia, 1861–1870.* 3 vols. Milan: Hoepli, 1888–90.

Hubner, Comte de. *Neuf ans de souvenirs d'un Ambassadeur d'Autriche à Paris sous le Second Empire.* Paris: Plon, 1904.

King, H. Bolton. *A History of Italian Unity, being a Political History of Italy from 1814–1871.* 2 vols. London: Nisbet, 1912.

La Marmora, Alfonso. *Un po di luce.* Mangonza, 1873.

Lipparini, L. 'C. Nigra, Roma, e Venezia nei colloqui con Napoleone'. *Nuova Antologia,* XX (February 1942), 317–26.

Martinengo-Cesaresco, Evelyn. *The Liberation of Italy, 1815–1870.* Freeport, New York: Books for Libraries, 1972.

Massari, Giuseppe. *Il Generale Alfonso La Marmora.* Florence: G. Barbera, 1880.

Monti, Antonio. *Vittorio Emanuele II.* Milan: Garzanti, 1941.

Moscati, Ruggero. *Il ministero degli affari esteri, 1861–1870*. Milan: Giuffrè, 1961.

Orsi, Pietro. *Modern Italy, 1748–1898*. New York: Putnam's 1900.

Ollivier, Emile. *Journal, 1846–1869. Volume II, 1861–1869*. Paris: Julliard, 1961.

Passamonti, Eugenio. 'Costantino Nigra ed Alfonso La Marmora dal 1862 al 1866'. *Il Risorgimento Italiano*, 3rd series: xxii, 363–4, 1929.

Pflanze, Otto. *Bismarck and the Development of the German Empire: the Period of Unification, 1815–1871*. Princeton: Princeton University Press, 1963.

Salomon, Henry. *L'Ambassade de Richard de Metternich à Paris*. Paris: Firmin-Didot, 1931.

Schnerb, Robert. *Rouher et le Second Empire*. Paris: Armand Colin, 1931.

Zorzi, Alvisi. *Venezia Austriaca 1798–1866*, Bari: Laterza, 1986.

VII 'FOURTH WAR OF LIBERATION' AND ACQUISITION OF ROME

Althaus Fiedrich (ed.). *The Roman Journals of Ferdinand Gregorovius, 1852–1865*. Trans. Mrs Gustavus W. Hamilton. London: George Bell and Sons, 1907.

Amabile, G. *La Legge delle Garantigie*. Catania: Gianotta, 1897.

Bartoccini, Fiorella. *La 'Roma dei Romani'*. Rome: Istituto per la Storia del Risorgimento Italiano, 1971.

Bartoccini, Fiorella. *Roma nell' Ottocento. Il Tramonto della 'Città Santa', nascita di una capitale*. Bologna: Cappelli, 1985.

Bastgen, Hubert. *Die Romische Frage: Dokumente und Stimmen*. Freiburg: Herder, 1917–19.

Blumberg, Arnold. 'George Bancroft, France, and the Vatican: some Aspects of American, French, and Vatican Diplomacy: 1866–1870', *Catholic Historical Review*, l (January 1965), 475–93.

Bolton, Glorney. *Roman Century: a Portrait of Rome as Capital of Italy, 1870–1970*. New York: Viking Press, 1970.

Bonfanti, Giuseppe. *Roma capitale e la questione romana. Documenti e testamonianze di storia contemporanea*. Brescia: La Scuola, 1977.

Bourgeois, Emile and E. Clermont. *Rome et Napoleon III (1849–1870)*. Paris: Librarie A. Colen, 1907.

Bourne, Kenneth. 'The British Government and the Proposed Roman

Conference of 1867', *Rassegna Storica del Risorgimento, anno,* XLIII (October–December 1956), 759–63.

Case, Lynn M. *Franco-Italian Relations, 1860–65: the Roman Question and the Convention of September.* Philadelphia: University of Pennsylvania Press, 1932.

Coppa, Frank J. 'Italy, the Papal States and the American Civil War', *La Parola del Popolo* (November–December 1976), 364–7.

Dalla Torre, Paolo. *L'Anno di Mentana.* Milan: Martello Editore, 1967.

Di Nolfo, Ennio. 'Austria e Roma nel 1870', *Rassegna Storica del Risorgimento, anno* LVIII (July–September 1971), 409–36.

De Cesare, Raffaele. *Roma e lo stato del Papa dal Ritorno di Pio IX al XX Settembre, 1850–1870.* Milan: Longanesi, 1970; Abridged and translated into English as *The Last Days of Papal Rome.* Trans. Helen Zimmern, London: Archibald Constable and Co., 1909.

De Feo, Italo. *Roma 1870. L'Italia dalla morte di Cavour a Porta Pia.* Turin: Mursia, 1970.

Del Cerro, E. *Cospirazioni romane (1817–1868). Rivelazioni storiche.* Rome: Voghera, 1899.

Engel-Janosi, F. 'The Roman Question in the Diplomatic Negotiations of 1869–70', *Review of Politics* (1941), 101.

Gladstone, William. *Rome et le Pape.* Trans. Victor Oger. Paris: Edition Populaire, 1876.

Halperin, S. William. *Diplomat Under Stress: Visconti Venosta and the Crisis of July 1870.* Chicago: University of Chicago Press, 1939.

Jemolo, Arturo Carlo. *La questione romana.* Milan: Istituto per gli studi di publica internazionale, 1938.

Kanzler, Hermann. *La Campagna romana dell' esercito pontificio nel 1867 descrita dal gen. Kanzler e documentata.* Bologna: Liberia della Immacolata, 1871.

Leonardis, Massimo de. *L'Inghilterra e la Questione Romana, 1859–1870.* Milan: Università Cattolica del Sacro Cuore, 1980.

Mori, Renato. *Il tramonto del potere temporale, 1866–1870.* Rome: Edizione di storia e letteratura, 1967.

Ollivier, Emile. *Journal, 1861–1869.* Ed. Theodore Zeldin and Anne Troisier de Diaz. Paris: Julliard, 1961.

Roma capitale d'Italia nel primo centenario. Milan: Mondadori, 1971.

Scott, Ivan. *The Roman Question and the Powers, 1848–1865.* The Hague: Martinus Nijoff, 1969.

VIII MODERATES IN THE UNIFICATION OF ITALY

Bianchi, Nicomede. *La politica di Massimo D'Azeglio dal 1848 al 1859. I Documenti*. Turin: Roux e Favale, 1884.

Camerani, Sergio (ed.). *Carteggio di Bettino Ricasoli*. Rome: Istituto storico Italiano per l'età contemporanea, 1972.

Cappelletti, Licugo. *Storia di Vittorio Emanuele II*. Rome: Voghera, 1892–93.

Chiala, Luigi (ed.) *Lettere edite ed inedite di Camillo Cavour*. 6 vols, Turin: Roux e Favale, 1883–87.

—— *Ricordi di Michelangelo Castelli 1847–75*. Turin: Roux e Favale 1888.

Cognasso, Francesco. *Vittorio Emanuele II*. Turin: Unione Tipografico Editrice torinese, 1942.

Coppa, Frank J. *Camillo di Cavour*. New York: Twayne, 1973.

Coppa, Frank J. 'Realpolitik and Conviction in the Conflict between Piedmont and the Papacy during the Risorgimento', *Catholic Historical Review*, LIV (January 1969), 579–612.

D'Azeglio, Massimo. *Degli ultimi casi di Romagna*. Florence, 1946.

D'Azeglio, Massimo. *I miei ricordi*. Trans. into English by Count Massei. *Recollections of Massimo D'Azeglio*. London: Chapman and Hall, 1868.

Farini, Luigi Carlo. *Lo Stato Romano dall' anno 1815 al 1850*. 3rd edn Florence: Le Monnier, 1853.

Ghisalberti, A.M. *Massimo D'Azeglio, un moderato realizzatore*. Rome: Edizioni Ateneo, 1953.

Mack Smith, Denis. *Cavour*. New York: Alfred A. Knopf, 1985.

Mack Smith, Denis. *Victor Emmanuel, Cavour, and the Risorgimento*. New York: Oxford University Press, 1971.

Manzotti, Fernando. 'Il problema italiano nella corrispondenza di Luigi Carlo Farini sulle Press, sulla *Morning Post*, e sul *Continental Review*', *Rassegna Storica del Risorgimento*, anno IL (1959), 43–60.

Massari, Giuseppe. *Diario dalle cento voci*. Bologna: Cappelli, 1959.

Minghetti, Marco. *Miei ricordi*. 3rd edn, Turin: Roux, 1888.

Montale, Bianca. *Emanuele Pes di Villamarina 1777–1852*. Rome: Istituto per la storia del Risorgimento, 1973.

Nigra, Costantino (ed.). *Count Cavour and Madame de Circourt. Some Unpublished Correspondence*. Trans. Arthur John Butler. London: Cassell and Co., 1894.

Omodeo, Adolfo. *L'Opera politica del Conte di Cavour*. Florence: La Nuova Italia, 1945.

Orsi, Pietro. *Cavour and the Making of Modern Italy, 1810–1861*. New York: Putnam's Sons, 1914.

Pasolini, Giuseppe. *Memorie, 1815–1876*. Ed. Pietro Desiderio Pasolini. 3rd edn Turin: Bocca, 1887.

Pasolini, Guidi (ed.). *Carteggio tra Marco Minghetti e Giuseppe Pasolini.* Turin: Bocca, 1924.

Pincherle, Marcella. *Moderatismo politico e riforma religiosa in Terenzio Mamiani*. Milan: Giuffrè, 1975.

Politique de M. D'Azeglio accompagnée d'une introduction per E. Rendu. Paris: Didier et Cie, 1867.

Rava, Luigi (ed.). *Epistolario di Luigi Carlo Farini.* Bologna: Zanichelli, 1911.

Romeo, Rosario. *Cavour e il suo tempo.* 4 vols. Bari: Laterza, 1969–84.

Rossi, Ernesto and Gian Paolo Nitti (eds). *Banche, governo e Parlamento negli stati sardi. Fonti documentarie (1843–1861).* Turin: Fondazione Luigi Einaudi, 1968.

Salvadori, Max. *Cavour and the Unification of Italy.* Princeton: Van Nostrand, 1961.

Scapecchi, Piero. 'Un polemista risorgimentale. Carlo Lorenzini'. *Rassegna Storica Toscana* **28** (1982, n. 2), 309–11.

Thayer, William Roscoe. *The Life and Times of Cavour.* 2 vols. Boston: Houghton-Mifflin Co., 1911.

Virlogeux, Georges. 'La correspondence di Massimo d'Azeglio'. *Rassegna Storica del Risorgimento* **68** (1981, n. 3), 332–46.

Whyte, Arthur J. *The Political Life and Letters of Cavour, 1848–1861.* London: Oxford University Press, 1930.

IX THE RADICALS IN THE UNIFICATION OF ITALY

Adamoli, G. *Da San Martino a Mentana. Ricordi di un voluntario.* Milan: Treves, 1892.

Adams-Daniels, Elizabeth. *Jesse White Mario, Risorgimento Revolutionary.* Athens: Ohio University Press, 1972.

Armani, Giuseppe. 'Cattaneo e Garibaldi'. *Ponte* **38** (1982, nn. 11–12), 1164–79.

Barili, A.G. 'Con Garibaldi alle porte di Roma' (1867). *Ricordi e note di A.G. Barili.* Milan: Treves, 1895.

Bianco, Carlo Angelo. *Della guerra nazionale d'insurrezione per bande, applicata all' Italia. Trattato dedicato ai buoni italiani da un amico del paese.* Malta, 1830.

Coppa, Frank J. 'The Religious Basis of Giuseppe Mazzini's Political Thought'. *Journal of Church and State.* XII (Spring 1970), 237–53.

Crispi, Francesco. *L'Italia e il Papa ed altri scritti.* Milan: Istituto Editoriale Italiano, 1917.

Garibaldi, Giuseppe. *Autobiography of Giuseppe Garibaldi.* 3 vols. Trans. A. Werner. London: Walter Smith and Innes, 1889.

Grew, Raymond. *A Sterner Plan for Italian Unity: the Italian National Society in the Risorgimento.* Princeton: Princeton University Press, 1963.

Griffith, G.O. *Mazzini: Prophet of Modern Europe.* London: Hodder and Stoughton, 1932.

Hales, Edward E.Y. *Mazzini and the Secret Societies: the Making of a Myth.* New York: Kenedy, 1956.

Jean, Carlo. 'Garibaldi e il volontariato italiano nel Risorgimento'. *Rassegna Storica del Risorgimento,* **69** (1982), 399–419.

Ladolini, Armando. *Mazzini: Maestro Italiano.* Milan: Dall' Oglia, 1963.

Lovett, Clara M. *The Democratic Movement in Italy, 1830–1876.* Cambridge: Harvard University Press, 1982.

Luciolilli, Mario. 'Garibaldi entre le scylla de l'idéalisme et le charybde des réalités', *Revue des Deux Mondes* **10** (1982), 45–57.

Martini, Ferdinando (ed.). *Due dell' estrema. Il Guerrazzi e il Brofferio. Carteggio inediti (1859–1866).* Florence: Le Monnier, 1920.

Mazzini, tra insegnamento e ricerca. Rome: Edizioni Dell' Ateneo, 1982.

Morelli, Emilia. *Mazzini. Quasi una biografia.* Rome: Edizioni Dell' Ateneo, 1984.

Pacifici, Vicenzo G. 'Crispi e Mazzini. La rottura'. *Rassegna Storica del Risorgimento* **68** (1981, n. 2), 169–97.

Palamenghi-Crispi, Thomas, (ed.). *The Memoirs of Francesco Crispi.* Trans. Mary Richard Agnetti. New York: Hodder and Stoughton, 1912.

Posthumous Papers of Jesse White Mario: the Birth of Modern Italy. Ed. Visconti-Arese. New York: Scribner's Sons, 1909.

Roberts, William. *Prophet in Exile: Joseph Mazzini in England, 1837–1868.* New York: Peter Lang, 1989.

Settembrini, Luigi. *Ricordanze della mia vita.* Milan: Feltrinelli, 1961.

Tramarollo, Giuseppe. 'Tre cartelle per la Libertà', *Risorgimento* **36** (1984, n. 2), 219–26.

Trevelyan, George Macaulay. *Garibaldi and the Thousand.* London: Longmans, Green, 1909.

Ugolini, Romano. *Garibaldi: Genesi di un mito.* Rome: Ateneo, 1982.

Varni, Angelo. 'Alle origini del' partito risorgimentale. Il caso di Felice Foresti tra carboneria mazzinianesimo ed adesione alla società nazionale', *Risorgimento* 35 (1983, n. 3), 236–58.

X THE RISORGIMENTO AND COUNTER-RISORGIMENTO

Collodi, C. *Biografie del Risorgimento.* Florence: Casa Editrice Marzocco, 1941.

Coppa, Frank J. *Cardinal Giacomo Antonelli and Papal Politics in European Affairs.* Albany: State University of New York Press, 1990.

Coppa, Frank J. *Pope Pius IX Crusader in a Secular Age.* Boston: Twayne Publishers, 1979.

De Magistris, Ambosi R. and I. Ghiron (eds.). *Diario di Nicola Roncalli dal anno 1949 al 1870.* Turin, 1884.

Falconi, Carlo. *Il Cardinale Antonelli. Vita e carriera del Richelieu italiano nella Chiesa di Pio IX.* Milan: Mondadori, 1983.

Galazzo, Giuseppe, (ed.). *Antologia degli scritti politici di Carlo Cattaneo.* Bologna: Società editrice Il Mulino, 1962.

Garrone, Alessandro Galante. 'Risorgimento e antirisorgimento negli scritti di Luigi Salvatorelli', *Rivista Storica Italiano,* LXXXVIII (September, 1966), 513–43.

Gay, H. Nelson. *Scritti sul Risorgimento.* Rome: La Rassegna Italiana, 1937.

Ghisalberti, Alberto M. *Momenti e figure del Risorgimento Romano.* Milan: Guiffrè, 1965.

Gioberti, Vincenzo. *Del primato morale e civile degli Italiani.* Brussels, 1843.

Gioberti, Vincenzo. *Del rinnovamento civile d'Italia.* Turin: Bocca, 1851.

Gorresio, Vittorio. *Risorgimento scomunicato.* Florence: Parenti, 1958.

Gramsci, Antonio. *Sul Risorgimento.* Ed. Elsa Fubini. Rome: Editori Riuniti, 1967.

Guzzetti, Giovanni Battista. 'Il Sillabo di Pio IX nel suo contesto storico–dottrinale', *Pio IX, anno* V (September–December 1976), 366–81.

Hearder, Harry. *Italy in the Age of the Risorgimento 1790–1870.* Harlow: Longman, 1983.

Howell, Paul M. *Capitalism in the Risorgimento*. Berkeley: University of California, 1983.

Jacini, Stefano. *La crisi religiosa del Risorgimento. La politica ecclesiastica italiana da Villafranca a Porta Pia*. Bari: Laterza, 1938.

Martina, Giacomo. *Pio IX (1851–1866)*. Rome: Editrice Università Gregoriana, 1986.

Masse, Domenico. *Cattolici e Risorgimento* Edizione Paoline, 1961.

Mori, Renato. *La questione romana, 1861–1865*. Edizioni di storia e letteratura, 1967.

O'Clery, Patrick Keyes. *The Making of Italy*. London: Kegan Paul, 1892.

Omodeo, A. *Difesa del Risorgimento*. Turin: Einaudi, 1951.

Ramm, Agata. *The Risorgimento*. London: Routledge & Kegan Paul, 1962.

Rossi, Ernesto. *Il Sillabo*. Florence: Parenti, 1957.

Salvatorelli, Luigi. *Pensiero e azione del Risorgimento*. Turin: Einaudi, 1963.

Stillman, W.J. *The Union of Italy, 1815–1895*. Cambridge: Cambridge University Press, 1909.

Woolf, S.J. *The Italian Risorgimento*. New York: Barnes and Noble, 1969.

Glossary

Aspromonte: Site in southern Calabria where Garibaldi and his followers were stopped from marching on Rome by Italian troops in 1862.

Brigandage: Term which the Italian government used to describe the resistance to its authority in the decade after proclamation of the Italian Kingdom (1861) in the provinces carved out of the former Kingdom of the Two Sicilies. A brutal repression was used to pacify the region.

Carbonari: The best known of the secret societies which opposed the treaties of 1815 and worked for revolutionary change in the peninsula. The Carbonari played a key role in the revolutions of 1820–21, and 1830 in Italy, but failed in their attempts to push out the Austrians and unite Italy.

Carlo Alberto (1798–1849): During the revolutionary upheaval of 1821 while serving as Regent he conceded a constitution for which he was called to task by his uncle, the King, Carlo Felice. He assumed the throne in 1831 and in 1848 granted the Piedmontese a Constitution or *Statuto*. His defeat by the Austrians during the First War of Italian Liberation (1848–49) led to his abdication and exile.

Cavour, Count Camillo di (1810–1861): Known as 'the brain' of Italian Unification, this aristocrat served as the architect of unity. He entered the Cabinet in Piedmont in 1850 and in 1852 became Prime Minister, following his *connubio* or political alliance with Urbano Rattazzi. After the Crimean War he presented the Italian case at the Congress of Paris (1856) and at Plombières (1858) he obtained Napoleon III's support for a War against Austria. Following the Franco-Piedmontese war against Austria (1859), his scheming with revolutionaries in

Central Italy, and the expedition of Garibaldi (1860), the Kingdom of Italy was proclaimed in 1861.

Civiltà Cattolica: This semi-official review of the Papacy run by the Jesuits was founded by Carlo Curci in 1850. Established initially in Naples, it subsequently moved to Rome.

Connubio: This 'marriage' or political alliance between Cavour of the Centre-Right and Urbano Rattazzi of the Centre-Left in 1852 provided the basis for Cavour's parliamentary majority in the Piedmontese Parliament and paved the way for his becoming Prime Minister in 1852.

Consulta di Stato: Consultative assembly created by Pope Pius IX in 1847 to advise the Pope's government on matters of administration, the ordering of municipalities, and other public needs. It was superseded first by the revolutionary agitation of 1848 and then the restoration of 1849.

Counter-Risorgimento: The opposition to the unification movement in the peninsula. The main role was played by the Papal regime, under the astute leadership of the Cardinal Secretary of State, Giacomo Antonelli.

First War for National Liberation: Began with a cycle of revolutions in 1848 that commenced with the revolution in Palermo and then reached a critical stage with the Five Days of Milan (March 18–22, 1848) in which the people of that city forced out the Austrian forces of General Radetzky, encouraging the King of Piedmont to launch a campaign for the liberation of Northern Italy. The Piedmontese defeat in 1848–49 led to the restoration of 1849 in the peninsula.

Garibaldi, Giuseppe (1807–1882): This foremost guerrilla leader in the fight for Italian unity is known as 'the Sword' of Italian unification. Influenced initially by Mazzini whose Young Italy organization he joined, he was forced into exile following the abortive revolution of 1833 in Savoy. He played a key role in the first War for National Liberation in 1848, and acted as defender of the Roman Republic. Subsequently he joined the National Society and during the Second War for National Liberation (1859), coordinated the activities of the volunteer troops. He and his Red Shirt volunteers are perhaps best known for the expedition of the thousand which overturned Bourbon rule in Sicily and Naples and brought the Italian south into the Kingdom of Italy proclaimed in 1861.

Gioberti, Vincenzo (1801–1852): This Risorgimento priest and states-man was the author of *Del Primato Morale e civile degli Italiani* (1843) which popularized the Italian cause, rendering respectable, even among a number of conservatives, the notion of some form of Italian unification.

Gioia, Melchiore (1767–1829): His essay on the theme of the best form of government for Italy won the prize awarded by the Cisalpine government. He called for a unitary republic.

Giovane Italia or Young Italy: This society was formed by Giuseppe Mazzini in Marseilles in 1831. Although a secret organization it hoped to spread national and democratic ideals among the masses and called for a republican Italy with Rome as its capital. It was more successful in popularizing national goals than in effecting revolutionary change, although it played an important role in bringing about the revolution-ary upheaval of 1848.

Italia Irredenta or Unreedemed Italy: Refers to the territories such as Trent and Trieste which remained under Austrian control following the Third War of Italian Liberation in 1866. This inspired irredentism or the movement for the redemption of these Italian speaking areas, which strained relations between Austria and Italy from 1866 to 1914. In 1915 Italy entered World War I, which became a fifth and final war of national liberation, and these territories were finally obtained.

Mazzini, Giuseppe: The 'soul' or 'heart' of Italian unification, Mazzini sought both a religious regeneration for the Italians who he claimed could be a 'messiah people' to awaken the nationalism of the peoples of Italy and Europe. In 1831 he founded Giovane Italia which aimed for a unitary republic in Italy with Rome as capital. He inspired a series of revolutions which were suppressed, and in 1849 provided leadership for the Roman Republic which emerged following the flight of Pope Pius IX. Mazzini served to inspire countless Italians, not least of whom was Garibaldi who considered him the master.

Metternich, Prince Clement von (1773–1859): This Austrian diplomat was largely responsible for the Vienna settlement of 1815 which brought Lombardy and Venetia under direct Habsburg control while much of the peninsula was under Austrian influence. Like the Austrian Emperor, Metternich championed the status quo in Italy and Europe and considered Italy no more than a 'geographical expression.'

Mezzogiorno: The Italian South, primarily the land which formerly belonged to the Kingdom of the Two Sicilies and which was integrated into the Kingdom of Italy proclaimed in 1861. It was here that 'brigandage' was strongest.

Muratism: Movement which hoped to restore a descendant of Joachim Murat, the former King of Naples and brother-in-law of Napoleon, to the throne of Naples.

Napoleon III (1808–1873): This nephew of Napoleon I served as President of the Second Republic (1848–52), which he transformed into the Second Empire which he ruled from 1852 to 1870. At Plombières he plotted with Cavour to wage a war against Austria, (Second War of National Liberation) and for compensation took Nice and Savoy as the Kingdom of Italy was proclaimed.

National Society: This organization founded in 1857 by Daniele Manin and Giorgio Pallavicino and Giuseppe La Farina brought popular support and led many former radicals and republicans to work with Cavour and Piedmont to achieve Italian independence.

Non expedit: Position announced by Pius IX that it was not expedient for Catholics to participate in the national political life of the state that had despoiled the Catholic Church and the Papacy of the temporal power. Later it was converted into a vital prohibition.

Orsini, Felice (1819–58): This Romagnol revolutionary and follower of Giuseppe Mazzini attempted to take the life of Napoleon III for his failure to champion the Italian cause (January 1858). Before his execution he issued a personal appeal to the French Emperor, which may have solidified Napoleon's resolve to do something for Italy.

Papal Allocution of April 1848: This formal message issued by Pius IX made it clear that the Pope could not and would not join the national crusade and First War of National Liberation against Austria. It led to the collapse of the constitutional Antonelli ministry, the revolution in Rome, and the Pope's flight into exile.

Papal Guarantees, Law of: This law of 1871 sought to regulate relations between the Kingdom of Italy and Holy See after the Italians seized Rome from the Pope (in the fourth War of National Liberation) as well as regulate relations between Church and State in Italy. Pius IX, who refused to recognize the loss of the temporal power, did not recognize its validity thus creating the Roman Question which plagued Italy until 1929.

Pius IX (or Pio Nono in Italian) (1792–1878): This longest reigning Pope (1846–1878), commenced his career as a reformer, but abandoned his liberal programme following the revolutions of 1848 and the restoration of 1849. Determined to preserve the Papal States (the Pope's temporal power), he and his Secretary of State Cardinal Giacomo Antonelli led the Counter-Risorgimento. He condemned liberalism and nationalism in his Syllabus of Errors. The Vatican Council which Pius called, defended the dogma of Papal Infallibility in 1870.

Quadrilateral: This strategic zone in northern Italy was guarded by the four fortresses of Mantua, Peschiera, Verona and Legnano. They played a key role in the First and Second Wars of National Liberation and fell into Italian hands only after 1866 and Third War of National Liberation.

Red Shirts: The irregular and volunteer military forces of Garibaldi who like their leader wore red shirts as a uniform of sorts. They played a part in the First, Second, and Third Wars of Italian unification.

Risorgimento: The nineteenth century movement which led to the unification of Italy. The Italian word for resurgence was also the name chosen by Cavour for his newspaper founded in December 1847. Initially the word had a predominantly literary or cultural significance and only later assumed a political-territorial meaning as well.

Sanfedisti: Name first applied to Cardinal Ruffo's Army of the Holy Faith or Santa Fede which overturned the French satellite Republic in Naples in 1799. After the Congress of Vienna it was applied to those ultra conservative secret groups who championed throne and altar against liberal pollution.

Second War of Italian Unification: This war of 1859 was fought by the Franco-Piedmontese forces, aided by volunteers, who defeated the Habsburg armies in northern Italy following the Plombières agreement of 1858. Cavour had hoped that the whole of northern Italy would be liberated, but by the armistice at Villafranca only Lombardy was ceded by Austria, which retained Venetia. This led to the Third War of Italian Liberation.

Statuto: The Constitution of 1848 which Carlo Alberto granted the Piedmontese. It was one of the few Italian constitutions which survived the restoration of 1849, and in modified form became the Constitution of the Italian Kingdom in 1861.

Syllabus of Errors: It was appended to Pius IX's encyclical Quanta cura issued in 1864. In the Syllabus the Pope condemned not only pantheism, naturalism and secularism, but liberalism, nationalism, contemporary civilization, and the separation of Church and state.

Third War of Italian Unification: This war of 1866 fought alongside Prussia against Austria resulted in the liberation of Venetia from Austrian rule and brought the Quadrilateral under Italian control.

Vittorio Emanuele II (1820–1878): He was the last King of Sardinia and the first of Italy. He came to power following his father's defeat in the First War of Italian Unification (1849), collaborated with Cavour and Napoleon to wage the Second War of 1859, which resulted in the proclamation of the Kingdom of Italy in 1861. In 1866 he brought Italy into the Third War and acquired Venetia. Finally in the Fourth War, in 1870, his troops seized Rome making it the Italian capital.

Maps

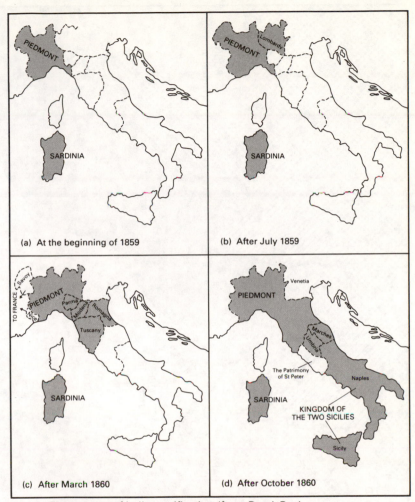

(a) At the beginning of 1859

(b) After July 1859

(c) After March 1860

(d) After October 1860

Map 1: The process of Italian unification (from Derek Beales,
The Risorgimento and Italian Unification, 1971)

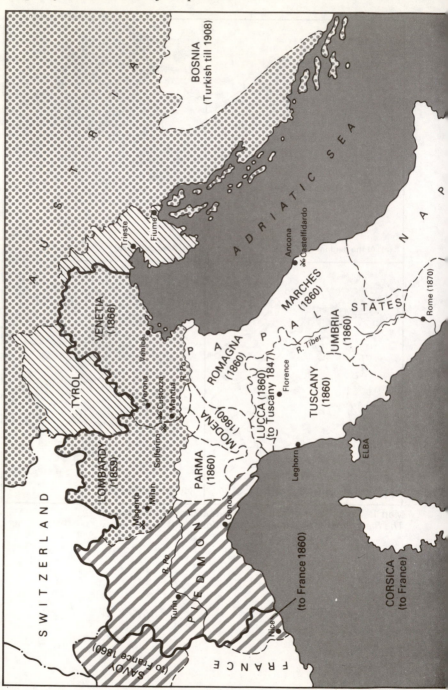

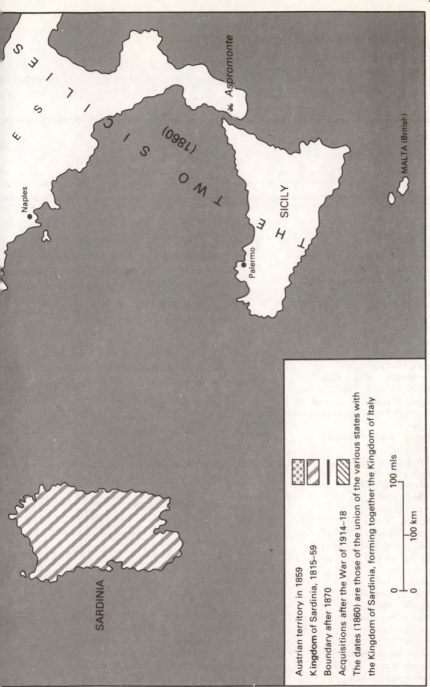

SICILIES

Aspromonte

TWO SICILIES (1860)

Naples

Palermo

SICILY

MALTA (British)

SARDINIA

Austrian territory in 1859

Kingdom of Sardinia, 1815–59

Boundary after 1870

Acquisitions after the War of 1914–18

The dates (1860) are those of the union of the various states with
the Kingdom of Sardinia, forming together the Kingdom of Italy

0   100 km
0   100 mls

Map 2: Italy in the later Nineteenth Century

Index